Hymnwriters 1

Bernard Braley

STAINER & BELL - LONDON

© 1987 Bernard Braley
First published in Great Britain by
Stainer & Bell Ltd, 82 High Road, London N2 9PW

British Library Cataloguing in Publication Data

Braley, Bernard
    The hymnwriters
    1
    1. Hymn writers — Biography
    I. Title
    264'.2'0922   BV325

    ISBN 0 — 85249 — 667 — 2
    ISBN 0 — 85249 — 678 — 8 Pbk

Printed and bound in Great Britain
at the University Press, Oxford by
David Stanford, Printer to the University.

Contents

Preface

This book is first of all just to be enjoyed in the reading of it. For many though, its usefulness will go far beyond a good read. It provides an opportunity for an evening singing an author's hymns as his story is told. Many suggested tunes are quoted that will be found in a wide range of hymnbooks: and others are possible, too. The especially imaginative will see chances for dramatisation and costume. Those constructing sermons will find many useful illustrations besides a wealth of stimulating ideas.

If you ask why these five hymnwriters in the first book of the series, I can only counter by asking why not! They do share the common office of clergymen in the Church of England — but that was by accident rather than design. I chose to avoid for Volume 1 those like Wesley and Watts whose stories are perhaps best known — and Thomas Ken, William Cowper, Reginald Heber, John Ellerton and William Walsham How spanning several centuries and such varied experiences seemed to add up to a rounded package. Volume 2 includes writers of other denominations including one of the twentieth century.

In quoting freely from the writings of the hymnwriters, I have been less profuse where anthologies are widely available. The complete poems and hymns of William Cowper, for instance, are widely available in libraries throughout the world.

I am obviously indebted to earlier biographers in preparing these chapters. I am especially grateful to Mrs. Jean Lowe and Mr. Keith Wakefield for their extensive work in layout and design. Mr. Wakefield's expertise in the field of photography has been especially valued. I hope that no rights of copyright owners have been overlooked in the following acknowledgements and will of course be pleased to correct any oversight brought to notice.

Thanks are especially due to the staff of the British Library, of Haringey Public Libraries, of the Cheshire Record Office, of the Essex Record Office, of the Surrey Record Office and of the Record Offices of East and West Sussex, and of the Archivist at Church House, Westminster. Special thanks are due to Miss Sylvia Bull, the Curator, and to the Trustees of the Newton and Cowper Museum, Olney, for access to many papers and permission to make and publish photographs of exhibits, and to the Vicar of Olney for permission to photograph stained glass. Readers are warmly commended to visit the church and museum at Olney if they can.

I am indebted to the Proprietor of Hymns Ancient and Modern and especially to Mr. Gordon A. Knights for access to archives and in particular to print the following letters:

From Revd. John Ellerton to Revd. G. Cosby White about a line in Isaac Watts' paraphrase of Psalm 118.
From Revd. John Ellerton to Revd. G. Cosby White about alterations to established Ellerton texts.
From Revd. John Ellerton to Sir Henry Baker, Bart., about Ellerton's text 'God of the living'.
From Revd. John Ellerton to Sir Henry Baker, Bart., about the principle of copyright.
From Revd. John Ellerton to the Proprietors of Hymns Ancient and Modern about Ellerton's translation of the 'Alleluia Perenne'.
From Revd. William Walsham How to Sir Henry Baker, Bart., about principles of copyright.
From Revd. William Walsham How to Sir Henry Baker, Bart., about Hymn Tunes.
From Bishop How to Revd. G. Cosby White about the plans of the compilers of 'Hymns Ancient and Modern' for a new edition.

I am further indebted to the Proprietors of Hymns Ancient and Modern and especially to Mr. Gordon A. Knights for permission to print an autograph of Bishop How's notes on 'Hymns for the Days of the Week', an autograph of Revd. John Ellerton's 'Saviour, again to Thy dear name we raise' and to reproduce photographs in the 1909 Historical Edition of 'Hymns Ancient and Modern'.

Thanks are due to the Society for Promoting Christian Knowledge for access to their archives and for permission to quote from Henry Housman's book on the life of John Ellerton. I am grateful to Pitman Publishing Limited for permission to quote from F. D. How's biography of his father; to the Methodist Publishing House for permission to quote from the Methodist Covenant Service; and to the Cambridge University Press to quote verses from Habakkuk in the New English Bible, Second Edition, © 1970 Oxford and Cambridge University Presses.

The publishers would like to thank the following for their kind permission to reproduce the photographs in this book:

National Portrait Gallery, London: 19, 25
London Borough of Hackney, Archives Department: 127
Passmore Edwards Museum: 130
London Transport Museum: 133
Keith Wakefield: 34 below, 126, 142, 151, 152, 160, 179, 188

Thanks are also due to the following:

Revd. Dr. O. A. Beckerlegge for advice on a text of a Wesley hymn in use during Revd. William Walsham How's time.
Revd. Canon Dr. Gareth Bennett for information in a lecture about Thomas Ken given on 25th September 1985.
Revd. G. A. H. Atkins, Vicar of Hinstock, for local information.
Miss C. Jenkins for information about the inscription on John Ellerton's grave.
Mr. G. R. Pimlett, the Principal Librarian of Crewe Public Library for access to the Minute Books of the Mechanics Institute and for data about Crewe Hall.
Revd. Canon Simonsen, Rector of Barnes, for permission to quote from Vestry Minutes and to take photographs in the church.
Revd. Exell for the loan of books.
Revd. David W. Smith, Vicar of Crewe Green, for information from the Register of Baptisms.
Revd. David B. Evans, sometime Vicar of Easebourne, for information about Easebourne Priory.
Revd. Canon D. R. Vicary, Precentor of Wells, for information about Thomas Ken.
Revd. Canon Dominic Walker O.G.S. Vicar of Brighton, for permission to print Minutes of Vestry Meetings and for helpful local data.
Professor J. Richard Watson, Professor of English at the University of Durham, and the Hymn Society of Great Britain and Ireland for permission to quote from a paper on John Ellerton printed in the Hymn Society Bulletin.

Bernard Braley
June 1987

List of Illustrations

A tune set to Ken's Hymns, about 1750, to be sung to the
lute-harp arranged by C. W. Lavington, the organist and choirmaster of Wells Cathedral, for use with the *Evening Hymn* sung
on 29th June, 1885, the bicentenary year of Bishop Ken's
consecration and the anniversary of the Trial of the Seven
Bishops. On that occasion, the window commemorating Ken
in the north aisle of the choir was seen by the public for the
first time.

Thomas Ken

Thomas Ken was born at Little Berkhamsted in July 1637, the son of another Thomas, attorney in the Court of Common Pleas in London and a member of the Company of Barber Surgeons. Then, as in later times, this membership probably had no occupational connection but was a means of acquiring the Freedom of the City of London. He was also one of the Clerks of the House of Lords, and of the Great Assizes of the Courts of Glamorgan, Brecon and Radnor. Thomas senior, by an earlier marriage to Jane Hughes, had fathered four children, of whom Anne, the youngest, plays a significant role in our story.

The older Thomas' second marriage was to Martha, the daughter of Ion Chalkhill, a poet and friend of Edmund Spenser. There were four children born to Martha, of whom the second was another Ion, who became Treasurer of the East India Company. Next came our Thomas: four years later, Martin lived only briefly and his mother died in childbed. So it fell to step-sister Anne to look after Thomas and keep house for her father.

Thomas was to live in troubled and momentous times. In the year of his birth, when Charles I had already reigned for eight years without summoning Parliament, Archbishop William Laud sought to impose the use of the New Prayer Book on the Scots and had provoked revolts. By 1640, the Archbishop had been impeached by Parliament and imprisoned in the Tower of London, to be beheaded in 1645. Civil War began in 1642: the King suffered the Archbishop's fate when condemned to death in 1649.

> Oh the gallant fisher's life,
> It is the best of any.
> 'Tis full of pleasure, void of strife
> And 'tis beloved of many:
> Other joys
> Are but toys,
> Only this
> Lawful is,
> For our skill
> Breed no ill,
> But content and pleasure.
>
> — — — — —
>
> If the sun's excessive heat
> Make our bodies swelter,
> To an osier hedge we get
> For a friendly shelter,
> Where in a dike
> Pearch or pike,
> Roach or dace
> We do chase,
> Bleak or Gudgion
> Without grudging,
> We are still contented.
>
> *Ion (John) Chalkhill*

Anne Ken had meantime fallen in love with Isaak Walton, whose first wife had been a great-niece of the martyred Archbishop Cranmer, famed for his work on the English Prayer Book. Anne and Isaak married in 1647, and on the death of Thomas Ken, senior, they provided young Thomas a home and exercised an informal guardianship. For a mere middle class tradesman, the author of *The Compleat Angler*, had a remarkable circle of friends: there was scarcely a theologian or man of letters with whom Walton did not correspond on friendly and familiar terms.

2

O Sir, doubt not but that Angling is an Art, and an Art worth your learning: the Question is rather whether you will be capable of learning it? for Angling is somewhat like Poetry, men are to be born so: I mean, with inclinations to it, though both may be heightened by practice and experience: but he that hopes to be a good Angler must not only bring an inquiring, searching, observing wit, but he must bring a large measure of hope and patience, and a love and propensity to the Art itself, but having once got and practised it, then doubt not but Angling will prove to be so pleasant, that it will prove like Virtue, a reward to itself.

Isaak Walton. The Compleat Angler

How happy is he born and taught,
That serveth not another's will;
Whose armour is his honest thought,
And simple truth his utmost skill.
Henry Wotton: The Character of a Happy Life

Prayer the Church's banquet . . .

Exalted manna, gladness of the best,
Heaven in ordinary, man well drest,
The Milkie Way, the bird of Paradise . . .

The land of spices; something understood.
George Herbert: Prayer

Through his foster-father, Thomas had access to a remarkable library, and would have been guided when he was walking the riverbank to observe every detail of the natural world. Isaak's heroes are evident in the biographies he chose to write: author and diplomat Sir Henry Wotton; poet and pastor, the Reverend George Herbert; poet and preacher, the Reverend John Donne; and the Reverend Richard Hooker, theologian and defender of the episcopate.

What if this present were the world's last night?
John Donne:
Holy Sonnets (1633):
Divine Meditations.

Of Law there can be no less acknowledged, than that her seat is the bosom of God, her voice the harmony of the world: all things in heaven and earth do her homage, the very least as feeling her care, and the greatest are not exempted from her power.
Richard Hooker

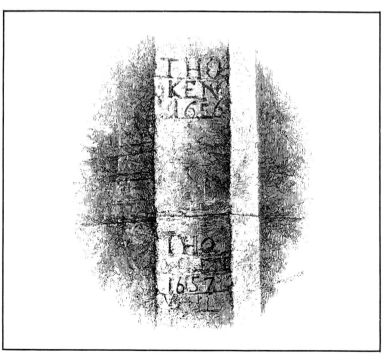

KEN'S NAME IN CLOISTERS, WINCHESTER

When Thomas entered Winchester College in 1652, the Prayer Book he had been taught to cherish was banned: and the Westminster Catechism replaced that of the Church of England. At Winchester, the boys were woken from their truckle-beds at five. He probably suffered schoolday trials for conscience's sake as he followed the religious devotions he had been taught at home. Perhaps he shared these with fellow-scholar Francis Turner, like Thomas, a poet and hymn-writer and who, in later life, as Bishop of Ely, was to be remanded with Bishop Ken to the Tower of London. The normal Cathedral and College services were suspended, but the college accounts for the period of the Parliamentary and Commonwealth regimes suggest some form of musical service. Holy Communion was administered at Christmas, Easter and on All Saints Day.

WINCHESTER COLLEGE

In May, 1647, Parliament passed an ordinance for the *Visitation and the Reformation of the University of Oxford, and the several Halls and Colleges therein.* Oxford had been staunchly Royalist: the Divine Right of Kings had been staunchly preached. The Visitors required absolute allegiance to the new regime: otherwise for Vice-Chancellor or college cook, dismissal was inevitable. At New College, conscience compelled fifty-three out of fifty-four fellows and all eight chaplains to refuse to submit. Seventy-five new appointments left New College the most deeply-dyed with Puritanism in the whole of Oxford. By 1654, the Visitors had turned to more positive activity, directing that fellows and students should at their meals in Hall, speak Latin or Greek so that *their ignorance in this matter might not bring discredit on the University in their public discourses with foreigners.* They also established sermons and lectures on divinity in many colleges: and probably the new fellows were more devout, if less learned, than many who had been dismissed. By the time Thomas Ken went up to New College in 1657, the new Vice-Chancellor, sometime Chaplain to Oliver Cromwell, and a great opponent of set forms of worship, nevertheless allowed the holding of Church of England services, including Holy Communion, in a house opposite Merton Chapel. In 1656 a musical society was allowed, meeting in the house of the former organist of St. John's College, William Ellis. He had an organ in his dwelling, and instrumentalists and singers gathered there weekly. The 1658 membership list includes the name of Thomas Ken.

When the monarchy was restored, Oxford went mad. Liberty and licence are separated but by a hair's breadth: the services of the Church of England were no longer confined to an Upper Room but in reacting against Puritan restraints, many threw out that essential piety which for Thomas Ken was a certain ingredient of true religion. It is recorded of Ken's college days that he willingly disbursed the loose coins in his pocket to the needy as he travelled round Oxford: his lack of concern for wealth shows itself throughout his life story, even to the extent of giving away sometimes more than he had!

In 1661, Thomas Ken obtained his degree; the following year he was admitted deacon in the Church of England; in 1663, he was appointed to the Rectory of Little Easton in Essex. Whilst Ken in no way neglected his duties in his first parish, he found time for frequent visits to Bishop Morley, who had been appointed to Winchester in 1661, and who had a London house in Chelsea opposite the pier on the Thames. The Bishop had been chaplain to Charles II and had kept up the services of the English Church during his exile. In theology, he was at once a Calvinist and a High Churchman. Though siding with the High Church party in the Act of Uniformity and other measures, he showed dissenters much personal kindness.

> Thine, Lord; Thou by creation hast the right
> To rule the work of thy all-quick'ning might;
> Thine, Lord; Thou art the Potter, I, the clay,
> Cannot the form Thou givest me gainsay . . .
> *Hymns on the Festivals: Resignation of Jesus*

The patron of Ken's first living was Lord Maynard, of Easton Lodge, then aged about thirty-five, a widower with two children, who had just married his second wife, Margaret. Margaret's father had been in exile during the Commonwealth: but her sister had married the Duke of Lauderdale, an ardent persecutor in Scotland — it was even rumoured she had been Cromwell's mistress. In contrast, Margaret seems to have been attracted to the ways of the

Church and to have looked for considerable guidance from her priest. Lord Maynard had played a significant part in bringing about the Restoration, and was to be Comptroller of the Household to Charles II and a Privy Counsellor. So Thomas Ken made his first contacts with those who served at Court.

When Isaak Walton's wife Anne died, Bishop Morley invited his old friend, then aged seventy, to make his home in the Bishop's quarters at Winchester. In 1665, Ken resigned the living at Easton and became a chaplain to the Bishop, which involved working in Winchester, at Farnham Castle, and at the Chelsea house annexed as part of the see. For many years, the two men who most influenced our hymnwriter's life, were to share the same home.

There was a neglected parish on the outskirts of Winchester known as St. John-in-the-Soke, where the living was so small it was difficult to find an incumbent. In 1665 Ken undertook duties here gratis and gave particular attention to the Office of Adult Baptism, so many of the parishioners not having been baptized as infants during the Commonwealth. In 1666, the Old Wykehamist became a Fellow of Winchester. In 1667 he added to his duties those of Rector of Brighstone in the Isle of Wight. This village was about six miles from Carisbrooke, which Ken would have remembered as a place of Charles I's imprisonment and attempted escape. The diary of Lady Warwick records her visits about this time to the Old Church at Chelsea and the impressions made upon her by Ken's sermons. They moved *her heart to long after the blessed feast* of the holy communion; to *weep bitterly*; to *bless God and have sweet communion with Him*. They stirred her up to speak to her husband *about things of everlasting concernment* to *persuade him to repentance and make his peace with God. With strong desires and tears* when Ken preached on the words: *Sin no more, lest a worse thing come unto thee*, she was *able to beg power against sin for the time to come.*

In 1669, he relinquished Brighstone, probably at the Bishop's request, and was appointed to the Rectory at East Woodhay in Hampshire. The Register at Woodhay records the birth of Rose Ken, daughter of Ion Ken in 1670, presumably during a visit by his brother's family. In 1672, he characteristically resigned East Woodhay so it could provide a home for Oxford friend, Dr. George Hooper, who needed an urgent

Pray'r often errs; Praise is that Grace alone
Which true Infallibility may own.
Thomas Ken of Prayer and Praise

Shou'dst Thou, thy face, a while to hide,
Retire to thy celestial Bride,
And while Thou dost from me recede
On lilies feed.

Thither I after Thee will fly,
And hymning Thee, will prostrate lie,
In hope to pluck a lily sweet
Kiss'd by thy feet.
Thomas Ken: From 'Christophil'

. . . he strictly accustomed himself but to one sleep, which often obliged him to rise at one or two o'clock in the morning, and sometimes sooner: a practice which grew so habitual, that it continued with him almost till his last illness. So lively and cheerful was his temper, that he would be very entertaining to his friends in the evening, even when it was perceived that with difficulty he kept his eyes open; and then seem'd to go to rest with no other purpose than the refreshing and enabling him with more vigour and cheerfulness to sing his morning-hymn, as he then used to do to his lute before he put on his clothes.

W. Hawkins: A Short Account of the Life of Thomas Ken, 1733

Some sins we for good ends commit,
Some for our callings are thought fit;
Some trivial seem, and are too small,
Under an endless wrath to fall;
To Sin we destin'd are by God's decree,
And irrespective Fate will be our plea.

From 'God's Attributes: God's Grace'

E'er since I hung upon my mother's breast,
Thy love, my God, has me sustained and blest;
My virtuous parents, tender of their child,
My education pious, careful, mild,
My teachers, zealous well to form my mind,
My faithful friends and benefactors kind,
My creditable station and good name,
My life preserved from scandal and from shame,
My understanding, memory, and health,
Relations dear and competence of wealth;
All the vouchsafements thou to me hast shown,
All blessings, all deliverances unknown, —
To hymn thy love my verse for ever bind,
And yet thy greatest love is still behind.

From 'Hymnotheo' in which Ken tells the story, first related by Clement of Alexandria, of St. John and the catechumen of Smyrna. Some scholars feel this particular passage may have an autobiographical ring about it as regards Ken's own life

---

move on health grounds.

For the next three years, Ken's duties were limited to those of Chaplain to the Bishop, as a Fellow of Winchester College and as pastor to St. John-in-the-Soke. Ken baptized a boy of that parish who was subject to fits and unable to walk at five years old. A few days later, when called by his nickname, the lad, previously dumb, replied 'My name is not Tattie: my name is Matthew, Dr. Ken has baptized me'. From then on, the lad could walk.

Ken next wrote his *Manual for Winchester College*, later used by many other schools, one as far afield as Philadelphia. He named his ideal boy Philotheus, one who loves God, one who is the friend of God. His instruction is precise. A boy with his own room should pray there but the choristers, housed in dormitories, should go for greater quietue to the chapel *between the first and second peal of the morning* (the half-hour after 5 a.m.). In the evening, the warden, fellows, masters, clerks, scholars and choristers processed round the cloisters before supper and Evensong. Individuals should say their prayers as they *went circum*, to use the chosen phrase for the procession. Guidance in the manual includes daily self-examination as to the sins of *idleness, unchastity, lying, stubbornness and quarrels*. Those sleeping badly should guard . . . *against idle and unclean thoughts* by repeating Psalms 138 and 139. Each boy is to look to *the receiving of the blessed sacrament* as *the most divine and solemn act of religion*. He speaks of the usefulness of the confessional, though not as an essential pre-requisite to forgiveness by God. The lad is not to neglect the *orders or duties of the school* on the plea of devotion.

Ken then travelled with his nephew, the young Isaak Walton, on the Grand Tour of Europe. Records of the trip are scanty: but on visiting Rome, he noted the clergy were given to Mammon worship. He was troubled, too, by the oppressive nature of papal taxation: nepotism was rife. Then, back to three happy years at Winchester. He had his own organ in his college rooms, friend-

ship with his Bishop, and conversation
with the octogenarian Isaak Walton, as
well as with his travelling companion
Isaak. A library of writers in mystical
and ascetic theology was close at hand.
On 6th July 1678, Ken became a
Bachelor of Divinity, and in June of the following year, he
was awarded a doctorate.

No wonder, said my Guardian, then,
God should transcend the thoughts of mortal men;
We Angels, who of God have blissful view,
Can his Idea form, no more than you . . .
From 'God's Attributes: Incomprehensibility'

Just when Ken wrote his Morning, Evening and Midnight
Hymns has never been definitely established. The directions
in the *Manual* encourage the singing of the Morning and
Evening Hymns in the scholar's room. But whether, as seems
likely, it was Ken's text or another is not absolutely resolved.
Mostly, we are familiar only with the verses culled for
modern hymnbooks: the full texts are printed as given in the
1697 edition of the *Winchester Manual*. At once full of
theology, about the everyday and the world of the angels,
they are essentially addressed to God who deserves the
worship of all his creatures. Tunes used for the extracts we
often sing are MORNING HYMN and TALLIS' CANON.

In 1679, Thomas Ken was invited to succeed his friend
George Hooper as Chaplain to the Princess Mary at the
Hague. The marriage, borne of politics rather than affection,
between William of Orange and his cousin, took place on
4th November 1677, when his young bride was fifteen. Her
first chaplain had allowed her to attend the services of Dutch
Congregationalists. Hooper had weaned her back towards the
Church of England by setting her to read Hooker and
Eusebius: and also tried to dissuade her from the sin of
playing cards on Sunday! But he reported to England that
Mary was harshly treated by her husband who also made fun
of the Communion Table installed in her quarters, there
being no chapel in William's residence.

Ken was to show himself willing throughout his life to speak
his mind in high places; he took William to task about his
treatment of his wife, about his liaison with a member of the
Princess' household, and about a scandal in which Count
Zulestein, a cousin of the Prince had seduced one of the
maids of honour under promise of marriage he never
intended to keep. Ken insisted he did. All this did not please
Prince William who threatened him with dismissal. Ken
resented the threats and would not accept dismissal at the
hand of someone who had not appointed him, but was ready
to resign with leave from the Princess. In the end, the Prince
regretted his hasty response and, for the sake of goodwill he
thought he would need later from the English, pleaded with

Ken to stay. He did for just a year, during which time he was asked by Bishop Compton of London to take soundings about a possible union of Dutch and English Protestants, one of a series of abortive attempts to bring about the Union of Protestant Christendom.

A MORNING HYMN

Awake my Soul, and with the Sun,
Thy daily stage of Duty run;
Shake off dull Sloth, and early rise,
To pay thy Morning Sacrifice.

Redeem thy mispent time that's past,
Live this day, as if 'twere thy last:
T'improve thy Talent take due care,
Gainst the great Day thy self prepare.

Let all thy Converse be sincere,
Thy Conscience as the Noon-day clear;
Think how all-seeing God thy ways,
And all thy secret Thoughts surveys.

Influenc'd by the Light Divine,
Let thy own Light in good Works shine:
Reflect all Heaven's propitious ways
In ardent Love, and chearful Praise.

Wake and lift up thyself, my Heart,
And with the Angels bear thy part,
Who all night long unwearied sing,
Glory to the Eternal King.

Awake, awake, ye Heavenly Choire,
May your Devotion me inspire,
That I, like you, my Age may spend,
Like you, may on my God attend.

May I, like you, in God delight,
Have all day long my God in sight,
Perform, like you, my Maker's will;
O may I never more do ill!

Had I your Wings, to Heaven I'd flie,
But God shall that defect supply,
And my Soul wing'd with warm desire,
Shall all day long to Heav'n aspire.

Glory to Thee who safe hast kept,
And hast refresht me whilst I slept.
Grant, Lord, when I from death shall wake,
I may of endless Light partake.

I would not wake, nor rise again,
Ev'n Heav'n itself I would disdain,
Wert not Thou there to be enjoy'd,
And I in Hymns to be imploy'd.

Heav'n is, dear Lord, wheree'r Thou art,
O never then from me depart;
For to my Soul 'tis Hell to be,
But for one moment without Thee.

Lord, I my vows to Thee renew,
Scatter my sins as Morning dew,
Guard my first springs of Thought, and Will,
And with Thy self my Spirit fill.

Direct, controul, suggest this day,
All I design, or do, or say;
That all my Powers, with all their might,
In Thy sole Glory may unite.

Praise God, from whom all blessings flow,
Praise Him, all Creatures here below,
Praise Him above, y'Angelick Host,
Praise Father, Son, and Holy Ghost.

The version of Ken's 'Morning Hymn' printed
in the Winchester 'Manual' of 1697

On his return to England, Ken was appointed, probably on the recommendation of Princess Mary, as a Chaplain to the King, before whom he preached in October 1680. He had, over the years, kept in touch with the Maynard family, his first contacts with those at court, and was saddened by Lady Margaret's death, preaching at her funeral service in June 1682.

King Charles II, whose country residence at Newmarket had been gutted, determined to build a new palace at Winchester. Sir Christopher Wren's design was to rival Versailles. A stately street was to connect the palace to the cathedral. It was to contain 160 rooms, with a cupola. The Grand Duke Cosimo of Tuscany presented marble pillars. As the plans were made, the Court visited Winchester, and the Royal Harbinger, seeking the necessary accommodation, chose Ken's prebendal house, for Eleanor Gwynn, better known as Nell, one of the

King's mistresses. Thomas Ken, as always unfrightened of the consequences of standing up to authority, refused saying *a woman of ill-repute ought not to be endured in the house of a clergyman, least of all in that of the King's Chaplain.* Dean Meggot, known for his excessive obeisance as the 'bowing dean' was more helpful: he built a room for Nell in the south end of his Deanery, which was pulled down in 1835 by a later occupant of that office to avoid perpetuating an unsavoury reputation.

Back in 1661, the Portuguese settlement at Tangier had become British as part of the marriage dowry of Catherine of Braganza. The gift proved to be a constant drain on English funds, and eventually in 1683, it was decided to demolish the fortifications and leave the city to be occupied by the local population of Moors. Samuel Pepys, one of the Commissioners of the Tangier territory, suggested Ken as Chaplain for the expedition to carry through this decision. Lord Dartmouth, in overall command looked for *piety, authority and learning* as necessary qualifications. Pepys and Ken had several heated arguments during the journey on points of theology but on arrival at Tangier agreed that they *had a great deal of discourse on the viciousness of the place, and it being time for Almighty God to destroy it.* Colonel Percy Kirke, the Governor of Tangier, had put a drunken and profligate priest, the brother of his mistress, in charge of the spiritual affairs of the garrison and now sought an appointment for him on one of the Naval vessels. Ken opposed rigorously. Perhaps the only real benefit from an unhappy time on the North African coast was the opportunity to see life in the town under the influence of another of the world's great religions.

> A Priest was to each Regiment assign'd,
> All were to hear the daily Prayers enjoyn'd,
> All taught that Soldiers best grim Death defy,
> Who go to Field the best prepar'd to die:
> No Soldier durst his Captain disobey,
> No Captain robb'd his Soldiers of their Pay:
> Well pay'd themselves, their Quarters they defray'd,
> And Towns a gain of quart'ring Soldiers made.
>
> *Thomas Ken: From 'Edmund'*

AN EVENING HYMN

Glory to Thee, my God, this night,
For all the Blessings of the Light;
Keep me, O keep me, King of Kings,
Under Thy own Almighty Wings.

Forgive me, Lord, for Thy dear Son,
The ill that I this day have done,
That with the World, my self, and Thee,
I, ere I sleep, at peace may be.

Teach me to live, that I may dread
The Grave as little as my Bed;
Teach me to die, that so I may
Triumphing rise at the last day.

O may my Soul on Thee repose,
And with sweet sleep mine Eye-lids close;
Sleep that may me more vig'rous make
To serve my God when I awake!

When in the night I sleepless lie,
My Soul with Heavenly Thoughts supply;
Let no ill Dreams disturb my Rest,
No powers of darkness me molest.

Dull sleep of Sense me to deprive,
I am but half my days alive;
Thy faithful Lovers, Lord, are griev'd
To lie so long of Thee bereav'd.

But though sleep o'er my frailty reigns,
Let it not hold me long in chains,
And now and then let loose my Heart,
Till it an Hallelujah dart.

The faster sleep the sense doth bind,
The more unfetter'd is the Mind;
O may my Soul from matter free,
Thy unvail'd Goodness waking see!

O, when shall I, in endless day,
For ever chase dark sleep away,
And endless praise with th'Heavenly Choir
Incessant sing, and never tire?

You, my blest Guardian, whilst I sleep,
Close to my Bed your Vigils keep,
Divine Love into me instil,
Stop all the avenues of ill;

Thought to thought with my Soul converse,
Celestial joys to me rehearse,
And in my stead all the night long,
Sing to my God a grateful Song.

Praise God from whom all Blessings flow,
Praise Him all Creatures here below,
Praise Him above y'Angelick Host,
Praise Father, Son, and Holy Ghost.
The version of Ken's 'Evening Hymn' printed in the
Winchester 'Manual' of 1697

Throughout his life, Ken had a great sense of the attributes of
God, which he made the subject of a series of poems. Just

when he wrote these texts is unknown: it may well have been later in life when freed from other duties. But its contents tell us something of the man's beliefs which determined his actions throughout his life. The poems, sometimes more than one on the same theme see, as God's attributes, infinity, eternity, incomprehensibility, immensity, immutability, unity, spirituality, omnipotence, independance, all-sufficiency, wisdom, truth, holiness, omniscience, justice, goodness and providence. Other poems tell of God's will, God's grace and God's benignity, tell of angels, remind us our God is a Father, and a Friend, and that God is Love. Another series of poems dwell on Jesus, with Jesus, our Retreat, set against poems on Jesus as Prophet, Prince and King. Other poems follow the Church calendar or celebrate the lives of various saints.

> Ere the Intelligence from Nothing rear'd,
> To spin succession on the sphere appear'd,
> To give Duration drop by drop, to move
> Frail Man, each fleeting minute to improve;
> Thou self-originated Deity,
> In indivisible Eternity;
> Thou Self-sufficient, by thy Self didst reign,
> And with thy Self, thy Self didst entertain;
> No rival Infinite could share thy throne,
> There no more infinites can be but one;
> For were there more, each would each other bound,
> All join'd, an infinite could ne're compound;
> All parts are bounds, the thing compounded piece,
> And bounds to boundless never can increase . . .
>
> *Thomas Ken: Opening lines of his sequence*
> *of poems on 'God's Attributes'*

> In ev'ry herb, plant, flower, or tree,
> Thought read the providential Deity;
> Thought saw the Earth impregnated with juice,
> From buried seeds all living plants produce;
> How they shot out in roots, stalk, leaves, and flow'r
> Endew'd with plastick pow'r;
> Still to assimulate to every kind
> The taste, form, colour, smell, Heav'n first assign'd,
> Their growth God governs, and promotes,
> For medicine, food, perfume, and antidotes;
> Even pois'nous plants which in the soil are nurs'd,
> Memorials of the Earth for sin accurs'd;
> To various creatures are for food assign'd,
> And medicinal to Mankind.
>
> *From 'God's Attributes: Providence'*
> *Isaak Walton had encouraged the young*
> *Thomas to observe Nature with care*

While Ken was away, his aged foster-parent Isaak Walton died at the age of ninety. A bequest in the will reads ' . . . to my brother Dr. Ken, a ring, with this motto, A Friend's Farewell, I.W. obit. 15 Dec 1683'.

Towards the end of 1684, Ken was summoned to the death-bed of Bishop Morley. His friend and mentor, like Ken himself, had chosen the celibate life and practised an ascetic austerity, eating but one meal a day. Until after his eighty-sixth birthday, he had risen summer and winter at five, and, even on the coldest of mornings, declined a fire. Now began the most eventful years in Thomas Ken's life.

Few years will wash away unwilful Taints; Religious Children soon grow aged Saints.
Thomas Ken of Youthful Piety

October 29, 1684   Bishop Morley of Winchester died.

November 4, 1684 Letter sent to Bishop Mews translating him from Bath and Wells to Winchester. The King had decided to offer Bath and Wells to Ken, remembering him as the little black fellow who would not give poor Nelly a lodging.

December 16, 1684 The Great Chapter of Bath and Wells confirmed the King's choice.

January 25, 1685   Bishop Ken was consecrated at Lambeth Palace.

February 2, 1685   King Charles II had apoplectic fit.

February 4, 1685 Of the Bishops called to the King's bedside, it fell to Ken to try to win a confession from the monarch so absolution could be granted. He first insisted on the Duchess of Portsmouth, the King's other mistress, leaving the bedside; and persuaded the King to seek his wife's forgiveness for many sins. Charles was not persuaded to take Holy Communion, but said he would think about doing so. The new Bishop decided the King's demeanour was just sufficient for him to speak the words of absolution. Some-time in the next hours, the King commended all his children (save the Duke of Monmouth in exile) to his brother's care. He gave each of them a parting embrace and blessing. The bishops needed the King's blessing, too. They asked *as he was the Lord's Annointed and the father of his country, they also, and all that were there present, and in them the whole body of his subjects, had a right to ask his blessing.* According to Bishop Burnet's account: *They all knelt down, the King raised himself on his bed, and solemnly blessed them all.*

'Know', Socrates reply'd, 'I for the one true God a Martyr dy'd; I knew great God by native Light, And Conscience told me what was right . . .
In 'Hymnarium', Ken shows his sharing in the wider hope for those not of specific Christian belief in the world beyond death

February 5, 1685   The Duchess of Portsmouth, believing Charles to be a Romanist at heart and anxious for his mortal soul, persuaded him to receive a Roman Catholic priest to whom the King confessed, received absolution and the Holy Sacrament of the Eucharist.

February 6, 1685   On the day Charles II died, Bishop Ken was enthroned by proxy, with the Chancellor of the Cathedral acting out the Bishop's role in the ceremonial. Ken's public prominence at this time led people to look to him for guidance as how to react to James II's Roman Catholicism. His personal view was that subjects do not choose their King. They obey the sovereign whom the providence of God has placed over them.

March 2, 1685   When Ken had scarcely reached Wells from London, he persuaded the Chapter to send a loyal address to the new King. Significantly, it refers to Charles II's deathbed blessing of the bishops. It is Ken's duty to serve and obey his sovereign.

Learn from Daniel a universal obligingness and benignity, an awful love to your Prince, a constant fidelity, an undaunted courage, an unwearied zeal in serving him. Learn from Daniel an equal mixture of the wisdom of the serpent and of the innocence of the dove, an unoffending conversation, a clean integrity, and an impartial justice to all within your sphere. Learn from the man *greatly beloved*, to reconcile policy and religion, business and devotion, abstinence and abundance, greatness and goodness, magnanimity and humility, power and subjection, authority and affability, conversation and retirement, interest and integrity, Heaven and the Court, the favour of God, and the favour of the King, and you are masters of Daniel's secret . . .
    A Sermon at Whitehall, 1685

March 8, 1685   Ken preached in Whitehall (London) for the first Sunday in Lent. He spoke out against the surfeits of intemperance expected in the Court.

April 23, 1685   It fell to Ken, in conformity with custom, to walk at the King's side in the Coronation procession from Westminster Hall, and to support him on the steps of the throne in Westminster Abbey.

June 13, 1685   Rebellion in Somerset. The miners of the Mendips and the Puritan traders of Taunton and Bridgwater supported the rebellion of the Duke of Monmouth; by 13th June, the King's troops were starving and deserting to the rebels. What else could the Chapter, which had so recently sent a loyal address, do but provide emergency funds to the King?

July 1, 1685   The rebels swarmed into the cathedral and severely damaged the organ. The previous night, the nave had provided stabling for their horses. The altar was defended from sacrilege, Lord Grey standing with drawn sword before it. The Chancellor determined to hold the Chapter meeting on his own, and after recording the devastation, adjourned!

July 8, 1685   Bishop Mews preached at Wells before the execution of several rebels.

July 14, 1685   James II, finding the Roman Catholic

priests he had sent rejected, directed Ken to the Tower to prepare the Duke of Monmouth for his death by execution. He and Bishop Turner watched with him through the night.

July 15, 1685   Ken was amongst the divines accompanying the Duke of Monmouth to the scaffold.

August 9, 1685   Despite all these events, Ken had found time for his pastoral work and now published his *Practice of Divine Love, being an Exposition of the Church Catechism.* This major work began his campaign towards the restoration of training in the Christian religion as understood by the Church of England. Later the same year, he found time to prepare and issue Directions for Prayer for the Diocese of Bath and Wells.

Thou shalt not Kill

O my God, O my Love, I renounce, and detest, and bewail, as odious and offensive to thee, as directly opposite to thy love, and to the love of my neighbour, for thy sake:

All duels and unlawful war;

All doing hurt to the body and life of my neighbour, directly by wounding or murdering him, indirectly by contriving or employing others to harm him;

All the ways of procuring abortion;

All malice and envy, hatred and revenge, contention and cruelty;

All injury and violence, all rash, causeless, immoderate or implacable anger, or contumelious speaking or reviling;

All wilful vexing, grieving or disquieting him,

All threatening, ill wishes or curses;

All needless endangering ourselves, and self-murder,

All murdering of souls by encouraging, ensnaring, tempting, commanding them to sin.

All the least tendencies towards any of these impieties. From all these and the like hateful violations of thy love, and of the love of my neighbour, and from the vengeance they justly deserve, O my God, O my Love, deliver me, and all faithful people.

O my God, O my Love, I earnestly pray that thy love, and the love of our neighbour, may so prevail over our hearts, that we may sadly lament and abhor all these abominations, and may never more provoke thee.

O my God, O my Love, let thy unwearied and tender love to me make my love unwearied and tender to my neighbour and zealous to procure, promote and preserve his health and safety and happiness and life that he may be better able to serve and to love thee.

O my God, O my Love, make me like thy own self, all meekness and benignity, all goodness and sweetness, all gentleness and long suffering.

Fill me full of good wishes and compassions, of liberality in alms-giving, according to my abilities, and of readiness to succour and relieve, and comfort, and rescue, and pray for all, whom thy love, or their own necessities, or miseries, or dangers recommend to my charity.

O let thy love, thou God of love, make me peaceful and reconcilable, always ready to return good for evil, to repay injuries with kindness, and easy to forgive, unless in those instances where the impunity of the criminal would be injustice or cruelty to the public.

O thou Lover of souls, let thy love raise in me a compassionate zeal to save the life, the eternal life of souls; and by fraternal, and affectionate, and seasonable advice or exhortation, or correction, to reclaim the wicked, and to win them to love thee.

O my God, O my Love, let thy all-powerful love abound in my heart, and in the hearts of all that profess thy name, that in all these, and in all other possible instances of duty, our lives may be continually employed to love thee, and for thy sake to love our neighbour, and to excite our neighbour to love thee.

From 'An Exposition on the Church Catechism
or The Practice of Divine Love'

September 1685   Wells Assizes was presided over by Judge Jeffreys. Of 500 prisoners, 97 were condemned to death and 385 to transportation. Ken interceded with the Judge in vain. Earlier he had some success by appealing to the King to stop some of the brutalities of martial law as enforced, amongst others, by Colonel Percy Kirke, with whom Ken had crossed swords at Tangier. Now, the Bishop did what he could to relieve the worst suffering of prisoners awaiting death or transportation.

My Lords, in King James's time, there were about a thousand or more imprison'd in my Diocese, who were engag'd in the rebellion of the Duke of Monmouth; and many of them were such which I had reason to believe to be ill men, and void of all religion; and yet for all that, I thought it my duty to relieve them. 'Tis well known to the Diocese, that I visited them night and day, and I thank God I supply'd them with necessaries myself, as far as I could, and encouraged others to do the same; and yet King James never found the least fault with me.

Ken describes the help he gave in 1685 to relieve the suffering of the imprisoned rebels. The passage occurs in his answer to the charge that he has done wrong a decade later in making a charitable appeal for the needs of dispossessed clergy and their families. He was summoned before the Privy Council.

October 6, 1685　　Rev. John Hickes, a Dissenting Minister, and brother of the Dean of Worcester, was executed at Glastonbury. Thomas Ken allowed burial in the church there.

October 18, 1685　　The Edict of Fontainebleau revoked the Edict of Nantes which had allowed freedom of worship to the French Hugenots. A flood of refugees fled to England and Ken was active in assisting their relief.

The events set out in diary form all occurred in the short space of twelve months: and stormy times were ahead. Meantime, life at the Bishop's Palace was very different from that in the days of Bishop Mews. No inaugural banquet for local notables marked Ken's accession: instead, he sent the funds saved towards the rebuilding of St. Paul's Cathedral in London. His predecessor had entertained the gentry with liberal hospitality: Ken invited twelve poor people of Wells to Sunday lunch when he was in residence. He set up schools in the towns so that children could learn the catechism; he provided books so the clergy had no excuse for not doing their job. He tried, but failed, to set up a workhouse, which he thought would help relieve some of the worst poverty and idleness. He took seriously the *Articles of Visitation and Enquiry*, which sought to ensure that there was done what should be done by the Church of England in every parish. He continued to preach in London from time to time, usually controversially.

His majesty in these his letters patent, which I now send you, having given a fresh and great assurance of his graciousness to his own subjects, in showing himself so very gracious to Protestant strangers, and having required me to give a particular recommendation and command to my brethren of the clergy within my diocese, to advance this so pious and charitable a work; I think it my duty, with my utmost zeal to further so godlike a charity; and I do therefore strictly enjoin you, that you most affectionately and earnestly persuade, exhort, and stir up all under your care to contribute freely and cheerfully to the relief of these distressed Christians . . .

From Bishop Ken's encyclical letter of 1686 on behalf of the Relief Fund for French Protestant refugees.

> By various names we thy Perfections call,
> But pure, unfathom'd Love, exhausts them all;
> By Love all things were made, and are sustain'd,
> Love all things, to allure man's love, ordain'd;
> Love vengeance from laps'd human race suspends,
> Love, our salvation, when provok'd, intends . . .
> 　　　　　*From 'God's Attributes: God is Love'*

In April 1687, a little more than two years after his enthronement, King James II issued his first *Gracious Declaration to All His Loving Subjects for Liberty of Conscience*. Anabaptists, Quakers, and other Dissenters thanked the King for his indulgence. James II had also been busy appointing Romanists to positions of influence. The following Lent, Ken preached a stunning sermon critical of many different political ploys being carried on by different pressure groups. In April 1688, the King issued a second letter of indulgence, directing it should be read in churches and chapels through the land. Many were to refuse, including Bishop Ken. His reason was not concerned with its content but its legality.

For after all the frequent and pressing Endeavours that were used in each of (the four last reigns), to reduce this Kingdom to an exact conformity in Religion, it is visible the Success has not answered the Design, and that the difficulty is invincible; We therefore out of our Princely Care and Affection unto all Our Loving Subjects, that they may live at Ease and Quiet, and for the increase of Trade, and incouragement of Strangers, have thought fit by vertue of Our Royal Prerogative, to issue forth this Our Declaration of Indulgence; making no doubt of the Concurrence of Our Two Houses of Parliament, when We shall think it convenient for them to Meet.

From 'Gracious Declaration to All His Loving Subjects for Liberty of Conscience'

The King was using a power which had been deemed illegal by Parliament. The Archbishop of Canterbury, with Ken and five other bishops petitioned the King. The King called the Petition an act of rebellion. 'I will have my Declaration published'. 'We have two duties to perform,' answered Ken 'our duty to God and our duty to your Majesty. We honour you, but we fear God'. 'Have I deserved this?' said the King. 'I, who have been such a friend to your Church! I did not expect this from some of you. I will be obeyed. My Declaration shall be published. You are trumpeters of sedition. What do you do here? Go to your dioceses and see that I am obeyed!'

'Tis Theodorodunum, near whose Wells
Edmund's best friend and God's dear Fav'rite dwells;
The city by proud Mendippe Hills surveyed,
Its treasure, shelter, pasture, and its shade;
In ancient time Arviragus there reign'd,
Against the Roman force his Crown maintain'd;
That Town Arimathean Joseph bless'd,
Before he was of Avalon possess'd.
There first the Sun of Righteousness arose,
For saving Truth the Island to dispose;
The City, for refreshing Springs renown'd,
Which fertilise the neighbouring Country round;
Heaven in that Type would to all Albion shew,
That living Waters thence should overflow:
King Ina there a goodly Temple rear'd,
To the bless'd Andrew's name, which he rever'd.

Thomas Ken: From 'Edmund'. In the story of this East Anglian prince, Ken tells of a visit to Wells, where he falls in love with the saintly Hilda. Theodorodunum is an ancient name for Wells, whose Cathedral Church, dedicated to St. Andrew, was founded by King Ina.

Stripes, labours, prisons, stonings, blows,
Deaths frequent, confluential woes,
Thieves, *pagans*, the apostate crew,
And spiteful *Jew*.

– – – – –

Fatigues, and shipwrecks on the deep,
Cold, nakedness, and want of sleep,
Thirst, hunger, all the grievous ills,
Which *Hell* instills.

Thomas Ken: From 'Of St. Paul'

Meanwhile someone had leaked the text of the Bishops' petition to the general public. The following Sunday, the Declaration was read in but four churches throughout London. The King decided to prosecute the seven petitioners for seditious libel. They were summoned to appear before the King (with Judge Jeffreys of the Bloody Assizes assisting) on June 8th. The proceedings led to a formal warning they would be prosecuted for a misdemeanour and must appear before the Court of the King's Bench. They were directed to provide their own recognizances, but refused, saying that as Peers of the Realm, all they need do was to give their word of honour to appear. They were resolved *to maintain the rights of the Peerage, as well as those of the Church; being equally bound to oppose all innovations, both in Government and Religion.* Judge Jeffreys threatened them with the Tower. They replied *they were ready to go withersoever the King might be pleased to send them, that they hoped that the King of kings would be their protector and their judge; they feared nothing from men; for, having acted according to law and their own consciences, no punishment should be able to shake their resolution.*

So the seven were ferried by river, for fear of riots in the streets, in one of the King's barges to the Tower. They went there not in fact for refusing to read the Declaration of Indulgence, or even for refusing to withdraw their petition: but on the technicality of their privileges as peers. When, a week later, the Court ruled they were mistaken on this count, then they willingly agreed to enter recognizances. But the general public were not so concerned with the minutiae of the law: they were almost all on the side of the Bishops. The men of Cornwall revived the burden of an old ballad:

'And have they fixed the where and when,
And must Trelawney die?
Then thirty thousand Cornishmen
Will know the reason why.'

THE SEVEN BISHOPS COMMITTED TO THE TOWER IN 1688

Bishop Trelawney of Bristol was one of the accused when the trial took place on the 29th June when the Lesson for the Day told of the Apostle Peter who, because he had said he must obey God rather than man, had been cast into prison and had been delivered by the ministration of an angel. The angel took the form of the jury who declared them 'Not Guilty' on the second day of the trial. The populace were overjoyed. Portraits of the Bishops became best-sellers overnight. No less than eight different medals were struck to commemorate their acquittal.

A MIDNIGHT HYMN

Lord, now my Sleep does me forsake,
The sole possession of me take;
Let no vain fancy me illude,
No one impure desire intrude.

Blest Angels! while we silent lie,
Your Hallelujahs sing on high,
You, ever wakeful near the Throne,
Prostrate, adore the Three in One.

I now, awake, do with you joyn,
To praise our God in Hymns Divine:
With you in Heav'n I hope to dwell,
And bid the Night and World farewell.

My Soul, when I shake off this dust
Lord, in Thy Arms I will entrust;
O make me Thy peculiar care,
Some heav'nly Mansion me prepare.

Give me a place at Thy Saints' feet,
Or some fall'n Angel's vacant seat;
I'll strive to sing as loud as they,
Who sit above in brighter day.

O may I always ready stand,
With my Lamp burning in my hand;
May I in sight of Heav'n rejoyce,
Whene'er I hear the Bridegroom's voice!

Glory to Thee in light arraid,
Who light Thy dwelling place hast made,
An immense Ocean of bright beams,
From Thy All-glorious Godhead streams.

The Sun, in its Meridian height,
In very darkness in Thy sight:
My Soul, O lighten, and enflame,
With Thought and Love of Thy great name.

Blest Jesu, Thou, on Heav'n intent,
Whole Nights hast in Devotion spent,
But I, frail Creature, soon am tir'd,
And all my Zeal is soon expir'd.

My Soul, how canst thou weary grow
Of ante-dating Heav'n below,
In sacred Hymns, and Divine Love,
Which will Eternal be above?

Shine on me, Lord, new life impart,
Fresh ardours kindle in my Heart;
One ray of Thy All-quick'ning light
Dispels the sloth and clouds of night.

Lord, lest the Tempter me surprize,
Watch over Thine own Sacrifice,
All loose, all idle Thoughts cast out,
And make my very Dreams devout.

Praise God, from whom all Blessings flow,
Praise Him, all Creatures here below,
Praise Him above y'Angelick Host,
Praise Father, Son, and Holy Ghost.

The version of Ken's 'Midnight Hymn' printed in the
Winchester 'Manual' of 1697

That 30th June marked another event memorable in the history of England and significant in the life of Bishop Ken. Some of the chief nobles and statesmen (though but one Bishop) sent a memorial to William of Orange in The Hague, begging him to come and defend their religion and their liberties.

At the end of the summer, the King learned of the expedition William was preparing and sent for the Bishops. They had an inconsequential meeting on 28th September with their monarch: Ken was angered at its lack of content. The Bishops then presented the King on 3rd October with what amounted to nothing less than a Bill of Rights.

What steps the King took in response to this were too little and too late; on 18th December, James was forced to flee and William was lodged at St. James; the same William whom

Ken as a young man had dared to charge with abusing his wife. Archbishop Sancroft called the Bishops to London. What should they do? Ken's position was clear. He was bound by his oath of allegiance to James. He would go along with expediences provided James was not deprived of his throne.

On 22nd January 1689, the Convention to settle William's position met. Ken voted in every division for a Regency. Ken acquiesced in the unanimous address to the Prince, confirming him in the administration of affairs. On 31st January, Ken voted against the declaration that the throne was vacant.

In the end, when all the negotiations between Lords, Commons and William were completed, that question was put again to the Lords. The motion *that the throne was vacant* was carried by 62 to 47. The resolution *that William and Mary should be declared King and Queen* was carried without a division, but 37 peers including 12 bishops, of whom Ken was one, entered their protest against it. Ken remained in the Lords on the ensuing days, voting against the measures which followed from the principal resolution. On 12th February 1689, four years after his appointment, he left the House of Lords and public life.

> How God unchang'd could change ordain,
> Is not my duty to explain;
> Had I of God the blissful sight,
> I then should see how they unite;
> God in himself has taught in Holy Writ,
> Prescience, and liberty to co-admit.
> *From 'God's Attributes: Immutability'*

He did not hurry to leave his duties at Bath and Wells. He had until 1st August under the Act of Parliament to swear oaths to the new monarch before being suspended from exercise of office. He however remained at Wells able to exercise his great gift of pastoral caring until April 1691 when the Government finally lost patience and he, and those other bishops who had refused to swear the oath, were replaced. When Dr. Richard Kidder was nominated as the new bishop, Thomas Ken went into the Cathedral, took his place in the Bishop's chair and asserted his right as the true and canonical Bishop of Bath and Wells. A home was provided for him by Lord Weymouth at Longleat. So began an exile in his own native land. He refused to plot with the other bishops who had refused to take the oath and he respected those, including his host, who took a different view.

> Short of my Aim I infinitely fall;
> I love Thee, Lord, I love, and that is all.
> *Thomas Ken of Apparent Failure*

The Non-Jurors, as those who refused to take the oath were known, found Bishop Ken's unwillingness to fight for their cause weak-kneed and vacillating. Ken saw his role as trying to live at peace with all men, acting as a spiritual director to those non-jurors who sought his guidance. He occasionally accepted invitations to preach; but would not take part in the public prayers. In July 1695, he did join in a letter with the other deprived bishops seeking the goodwill of Christian people in providing funds for the families of all Christians deprived of their income through refusal to recognise the new King. He, himself, had little enough to live on, always having given away what came his way.

This letter led to his being summoned to appear before the Privy Council, who scented a plot against the authorities. He argued his intent was entirely charitable in regard to the needy, and was released from custody by an Order in Council. He went back to his quiet life, reading, writing some poetry, and visiting those friends in whose homes he was still welcome, including that of the Rev. Isaak Walton Junior at Poulshot near Salisbury, and an Anglican community established by two sisters known as the good ladies of Naish, in a house with fine views over the Bristol Channel. This was a home from home for him.

When Queen Anne succeeded William in 1702, she accepted Lord Weymouth's suggestion that Bishop Kidder who had succeeded Ken at Bath and Wells, should go to Carlisle, so Ken could be re-instated at Bath and Wells. Perhaps with the death of James II the previous year, he would feel able to accept. He declined the offer, saying he was too old and infirm to re-enter the episcopal fray. The following year Kidder and his wife were killed during a great gale when a stack of chimneys fell through the palace roof into their bedroom.

Did you subscribe this paper?

My Lords, I thank God I did, and it had a very happy effect; for the will of my blessed Redeemer was fulfilled by it; and what we were not able to do ourselves, was done by others; the hungry were fed, and the naked were clothed; and to feed the hungry, to clothe the naked, and to visit those who are sick or in prison, is that plea which all your Lordships, as well as I, as far as you have had opportunities, must make for yourselves at the Great Day. And that which you must all plead at God's tribunal for your eternal Absolution, shall not, I hope, be made my condemnation here.

Thomas Ken replies to the Privy Council

Nor eye, ear, thought can take the height,
To which my song is taking flight
Yet rais'd on humble wing,
My guess of heav'n I'll sing.
'Tis Love's reward; and Love is fir'd,
By guessing at the bliss desir'd.

Guess then, at saints' eternal lot,
By due considering what 'tis not.
No mis'ry, want, or care;
No death, no darkness there;
No troubles, storms, sighs, groans or tears
No injury, pains, sickness, fears.

There, souls no disappointments meet;
No vanities, the choice to cheat:
Nothing that can defile;
No hypocrite, no guile,
No need of pray'r, or what implies
Or absence, or vacuities.

There, no ill conscience gnaws the breast;
No tempters, Holy Souls infest
No curse, no weeds, no toil;
No errors, to embroil.
No lustful thought can enter in,
Or possibility of sin.

From all vexations here below,
The region of sin, death, and woe
Song to your utmost stress
Now elevate your guess:
Sing, what in sacred lines you read,
Of bliss for pious souls decreed.

They dwell in pure ecstatic Light,
Of God Triune have blissful sight;
Of fontal Love, who gave
God filial, Man to save:
Of Jesus' Love, who Death sustain'd,
By which the saints their glory gain'd.

Of Love co-breath'd the boundless source,
From which saints love derives its force,
Within the gracious shine
Of the co-glorious Trine,
The saints in happy mansions rest,
Of all they can desire posses'd.

Saints bodies there the sun out-vie,
Temper'd to feel the joys on high
Bright body, and pure mind,
In rapture unconfin'd,
Capacities expand, till fit
Deluge of Godhead to admit.

In all-sufficient bliss they joy,
Duration in sweet hymns employ:
With angels they converse
Their loves, and joys rehearse;
Taste suavities of Love immense,
Of all delights full confluence.

With God's own Son they reign co-heirs:
Each saint with him in glory shares;
Like Godhead, happy, pure,
Against all change secure,
In boundless joys they sabbatize;
Which Love Triune will eternise.

By boundless Love, for souls refin'd,
Are joys unspeakable design'd:
When I those joys imbibe,
I then may them describe,
Joys to full pitch will hymn excite
When from sensation I endite.

Thomas Ken: From
'Preparatives for Death: Heaven'

You short-liv'd, little, despicable Thing,
You that have nothing certain but your Sting.
Thomas Ken of the World

THOMAS KEN *attributed to F. Scheffer*

The See was offered to Ken's long-standing friend George Hooper. Ken had never recognised Kidder's bishopric: but now was ready to resign the position he maintained in canon law he still held. He did not share the view of many non-jurors that the whole of the Church of England had become heretical by adhering to a usurper to the throne. He was glad that the people of the Diocese would at last be cared for by a faithful pastor and teacher.

Know, son! 'tis not bare reading
I commend;
You must choice hours in
meditation spend.
From 'Hymnotheo'

His last years were made more comfortable by a pension of
£200 from the Government, in acknowledgement of which
he wrote a gracious letter to Queen Anne. In many ways
though, he remained an outcast, whom non-jurors thought
had betrayed the cause; and who had rejected the way of
the majority when William III was welcomed. He showed
however his ability still to enjoy friendship with those whose
views he did not share, including the young poet Elizabeth
Rowe, whose works were edited after her death by Isaac
Watts. He wrote a series of poems to two grand-daughters of
Lord Weymouth, whom he affectionately addressed as *Dear
Chickens*. His last years were of prolonged physical suffering,
which he recorded in a series of poems called *Anodynes*. The
adjective means *having the power to assuage pain*.

> O cruel Pain, you break the truce,
> And all your lambent fires unsluce;
> In vain, I strive from you to turn,
> By motion you more raging burn;
> Ten thousand atoms with sharp points
> Now poignard my resistless joints.

— — — — —

> My curtain oft I draw away,
> Longing to see the morning ray;
> But when the morning gilds the skies,
> The morning no relief supplies;
> To me, alas! the morning light
> Is as afflictive as the night.

— — — — —

> Pain, then exert your last effort,
> Since God proportions his support,
> I your insulting shall not dread,
> Though you torment me in my bed;
> The greater rage you on me vent,
> God will his aids the more augment.
>
> *Thomas Ken: From 'Anodynes'*

Just before his death, he encouraged other moderate non-
jurors to rejoin the Church of England and intended as a
symbolic act to return to his Cathedral at Wells to take Holy
Communion. Ill health prevented this. He died at Longleat on
19th March, 1711. He had entertained twelve poor men on
Sundays in the Bishop's Palace. Twelve poor men carried his
coffin, without pomp or ceremony beyond the Order for
Burial in the Liturgy of the Church of England, to his grave
at Frome, the nearest parish to Longleat in his old Diocese.

As for my Religion, I die in the Holy Catholick and Apostolick
Faith, professed by the whole Church before the disunion of East
and West; more particularly I dye in the Communion of the
Church of England, as it stands distinguished from our Papall and
Puritan Innovations, and as it adheres to the doctrines of the
Cross.

From Thomas Ken's Will

Ken's pictures of an ideal priest and an ideal bishop are found
in his poetry: they form an appropriate postscript.

Give me the priest these graces shall possess;
Of an ambassador the just address,
A father's tenderness, a shepherd's care,
A leader's courage, which the cross can bear,
A ruler's arm, a watchman's wakeful eye,
A pilot's skill the helm in storms to ply,
A fisher's patience and a lab'rer's toil,
A guide's dexterity to disembroil,
A prophet's inspiration from above,
A teacher's knowledge, and a Saviour's love.
Give me the priest, a light upon a hill,
Whose rays his whole circumference can fill,
In God's own Word, and sacred learning vers'd,
Deep in the study of the heart immers'd,
Who in such souls can the disease descry,
And wisely fit restoratives apply.

— — — — —

Bishops are priests sublim'd, are angels stiled,
And they should live, like angels, undefil'd;
In an enlighten'd love should spend their days,
In pure intention, love, obedience, praise.
Should here on earth be guardians to the fold,
And God, by contemplation still behold.
High priests had, on the plate fix'd on their breast,
For a memorial, the tribes' names imprest;
Thus every bishop on his breast should grave
The names of those whom he is charg'd to save,
That he may lead and warn them day and night,
And in his prayers their ghostly wants recite;
That he may ever lodge them near his heart,
And in their sorrows bear paternal part.
We, the more spirits we from dross refine,
In higher thrones and brighter rays shall shine.

JUBILATE   7.6.7.6. D.   C. H. H. PARRY, 1848-1918

A-men.

Sometimes a light surprises
  The Christian while he sings;
It is the Lord who rises
  With healing in His wings:
When comforts are declining,
  He grants the soul again
A season of clear shining,
  To cheer it after rain.

In holy contemplation,
  We sweetly then pursue
The theme of God's salvation,
  And find it ever new.
Set free from present sorrow,
  We cheerfully can say,
E'en let the unknown to-morrow
  Bring with it what it may:

It can bring with it nothing
  But He will bear us through;
Who gives the lilies clothing
  Will clothe His people too:
Beneath the spreading heavens
  No creature but is fed;
And He who feeds the ravens
  Will give His children bread.

Though vine nor fig-tree neither,
  Their wonted fruit should bear,
Though all the field should wither,
  Nor flocks nor herds be there,
Yet God the same abiding,
  His praise shall tune my voice;
For, while in Him confiding,
  I cannot but rejoice.

William Cowper, 1731 - 1800

William Cowper

William Cowper came of stock which had known trouble. His grandfather Spencer Cowper had been unjustly accused of the murder of a Quaker girl who had fallen in love with him: although he was found not guilty and his innocence was beyond doubt it was a traumatic experience for both grandfather and father, who was sometime chaplain to King George II.

WILLIAM COWPER *by Romney*

COWPER'S BIRTHPLACE – *Berkhamsted Rectory*

William was born on 15th November 1731 to the Reverend John Cowper and his wife Anne, a daughter of Ludham Hall in Norfolk, at the Rectory House at Great Berkhamsted. He was the fourth child of the marriage; but Spencer, Ann and John had died in infancy. William was a weakling of a child: but the earliest days seem to have been happy ones with his mother's care being a support remembered in later life. His mother's death in childbed following the birth of his brother John, left William bereft just before his sixth birthday. At Dr. Pitman's boarding school he suffered two years of severe bullying, leading to the expulsion of his chief tormentor. He was himself saved from further attendance by a condition in which his eyes were covered in specks: and this painful affliction led to residence in 1739 and 1740 with an eminent oculist, Mrs. Disney. The defect was to disappear as he recovered from an attack of smallpox in his early teens.

> Oh that those lips had language! Life has pass'd
> With me but roughly since I heard thee last.
> Those lips are thine — thy own sweet smiles I see,
> The same that oft in childhood solac'd me;
> Voice only fails, else, how distinct they say,
> 'Grieve not, my child, chase all thy fears away!'
>
> *Part of William Cowper's poem, 'On the Receipt of my Mother's Picture out of Norfolk', written when receiving a gift of her portrait from a cousin.*

When he was ten, he attended Westminster School, where he enjoyed some protection from fellow-scholar Warren Hastings, who was later to be impeached for and acquitted of corruption and cruelty during service as Governor-General of India. Cowper penned some lines on the historic trial of his schoolday associate. Whilst there is no evidence that he was especially unhappy at Westminster, he seems to have a poor view of English public schools according to his poem *Tirocinium* published in 1784. William described his school as the place where he learned to be *an adept in the infernal art of lying*, a necessary practice to explain to masters why work had not been done. The truth was that Cowper spent time intended for school preparation writing poems in English and Latin. Surprisingly for a lad of poor physique, he seems also to have enjoyed football and cricket.

> Hastings! I knew thee young, and of a mind,
> While young, humane, conversable, and kind,
> Nor can I well believe thee, gentle *then*,
> Now grown a villain, and the *worst* of men.
> But rather some suspect, who have oppress'd
> And worried thee, as not themselves the *best*.
> *To Warren Hastings, Esq.*

> Public schools 'tis public folly feeds . . .
> . . . . .
> If it chance, as sometimes chance it will,
> That, though school-bred, the boy be virtuous still.
> Lines from 'Tirocinium', concerned with recommending private tuition in preference to a school education.

He formed a friendship with the *slovenly, dirty and good-natured* fifth-form master Vincent Bourne. Later in life, he was to translate Bourne's Latin verse into English, including poems about glow-worm, jackdaw, parrot, robin, silkworm and snail. Charles Churchill, Robert Lloyd and Colman the Elder were all schoolfriends. He maintained a life-time correspondence with Walter Bagot (they met in Olney in 1785): but he was to mourn his best friend, who as Sir William Russell, died young. *Still, still I mourn, with each returning day* wrote Cowper on his death, a loss coupled in the poem with the solitude of permanent separation from his sweetheart.

> Belinda and her bird! 'tis rare
> To meet with such a well match'd pair,
> The language and the tone,
> Each character in ev'ry part
> Sustain'd with so much grace and art,
> And both in unison.
>
> When children first begin to spell,
> And stammer out a syllable,
> We think them tedious creatures;
> But difficulties soon abate,
> When birds are to be taught to prate,
> And women are the teachers.
> *From 'The Parrot'*

Leaving school at the age of seventeen he spent nine months at the old 'Pastoral House' as he called Berkhamsted Rectory, back in the woods and fields he loved. He was then articled to Mr. Chapman, an attorney, to learn all about practising the law. Much of his time was spent at his Uncle Ashley's home in Southampton Row with fellow-clerk Edward Thurlow, a future Lord Chancellor. However, to quote Cowper, they spent much of their time, supposedly at study, *constantly employed from morning to night in giggling and making giggle* with the daughters of the house. He fell in love with his cousin Theodora, but her father refused to allow them to marry. Both were to remain unmarried: there seems though little doubt that many anonymous gifts to William throughout his life came from his cousin.

William was once a bashful youth,
His modesty was such,
That one might say (to say the truth)
He rather had too much.

Some said that it was want of sense,
And others, want of spirit,
(So blest a thing is impudence,)
While others could not bear it.

But some a different notion had,
And at each other winking,
Observ'd that though he little said,
He paid it off with thinking.

Howe'er, it happen'd, by degrees,
He mended and grew perter,
In company was more at ease,
And dress'd a little smarter:

Nay, now and then would look quite gay,
As other people do;
And sometimes said, or tried to say,
A witty thing or so.

He eyed the women, and made free
To comment on their shapes,
So that there was, or seem'd to be,
No fear of a relapse.

The women said, who thought him rough,
But now no longer foolish,
The creature may do well enough,
But wants a deal of polish.

At length, improv'd from head to heel,
'Twere scarce too much to say,
No dancing bear was so genteel,
Or half so dégagé.

Now, that a miracle so strange
May not in vain be shown,
Let the dear maid who wrought the change
E'er claim him for her own.

                    Of Himself

32

> Wherefore with my utmost art
> I will sing thee,
> And the cream of all my heart
> I will bring thee.
> Though my sins against me cried,
> Thou didst clear me;
> And alone, when they replied,
> Thou didst hear me.
>
> *George Herbert*

He was in his early twenties when he suffered a fit of great depression. He turned in his melancholy to the poetry of George Herbert, and although he found this helpful, a relative dissuaded him from further study of this religious poet for fear it would turn him even more into himself. He tried other religious exercises: but the despair suddenly lifted while on a yachting expedition with Sir Thomas Hesketh, whose fiancée was Theodora's sister, Harriet.

Cowper had by then purchased rooms in the Inner Temple and on 14th June 1754 he was called to the Bar. He seems at this time not to have lacked friends (or at least associates). With six others, he formed the Nonsense Club, a group of Westminster men who dined together weekly. Two of them started *The Connoisseur* and William submitted a few papers. He also produced 'several halfpenny ballads, two or three of which had the honour to become popular'.

In 1756, his father died and he said goodbye for ever to the beloved parsonage of childhood days. The following year he translated two satires from Horace: but of briefs, there seem to be none. He obtained a small income from 1759 as a Commissioner of Bankrupts at £60 per year. He did little writing either though he read much. He translated some Voltaire in 1762 but his financial circumstances were by then straitened. No wonder then that at first he was delighted at the idea that his kinsman, Major Ashley Cowper should offer him the well-paid appointment of Clerk of the Journals of the House of Lords. Once he learned however that he would be obliged to qualify himself at the Bar of the House, he became terrified by the prospect. This time the breakdown was complete and there were three suicide attempts. He found succour at the Collegion Insanorum, a private mental hospital, kept by Dr. Nathaniel Cotton at St. Albans. The doctor was a poet as well as a medical man; and Cowper and Cotton struck up a good relationship which led to William staying on at St. Albans for several months after his condition had improved sufficiently to make a continued stay non-essential. In a sermon preached by Revd. Samuel Greatheed on Cowper's death, he indicated *How blest thy creature is, O God*, eventually published in *Olney Hymns*, as written under the influence of Cowper's conversion that year.

> I was not only treated by him with the greatest tenderness while I was ill, and attended with the utmost diligence, but when my reason was restored to me, and I had so much need of a religious friend to converse with, to whom I could open my mind upon the subject without reserve, I could hardly have found a fitter person for the purpose . . . The doctor was as ready to administer relief to me in this article likewise, and as well qualified to do it, as in that which was more immediately his province.
>
> *William Cowper describing Dr. Nathaniel Cotton to Lady Hesketh*

Cowper felt however that he must resign his Commissionership and, save for some rent from his chambers he became wholly dependant on friends and relatives, with the help of Mr. Joseph Hill, who guided him in money matters with great kindness. But what he needed even more than money was a home in the country. He chose Huntingdon, so as not to be too far from his brother John in Cambridge. A temporary lodging with the Unwin family intended for a fortnight was to last for twenty-two years. The Reverend Morley Unwin was 'a Parson Adams in simplicity' but it was his wife Mary who was to play so significant a part in Cowper's future life. The son of the house was also to carry on an extensive correspondence with the poet and hymn-writer. The therapy of gardening was often to help Cowper to recuperate after periods of despair, and he sought to increase the variety of flowers in the home of his adoption. It was here that Cowper wrote *Hark my soul! it is the Lord*; describing the 'she bear' hymn, Percy Dearmer stresses the need to avoid a sentimental tune. He used FREUEN WIR UNS in *Songs of Praise*. Other choices have included ST. BEES, PETERSFIELD, LANCASHIRE, SAVANNAH and CHRIST CHAPEL. The hymn was thought worthy of translation into Italian and Latin.

An honest man, close-button'd to the chin,
Broad-cloth without, and a warm heart within.
From Cowper's poem 'Epistle to Joseph Hill'

I am become a great Florist and Shrub-doctor. If the Major can make up a small paquet of seeds that will make a figure in a garden where we have little else besides Jessamine and Honeysuckle, such a paquet I mean as may be put in one's fob. I will promise to take great care of them, as I ought to value natives of the Park. They must not be such however as to require great skill in the management for at present I have no skill to spare.
William Cowper writing to a relative on 14th March, 1767.

Hark, my soul! it is the Lord;
'Tis thy Saviour, hear his word;
Jesus speaks and speaks to thee:
'Say, poor sinner, lov'st thou me?

I delivered thee when bound,
And, when wounded, healed thy wounds;
Sought thee wandering, set thee right;
Turned thy darkness into light.'

Can a woman's tender care
Cease toward the child she bare?
Yes, she may forgetful be;
Yet will I remember thee.

Mine is an unchanging love,
Higher than the heights above,
Deeper than the depths beneath,
Free and faithful, strong as death.

Thou shalt see My glory soon,
When the work of grace is done;
Partner of My throne shalt be,
Say, poor sinner, lov'st thou Me?'

Lord, it is my chief complaint
That my love is weak and faint,
Yet I love Thee, and adore.
O for grace to love Thee more.

Lovest thou Me?

To find those I love, clearly and strongly persuaded of evangelical truth, gives me a pleasure superior to any this world can afford me.

William Cowper to his cousin. 11th March 1767

MARY UNWIN

In 1767, the Revd. Morley Unwin was killed in a riding accident and his wife resolved to leave Huntingdon. Whilst considering where to make their new home, the Reverend John Newton called at the request of a friend of the Unwin's son. They wished to live in a town where they would be under an evangelical minister: who better than this remarkable slaver turned priest appointed three years earlier to a curacy at Olney? So Mrs. Unwin and her daughter and her lodger moved, first to stay with John Newton and his wife, Mary at the Vicarage and then to the house Orchard Side on the Market Square. The house is now a museum dedicated to Cowper and Newton.

Olney was described at the time as a rather low and dirty town, and there is no doubt that the lacemakers received very little pay. Over half of the inhabitants were paupers and gangs of ill-fed child savages roamed the streets. Cowper was to become a lay curate assisting John Newton in the parish work, especially active in visiting the sick and dying: he became Squire Cowper to the local community.

JOHN NEWTON – *stained glass window in Olney Parish Church*

Behind the house in Market Square is a delightful garden. A gravel path leads to a tiny building *not much bigger than a sedan chair* where Cowper spent many hours in what he called his Sulking Room. It had served a previous owner as a Smoking Room and, beneath a trap door in the floor, as a store for the bottles he used as an apothecary. Mrs. Aspray's orchard separated the poet's garden from that of the Vicarage.

THE SULKING ROOM

For more than a decade Cowper and Newton were frequent visitors to one another and they paid the owner of the orchard a guinea a year for the privilege of crossing his land rather than going round by the street. The area is known as Guinea Field to this day.

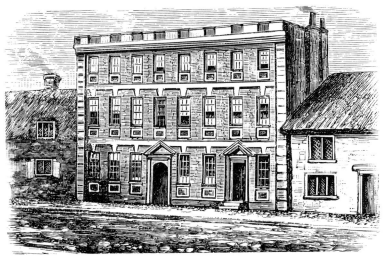

ORCHARD SIDE – *as it was in the days of William Cowper*

36

Oh! for a closer walk with God,
A calm and heav'nly frame,
A light to shine upon the road
That leads me to the Lamb!

The dearest idol I have known,
Whate'er that idol be;
Help me to tear it from Thy throne,
And worship only Thee.

From 'Walking with God'

I am no longer my own, but yours. Put me to what you will, rank me with whom you will; put me to doing, put me to suffering; let me be employed for you or laid aside for you, exalted for you or brought low for you; let me be full, let me be empty; let me have all things, let me have nothing; I freely and wholeheartedly yield all things to your pleasure and disposal. And now, glorious and blessed God, Father, Son and Holy Spirit, you are mine and I am yours. So be it. And the covenant now made on earth, let it be ratified in heaven. Amen.

*From the Methodist
Covenant Service*

Late in 1769 Mrs. Unwin was seriously ill and Cowper, awake before daybreak, and distressed that he might lose 'the chief of blessing I have met with in my journey' penned the text of *Oh! for a closer walk with God.* He explained his distress in a letter to a friend *O for no will but the will of my heavenly Father.* How many Methodists have struggled since the Annual Covenant Service with the difficulty of similar words of surrender! Cowper's hymn is commonly sung to CAITHNESS, CHESHIRE, BELMONT, and STRACATHRO.

Earlier that year, John Newton had moved the weekly prayer meeting to the great room in the great house, where 130 could be accommodated in comfort. For the first gathering in the new venue, Cowper wrote *Jesus, where'er thy people meet.* The line *Thy former mercies here renew* is a clear reference to the move and a verse, with its reference to the words from Isaiah *to stretch forth the curtains of thy habitation* has not survived for use in present-day house groups! Tunes used include REDHEAD No.4, ST. SEPULCHRE, ST. PETERSBURG, WAREHAM, WARRINGTON and SIMEON.

Jesus, where'er thy people meet,
There they behold thy mercy-seat;
Where'er they seek thee, thou art found,
And every place is hallowed ground.

For thou, within no walls confined,
Inhabitest the humble mind;
Such ever bring thee, where they come,
And going, take thee to their home.

Dear Shepherd of thy chosen few!
Thy former mercies here renew;
Here, to our waiting hearts, proclaim
The sweetness of thy saving name.

Here may we prove the power of prayer
To strengthen faith and sweeten care;
To teach our faint desires to rise,
And bring all heaven before our eyes.

Behold! at thy commanding word,
We stretch the curtain and the cord;
Come thou, and fill this wider space,
And bless us with a large increase.

Lord, we are few, but thou art near;
Nor short thine arm, nor deaf thine ear;
Oh rend the heav'ns, come quickly down,
And make a thousand hearts thine own!
On opening a place for social prayer

In 1770, William suffered the death of his young brother John whose will left William a small legacy. In 1771 John Newton was especially concerned with increasing signs of despondency in his friend, and, hopeful it would divert William's mind from his despair, suggested the extensive hymn-writing that would eventually become the volume of texts by the pair of them known as *Olney Hymns* published at the end of that decade. Many of Cowper's hymns were suggested by Newton's sermons: most were first sung either at the church or at the 'Great House'. One way in which Newton tried to keep up attendance at the weekly prayer-meeting there was by the promise of a new hymn each Tuesday!

. . . a desire of promoting the faith and comfort of sincere Christians . . . intended to perpetuate the remembrance of an intimate and endeared friendship.

From the preface to 'Olney Hymns' by Rev. John 'Amazing Grace' Newton.

THE GREAT HOUSE

Winter has a joy for me,
While the Saviour's charms I read,
Lowly, meek, from blemish free,
In the snow-drop's pensive head.
From 'I will praise the Lord at all times'

To keep the lamp alive
With oil we fill the bowl!
'Tis water makes the willow thrive,
And grace that feeds the soul.
From 'Dependance'

The saints should never be dismay'd
Nor sink in hopeless fear;
For when they least expect his aid,
The Saviour will appear.

This Abraham found, he rais'd the knife,
God saw, and said 'Forbear;
Yon ram shall yield his meaner life,
Behold the victim there.'

   · · · · ·

Wait for his seasonable aid,
And tho' it tarry wait:
The promise may be long delay'd,
But cannot come too late.

From 'Jehovah-Jireh,
The Lord will provide'

Heal us, Emmanuel, here we are,
Waiting to feel thy touch;
Deep-wounded souls to thee repair,
And Saviour, we are such.

From 'Jehovha-Rophi,
I am the Lord that healeth thee.'

God gives his mercies to be spent;
Your hoard will do your soul no good:
Gold is a blessing only lent,
Repaid by others giving food.

   · · · · ·

The joy that vain amusements give,
Oh! sad conclusion that it brings!
The honey of a crowded hive,
Defended by a thousand stings.

From 'Vanity of the world'

The Lord will happiness divine
On contrite hearts bestow:
Then tell me, gracious God, is mine
A contrite heart, or no?

   · · · · ·

Thy saints are comforted I know,
And love thy house of pray'r;
I therefore go where others go,
But find no comfort there.

Oh make this heart rejoice, or ache;
Decide this doubt for me;
And if it be not broken, break,
And heal it, if it be.

From 'The contrite heart'

'Write to Sardis, saith the Lord,
And write what he declares;
He whose Spirit, and whose word,
Upholds the seven stars:
All thy works and ways I search,
Find thy zeal and love decay'd:
Thou art call'd a living church,
But thou art cold and dead.'

From 'Sardis'

As much, when in the manger laid,
Almighty ruler of the sky;
As when the six days' works he made
Fill'd all the morning-stars with joy.

From 'Jehovah-Jesus'

O Lord, the pilot's part perform,
And guide and guard me thro' the storm;
Defend me from each threat'ning ill;
Control the waves, say, 'Peace, be still.'

Amidst the roaring of the sea,
My soul still hangs her hope on thee;
Thy constant love, thy faithful care,
Is all that saves me from despair.

. . . . .

Tho' tempest-toss'd and half a wreck,
My Saviour thro' the floods I seek;
Let neither winds nor stormy main,
Force back my shatter'd bark again.

From 'Temptation'

Sin enslav'd me many years,
And led me bound and blind;
Till at length a thousand fears
Came swarming o'er my mind.
Where, I said in deep distress,
Will these sinful pleasures end?
How shall I secure my peace,
And make the Lord my friend?

Friends and ministers said much
The gospel to enforce;
But my blindness still was such,
I chose a legal course:
Much I fasted, watch'd and strove,
Scarce would shew my face abroad,
Fear'd, almost, to speak or move,
A stranger still to God.

> Thus afraid to trust his grace,
> Long time did I rebel:
> Till, despairing of my case,
> Down at his feet I fell:
> Then my stubborn heart he broke,
> And subdu'd me to his sway;
> By a simple word he spoke,
> 'Thy sins are done away.'
>
> *The heart healed*
> *and changed by mercy*

There are no less than 348 texts in *Olney Hymns,* of which Cowper contributed 66, whilst Newton wrote 282. The volume is divided into three sections, the first linked to selected scripture passages, the second on seasons, ordinances, providences and creation, and the third on the rise, progress, changes and comforts of the spiritual life. Most of Cowper's texts were written in 1771 and 1772, the year he became engaged to Mrs. Mary Unwin.

Several of the hymn texts reveal Cowper's turmoil of mind and spirit. In January 1773, a new attack of lunacy led to the engagement being broken off. According to Greatheed's 1800 sermon, *our departed friend conceived some presentiment of this sad reverse as it drew near; and during a solitary walk in the fields, he composed a hymn.* In *God moves in a mysterious way* we catch a vivid picture of the storm of the battered mind with which Cowper craved a divine presence. Here was one of the fearful saints needing to find enough courage just to go on living. Here was experience of the bitter-tasting bud. Here was the feeble sense overwhelmed with the mystery of love, contradicted by his times of melancholia, yet ultimately trusted. Here was the crushing sense of guilt daring to hope for the smiling face behind a frowning providence.

> God moves in a mysterious way
> His wonders to perform;
> He plants his footsteps in the sea
> And rides upon the storm.
>
> .   .   .   .   .
>
> Ye fearful saints fresh courage take,
> The clouds ye so much dread
> Are big with mercy, and shall break
> In blessings on your head.

> Judge not the Lord by feeble sense,
> But trust him for his grace:
> Behind a frowning providence
> He hides a smiling face.
>
> His purposes will ripen fast,
> Unfolding every hour:
> The bud may have a bitter taste
> But sweet will be the flower.
>
> *From 'Light shining out of darkness'*

There was, too, plenty to be depressed about in Olney in the seventeen-seventies. The collapse of the hand-made lace trade led to even more terrible poverty amongst the cottagers and to business failures amongst householders. Nearly a century later, a story is told of a mill-girl singing the words *Ye fearful saints, fresh courage take* to fellow-workers in Lancashire when confronted with the news of factory closure during the cotton crisis of the eighteen-sixties. The tunes used for this hymn include LONDON NEW and IRISH.

The cattle fair at Olney took place in the Market Square outside Orchard Side. It was a noisy business and on the morning of the Easter Monday Fair, Cowper felt the strain of the bustle would be too much. He asked John Newton therefore whether he could come to the Vicarage to stay a short while and remained until the late spring of the following year.

At first, Cowper refused all medicine which might relieve his depression but eventually he acceded to remedies pressed on him by his cousin, Mrs. Judith Madan and was treated again by Dr. Cotton; eventually he was well enough to return to Orchard Side in May 1774. While away, Mrs. Unwin's daughter had married, and Mary and William had the house to themselves.

The Old Testament prophet Habakkuk had earlier provided Cowper with inspiration for a hymn which has comforted many Christians as they too emerge from a period of spiritual wilderness. Habakkuk's prayer for mercy remembers that although the Lord shows his wrath at a nation's misdeeds, he remains a God whose divine justice is matched with divine mercy. The prophet writes:

I have seen, O Lord, thy work.
In the midst of the years thou didst make thyself known,
and in thy wrath thou didst remember mercy.

and later:

He rises like the dawn,
with twin rays starting forth at his side;
the skies are the hiding-place of his majesty,
and the everlasting ways are for his swift flight.

So Cowper had written his hymn, *Sometimes a light
surprises*. Its last verse is a testimony to Cowper's expression
of ultimate trust in a loving and caring God who deserved
praise and adoration whatever life's journey might bring.
The old prophet wrote (using the New English Bible
translation)

Although the fig-tree does not burgeon,
the vines bear no fruit,
the olive-crop fails,
the orchards yield no food,
the fold is bereft of its flock
and there are no cattle in the stalls,
yet I will exult in the Lord
and rejoice in the God of my deliverance.

The hymn is usually sung to OFFERTORIUM, PETITION,
JUBILATE, LLANGLOFFAN, RHYDDID and BENTLEY.

It was however a gradual recovery. Cowper describes himself
in 1774 as *being much indisposed both in mind and body,
incapable of diverting myself with either company or books,
and yet in a condition that made some diversion necessary,
I was glad of any thing that would engage my attention
without fatiguing it*. The chosen diversion was a hare.
A leveret about three months old was the plaything of a
neighbour's children of which they had grown weary. Cowper
was soon offered several other hares and ended up in keeping
three.

Immediately commencing carpenter, I built them houses to sleep
in; each had a separate apartment, so contrived that their ordure
would pass through the bottom of it; an earthern pan placed
under each received whatsoever fell, which being duly emptied
and washed, they were thus kept perfectly sweet and clean. In
the day time they had the range of a hall, and at night retired
each to his own bed, never intruding into that of another.

Puss grew presently familiar, would leap into my lap, raise himself upon his hinder feet, and bite the hair from my temples. He would suffer me to take him up and to carry him about in my arms, and has more than once fallen fast asleep upon my knee. He was ill three days, during which time I nursed him, kept him apart from his fellows that they might not molest him, (for, like many other wild animals, they persecute one of their own species that is sick,) and by constant care and trying him with a variety of herbs, restored him to perfect health. No creature could be more grateful than my patient after his recovery; a sentiment which he most significantly expressed, by licking my hand, first the back of it, then the palm, then every finger separately, then between all the fingers, as if anxious to leave no part of it unsaluted; a ceremony which he never performed but once again upon a similar occasion. Finding him extremely tractable, I made it my custom to carry him always after breakfast into the garden, where he hid himself generally under the leaves of a cucumber vine, sleeping or chewing the cud till evening; in the leaves also of that vine he found a favourite repast. I had not long habituated him to this taste of liberty, before he began to be impatient for the return of the time when he might enjoy it. He would invite me to the garden by drumming upon my knee, and by a look of such expression as it was not possible to misinterpret. If this rhetoric did not immediately succeed, he would take the skirt of my coat between his teeth, and pull at it with all his force. Thus Puss might be said to be perfectly tamed, the shyness of his nature was done away, and on the whole it was visible, by many symptoms which I have not room to enumerate, that he was happier in human society than when shut up with his natural companions.

William Cowper, 28th May, 1784

After a long silence, Cowper began in 1776 to correspond again with his friends. Many of his letters from this date forward to his friend and adviser, Joseph Hill speak of the garden, of a little green-house, melons, cucumbers and pineapple, of crocus, pinks, sunflower and myrtle. In 1779 the *Olney Hymns* were published. In correspondence with Mary Unwin's son, William, now the parson at Stock in Essex, about the collection of tithes, he put these thoughts into verse in *The Yearly Distress* or *Tithing Time at Stock in Essex*, addressed to a country clergyman complaining of the disagreeableness of the day annually appointed for receiving the Dues of the Parsonage.

I will enclose a few Seeds of the plant called Broallia, a new flower in this Country. A few seeds were given me last year which have produced a Quantity. Gordon, I am told, sells it 2 Guineas an Ounce. We account it the most elegant Flower we have seen, and when Lord Dartmouth was here, he did it the Honour to think with us. I will send with it Directions for the Management of it.

From a letter written in 1777 to Joseph Hill

Come, ponder well, for 'tis no jest,
To laugh it would be wrong;
The troubles of a worthy priest
The burthen of my song.

44

This priest he merry is and blithe
Three quarters of the year,
But oh! it cuts him like a scythe
When tithing time draws near.

He then is full of frights and fears,
As one at point to die,
And long before the day appears
He heaves up many a sigh.

For then the farmers come jog, jog,
Along the miry road,
Each heart as heavy as a log,
To make their payments good.

In sooth, the sorrow of such days
Is not to be express'd,
When he that takes and he that pays
Are both alike distress'd.

Now all unwelcome, at his gates
The clumsy swains alight,
With rueful faces and bald pates —
He trembles at the sight.

And well he may, for well he knows
Each bumkin of the clan,
Instead of paying what he owes,
Will cheat him if he can.

So in they come — each makes his leg,
And flings his head before,
And looks as if he came to beg,
And not to quit a score.

'And how does miss and madam do,
The little boy and all?'
'All tight and well: and how do you,
Good Mr. What-d'ye-call?'

The dinner comes, and down they sit:
Were e'er such hungry folk?
There's little talking and no wit;
It is no time to joke.

One wipes his nose upon his sleeve,
One spits upon the floor,
Yet, not to give offence or grieve,
Holds up the cloth before.

I must beg your assistance in a design I have formed to cheat the glazier. Government has laid a tax upon glass, and he has trebled it. I want as much as will serve for a large frame, but am unwilling to pay an exorbitant price for it. I shall be obliged to you, therefore, if you enquire at a glass-manufacturer's how he sells his Newcastle glass, such as is used for frames and hot-houses.

William Cowper to William Unwin, 26th May 1779

The punch goes round, and they are dull
And lumpish still as ever;
Like barrels with their bellies full,
They only weigh the heavier.

At length the busy time begins,
'Come, neighbours we must wag' —
The money chinks, down drop their chins,
Each lugging out his bag.

One talks of mildew and of frost,
And one of storms of hail,
And one, of pigs that he has lost
By maggots at the tail.

Quoth one, A rarer man than you
In pulpit none shall hear:
But yet, methinks, to tell you true,
You sell it plaguy dear.

Oh, why are farmers made so coarse,
Or clergy made so fine!
A kick that scarce would move a horse
May kill a sound divine.

Then let the boobies stay at home;
'Twould cost him, I dare say,
Less trouble taking twice the sum,
Without the clowns that pay.

'The Yearly Distress' or
'Tithing Time at Stock in Essex'

I consider England and America as once one country. They were so, in respect of interest, intercourse, and affinity. A great earthquake has made a partition, and now the Atlantic Ocean flows between them. He that can drain that ocean, and shove the two shores together, so as to make them aptly coincide, and meet each other in every part, can unite them again. But this is a work for Omnipotence, and nothing less than Omnipotence can heal the breach between us.
William Cowper to John Newton, 31st March 1781

John Newton, before leaving Olney for St. Mary Woolnoth in the City of London, introduced William to the Reverend William Bull, an independent minister from nearby Newport Pagnall. Bull was an inveterate pipe smoker, and the hole in the ground beneath Cowper's Sulking Room became a hidey-hole for Bull's pipe and tobacco. Later generations have William Bull to thank for his success from time to time in persuading Cowper not to tear up his poetry in times of depression. Although at times the poet yearned for solitude, perhaps his greatest problem was his inability to live with himself. He needed friends and they served him well. Could this perhaps have led to his choice for a poem *Verses supposed to be written by Alexander Selkirk,* the sailor whose stranding on the island of Juan Fernandez inspired Daniel Defoe's *Robinson Crusoe.*

I am monarch of all I survey,
My right there is none to dispute;
From the centre all round to the sea,
I am lord of the fowl and the brute.
Oh, solitude! where are the charms
That sages have seen in thy face?
Better dwell in the midst of alarms,
Than reign in this horrible place.
William Cowper's 'Verses supposed to be written by Alexander Selkirk'

46

So began the period when Cowper greatly encouraged by Mary Unwin wrote the poetry which was to make him world-famous. Between December 1780 and March 1781 he wrote *The Progress of Error* (624 lines); *Truth* (589 lines); *Table Talk* (771 lines); and *Expostulation* (734 lines). Throughout 1781, the words continued to flow. By early 1782, a volume of poems was published but little noticed.

> Yon cottager, who weaves at her own door,
> Pillow and bobbins all her little store;
> Content, though mean; and cheerful, if not gay;
> Shuffling her threads about the live-long day,
> Just earns a scanty pittance; and at night
> Lies down secure, her heart and pocket light:
> She, for her humble sphere by nature fit,
> Has little understanding, and no wit,
> Receives no praise; but though her lot be such,
> (Toilsome and indigent) she renders much;
> Just knows, and knows no more, her Bible true —
> A truth the brilliant Frenchman* never knew;
> And in that charter reads, with sparkling eyes,
> Her title to a treasure in the skies.
> * Voltaire   *From 'Truth'*

John Newton's successor as curate at Olney was the Reverend Thomas Scott, the author of a best-selling comprehensive commentary on the whole Bible. He did not however receive any payment for this mammoth task which explains perhaps his need to let the first floor of the Vicarage to Lady Austen, who was also sister of the curate in the nearby village of Clifton-Reynes. At first, Cowper was very taken with the lady though they quarrelled early in 1782 to be reconciled that June. It was an amusing story told by this lady that sparked off the narrative poem *John Gilpin*. It was Lady Austen, who by 1783 had fallen in love with William Cowper, inspired the writing of his major work *The Task*. The poet might have been content to allow Lady Austen's friendship to grow into something more — he enjoyed her conversation and her company — were it not for the way Mrs. Mary Unwin had stood by him in all his years of sickness.

LADY AUSTEN

From an early edition of **JOHN GILPIN**

William Cowper certainly thought highly of another great epic poem, John Milton's *Paradise Lost*. *The Task* was not on such a scale, yet it was a major work and its eventual publication made its author famous. The ancient mansion of Throckmorton, Weston Hall, to the west of Olney, lay in attractive grounds, and the acquaintanceship at this time with the present residents, John and George Throckmorton, gave William Cowper access to them. The charming views from part of the estate find their place within *The Task*.

Now that I talk of authors how do you like Cowper? Is not *The Task* a glorious poem? The religion of *The Task*, bating a few scraps of Calvinistic divinity, is the religion of God and Nature: the religion that exults, that ennobles man.
Robert Burns writing to Mrs. Dunlop about 'The Task'

The night was winter in his roughest mood;
The morning sharp and clear. But now at noon
Upon the southern side of the slant hills,
And where the woods fence off the northern blast,
The season smiles, resigning all its rage,
And has the warmth of May. The vault is blue
Without a cloud, and white without a speck
The dazzling splendour of the scene below.
Again the harmony comes o'er the vale;
And through the trees I view th'embattled tow'r
Whence all the music. I again perceive
The soothing influence of the wafted strains,
And settle in soft musings as I tread
The walk, still verdant, under oaks and elms,
Whose outspread branches overarch the glade.
The roof, though moveable through all its length
As the wind sways it, has yet well suffic'd,
And, intercepting in their silent fall
The frequent flakes, has kept a path for me.
No noise is here, or none that hinders thought.
The redbreast warbles still, but is content
With slender notes, and more than half suppress'd:
Pleas'd with his solitude, and flitting light
From spray to spray, where'er he rests he shakes
From many a twig the pendent drops of ice,
That tinkle in the wither'd leaves below.
Stillness, accompanied with sounds so soft,
Charms more than silence. Meditation here
May think down hours to moments. Here the heart
May give an useful lesson to the head,
And learning wiser grow without his books.
Knowledge and wisdom, far from being one,
Have oft-times no connexion. Knowledge dwells
In heads replete with thoughts of other men;
Wisdom in minds attentive to their own.

Knowledge, a rude unprofitable mass,
The mere materials with which wisdom builds,
Till smooth'd and squar'd and fitted to its place,
Does but encumber whom it seems t'enrich.
Knowledge is proud that he has learn'd so much;
Wisdom is humble that he knows no more.

Extract from Book VI of 'The Task':
'The Winter Walk at Noon'

As to the King, I love and honour him upon a hundred accounts; and have, indeed, but one quarrel with him in the world; which is, that after having hunted a noble and beautiful animal, till he take it perhaps at last in a lady's parlour, he in a few days turns it up and hunts it again.

William Cowper to Lady Hesketh, 23rd November 1785

In 1784, Cowper began a translation of Homer, a full-time job of work. It was eventually to be published in 1791, with the translator being paid £1000 for the copyright. But in 1785 he needed help again from relatives to keep himself solvent. An anonymous donor settled an annuity of £50 a year on Cowper. The gift probably came from Lady Hesketh who rented Olney Vicarage from June until November 1786. Newton was beginning to show some concern about Cowper's life-style. Was he wasting his time and talents in dissipation? Theodora on the other hand was concerned that depression would set in again. She decided a change of abode would be helpful for the poet and rented a comfortable house for Mrs. Unwin and Cousin William in the middle of the village of Weston Underwood. The village retains its charm today — it has won the prize as Best Kept Village in the area many times — and adjoins the estate of Weston Hall. No sooner had they moved in, however, than news came of the death of Mary's son, William Unwin and the grief set off another period of derangement of mind. Six months later however, he was healed and resumed at once his Homeric task of translation.

On 9th March, 1786 a memorandum found amongst Cowper's papers records the last of his three hares *This day died poor Puss, aged eleven years eleven months. She died between twelve and one at noon, of mere old age, and apparently without pain.*

His dog Beau was Cowper's faithful friend, and he is immortalized in the poem *The Dog and the Water-Lily*, subtitled *No Fable* written in August 1788. The same month, he was visited by Mary and John Newton. John was now active in the fight for the abolition of slavery: perhaps this led to Cowper's submission of the lines *Pity for Poor Africans* published in the *Northampton Mercury* for 9th August.

The noon was shady, and soft airs
Swept Ouse's silent tide,
When, 'scap'd from literary cares,
I wander'd on his side.

My spaniel, prettiest of his race,
And high in pedigree,
(Two nymphs, adorn'd with ev'ry grace,
That spaniel found for me)

Now wanton'd lost in flags and reeds,
Now starting into sight
Pursued the swallow o'er the meads
With scarce a slower flight.

It was the time when Ouse display'd
His lilies newly blown;
Their beauties I intent survey'd;
And one I wish'd my own.

With cane extended far I sought
To steer it close to land;
But still the prize though nearly caught,
Escap'd my eager hand.

Beau marked my unsuccessful pains
With fixt consid'rate face,
And puzzling set his puppy brains
To comprehend the case.

But with a chirrup clear and strong,
Dispersing all his dream,
I thence withdrew, and follow'd long
The windings of the stream.

My ramble finish'd, I return'd.
Beau trotting far before
The floating wreath again discern'd,
And plunging left the shore.

I saw him with that lily cropp'd
Impatient swim to meet
My quick approach, and soon he dropp'd
The treasure at my feet.

Charm'd with the sight, the world, I cried,
Shall hear of this thy deed.
My dog shall mortify the pride
Of man's superior breed;

Beau seems to have objections against my writing you this morning that are not to be over-ruled. He will be in my lap, licking my face, and nibbling the end of my pen. Perhaps he means to say, I beg you will give my love to her, which I therefore send you accordingly.
William Cowper to Lady Hesketh, 13th September 1788

But, chief, myself I will enjoin,
Awake at duty's call,
To show a love as prompt as thine
To Him who gives me all.

The Dog and The Water-Lily

I own I am shock'd at the purchase of slaves,
And fear those who buy them and sell them are knaves;
What I hear of their hardships, their tortures, and groans,
Is almost enough to draw pity from stones.

I pity them greatly, but I must be mum,
For how could we do without sugar and rum?
Especially sugar, so needful we see?
What? give up our desserts, our coffee, and tea!

We are forbidden to trust in man; I will not therefore say I trust in Mr. Pitt's — but in his counsels, under the blessing of Providence, the remedy is, I believe, to be found, if a remedy there be.

William Cowper expresses his feeling about national affairs in a letter of 20th December 1788

Besides, if we do, the French, Dutch, and Danes,
Will heartily thank us, no doubt, for our pains;
If we do not buy the poor creatures, they will,
And tortures and groans will be multiplied still.

If foreigners likewise would give up the trade,
Much more in behalf of your wish might be said;
But while they get riches by purchasing blacks,
Pray tell me why we may not also go snacks?

Your scruples and arguments bring to my mind
A story so pat, you may think it is coin'd,
On purpose to answer you, out of my mint;
But, I can assure you, I saw it in print.

A youngster at school, more sedate than the rest,
Had once his integrity put to the test;
His comrades had plotted an orchard to rob,
And ask'd him to go and assist in the job.

He was shock'd, sir, like you, and answer'd — 'Oh, no!
What! rob our good neighbour! I pray you, don't go;
Besides, the man's poor, his orchard's his bread.
Then think of his children, for they must be fed.'

'You speak very fine, and you look very grave,
But apples we want, and apples we'll have;
If you will go with us, you shall have a share,
If not, you shall have neither apple nor pear.'

They spoke, and Tom ponder'd — 'I see they will go:
Poor man! what a pity to injure him so!
Poor man! I would save him his fruit if I could,
But staying behind will do him no good.

'If the matter depended alone upon me,
His apples might hang till they dropt from the tree:
But, since they will take them, I think I'll go too.
He will lose none by me, though I get a few.'

His scruples thus silenc'd, Tom felt more at ease,
And went with his comrades the apples to seize;
He blam'd and protested, but join'd in the plan,
He shar'd in the plunder, but pitied the man.

Pity for Poor Africans

One of Cowper's contemporaries was Samuel Teedon, a simple-minded and fervently religious Olney schoolmaster. He considered himself especially close and favoured by God, the very reverse of Cowper's relationship with his Maker, who thought himself an abomination to the Lord whom he let down so often. A curious relationship grew up between the two of them, with the gifted poet consulting the 'good man' in the manner of an oracle, especially when Cowper sought interpretation of his visions and dreams. It was therefore to Teedon he turned for advice on whether his next major task should be an edition of Milton's poetry. Samuel Teedon consulted with Heaven and said 'Yes'. The project was a complete failure: to work on it he set aside plans of May 1791 for a successor to *The Task*, a poem of similar length on *The Four Ages — Infancy, Youth, Manhood, and Old Age*. Only thirty-eight lines were ever written.

In December 1792, Mrs. Mary Unwin had a stroke. Whilst she soon recovered from the paralysis, it was the beginning of the end. In the following May, Cowper wrote the sonnet *Mary! I want a lyre with other strings* and as Mary's health further declined, his affection burned brighter and he penned the

Hayley, thy tenderness fraternal shown
In our first interview, delightful guest!
To Mary and me for her dear sake distress'd,
Such as it is has made my heart thy own,
Though heedless now of new engagements grown;
For threescore winters make a wintry breast
And I had purpos'd ne'er to go in quest
Of Friendship more, except with God alone.

But thou hast won me; nor is God my foe,
Who, ere this last afflictive scene began,
Sent thee to mitigate the dreadful blow,
My brother, by whose sympathy I know
Thy true deserts infallibly to scan,
Not more t'admire the Bard than love the Man.
To William Hayley

The French are a vain and childish people, and conduct themselves on this grand occasion with a levity and extravagance nearly akin to madness; but it would have been better for Austria and Prussia to let them alone. All nations have a right to choose their own mode of government . . .

> William Cowper to Lady Hesketh, 1st December 1792

stanzas *To Mary*. The one compensation for his decision to work on Milton's poetry was that it brought the poet in touch with William Hayley, then working on a *Life of Milton*. Lady Harriet Hesketh spent several months at Weston in the first half of 1794; and Hayley managed to arrange for Cowper to receive a pension of £300 a year.

The strain of watching Mary decline brought William Cowper again to the point of breakdown and his last years were spent in the twilight sadness of an enfeebled mind. A kinsman took the two invalids to Norfolk, hoping for therapy through change of scene but neither the parson's house at North Tuddenham, the coastal village of Mundesley, the stay at Durham Lodge nor the final residence at East Dereham brought relief. Just before Christmas in 1796, Mary died. Cowper's bleakness was complete though he did work from time to time on the second edition of Homer which he completed in 1799. Just before Christmas that year, he wrote from the depths of despondency his last poem *The Castaway*.

> Obscurest night involv'd the sky,
> Th'Atlantic billows roar'd,
> When such a destin'd wretch as I,
> Wash'd headlong from on board,
> Of friends, of hope, of all bereft,
> His floating home for ever left.
>
>   . . . . .
>
> I therefore purpose not, or dream,
> Descanting on his fate,
> To give the melancholy theme
> A more enduring date:
> But misery still delights to trace
> Its 'semblance in another's case.
>
> No voice divine the storm allay'd,
> No light propitious shone;
> When, snatch'd from all effectual aid,
> We perish'd, each alone:
> But I beneath a rougher sea,
> And whelm'd in deeper gulphs than he.
>
> *From 'The Castaway'*

We can end on a note, not of utter despair, but of triumph. The divine mystery and the unfathomable wonder of God's love for his creatures of which Cowper wrote so eloquently in his hymn about the wisdom of God assures us that he will have found his place amongst the saints.

PEARSALL   7.6.7.6. D.   St. Gall *Gesangbuch*, 1863

Ere God had built the mountains,	Thus wisdom's words discover
Or rais'd the fruitful hills;	Thy glory and thy grace,
Before he fill'd the fountains	Thou everlasting lover
That feed the running rills;	Of our unworthy race!
In me, from everlasting,	Thy gracious eye survey'd us
The wonderful I AM	Ere stars were seen above;
Found pleasures never wasting,	In wisdom thou hast made us,
And Wisdom is my name.	And died for us in love.
When, like a tent to dwell in,	And couldst thou be delighted
He spread the skies abroad;	With creatures such as we!
And swath'd about the swelling	Who when we saw thee, slighted
Of ocean's mighty flood;	And nail'd thee to a tree?
He wrought by weight and measure,	Unfathomable wonder,
And I was with him then;	And mystery divine!
Myself the Father's pleasure,	The Voice that speaks in thunder,
And mine, the sons of men.	Says, 'Sinner I am thine!'

BISHOP HEBER

Reginald Heber

Reginald Heber was born on 21st April 1783 into the luxury of lord of the manors and patron of the rectories of Marton and Hodnet in Shropshire. His birthplace was to the north across the Cheshire border where his father held a moiety of the living at the Church dedicated to St. Oswald, the Northumbrian missionary king who was martyred in battle when the heathen Penda took up arms against him. Tradition remembers how Reginald's father drove in a coach and four the many miles across mostly roadless country to hold services at Hodnet, where the Rectory stood in a spot regarded as unhealthy.

The name Heber is derived from Heyber(g) in Yorkshire whence the family came. Reginald's mother was daughter of a Yorkshire rector; and an elder half-brother Richard, the child of his father's first marriage, was a prolific book collector — after his death, the auction to sell off the collection of over 150,000 volumes lasted 216 days.

Twice in early childhood, Reginald almost died; but this did not stop his active brain so responding to his father's tuition in Latin and Greek that at the age of seven, he translated the fables of Phaedrus into verse. The remaining half of the Malpas living vested in Dr. Townson, who gave the child the run of his considerable library; his half-brother's avid interest in books spilled over on Reginald who needed but little encouragement to devour them. At the age of eight he went to Whitchurch Grammar School, where he wrote *The Prophecy of Ishmael* as a class exercise on the Battle of the Nile after Napoleon Bonaparte's invasion of Egypt.

> Dependant on thy bounteous breath
> We seek thy grace alone,
> In childhood, manhood, age and death,
> To keep us still thine own.
>
> *First Sunday after Epiphany:*
> *From 'By cool Siloam's shady rill'*
> *A tune used is WESTGATE*

Reginald Heber senior loved Holy Scripture and directed his son to read the Bible, not just in extracts, but in full. When around fourteen, he *borrowed* his mother's copy of a manual of preparation for Holy Communion: after three weeks he sought permission to attend Sacrament with her. So he grew into accepting the Christian faith: later in life he cautioned those who claimed that instantaneous conversion was the only road for a true Christian against presumptuously confining the grace of God to a single mode of operation. When he was fifteen, he was sent to Neasden, then on London's outskirts, to study with

> Bread of the world in mercy broken,
> Wine of the soul in mercy shed,
> By whom the words of life were spoken,
> And in whose death our sins are dead;
>
> Look on the heart by sorrow broken,
> Look on the tears by sinners shed;
> And be thy feast to us the token
> That by thy grace our souls are fed.
>
> *Sung to RENDEZ À DIEU and*
> *LES COMMANDEMENS*

. . . I fully agree with you respecting the stipends of the clergy. Were Queen Anne's bounty better regulated, and were it ordered that every clergyman of above £200 a year should, *bona fide*, pay the tenth of his benefices to that, or some other similar institution, and so on in such an ascending scale to the largest preferments, as might be thought right and equal, much of this evil, and all its attending mischiefs of non-residence, contempt of the ministry etc., might, I think, without inconvenience, be prevented. This it is thought was the intention of Queen Anne; but the death of that excellent woman (for I am tory enough to think highly of her), and the unfortunate circumstances which followed, threw obstacles in the way of the Church which I fear there is no probability of its being able to get over . . .

> Reginald Heber writing
> from Neasden on
> 24th June 1800

. . . I have been a much gayer fellow than usual of late, having been at a race, and also at, what I never saw before, a masquerade. This catalogue of jaunts, though not much perhaps for a girl, has been a great deal for me, and has indeed quite satisfied me. If these things are so little interesting even while they have the charm of novelty, I think I shall care very little indeed for them when that is worn off . . .

— — — — —

. . . We have some tumults in this neighbourhood. In Staffordshire, the mob proceeded to domiciliary visits with halters and agreements, forcing the farmers to the alternative. All is, however, quiet at present.

> Reginald Heber writing
> from Malpas in
> October 1800

a few others under a Dr. Bristow(e). There he met John Thornton, son of the Member of Parliament for Surrey. John and Reginald became firm friends: later a son of John's was to marry Reginald's youngest daughter.

On then to Brasenose College, Oxford while Thornton went to Cambridge. Heber's fellow commoners included a future President of the Board of Control, a future Chief Justice of Calcutta and another of Bombay, and Henry Hart Milman, later Dean of St. Paul's who was to contribute several hymns to Heber's collection including *Ride on! ride on in majesty* sung since to WINCHESTER NEW and PALM SUNDAY.

> Ride on! ride on in majesty!
> Hark! all the tribes Hosanna cry:
> Thine humble beast pursues his road
> With palms and scatter'd garments strew'd.
> *Opening verse of Henry Hart Milman's hymn*

At Oxford, Heber developed his interest in both landscape and architectural drawing, and learned to love Edmund Spenser's *The Faerie Queene*, with its knightly adventures, which became a constant companion. He had no appetite for sport but loved walking with only himself for company. In 1801, he recited the University Prize Poem on the *Commencement of the Nineteenth Century*.

> As when a weary traveller, that strays
> By muddy shore of broad seven-mouthed Nile,
> Unweeting of the perilous wand'ring ways
> Doth meet a cruel crafty crocodile,
> Which, in false grief hiding his harmful guile,
> Doth weep full sore, and sheddeth tender tears;
> The foolish man, that pities all this while
> His mournful plight, is swallow'd up unwares;
> Forgetful of his own, that minds another's cares.

— — — — —

> 'Fair Knight' quote he, 'Hierusalem that is,
> The New Hierusalem, that God has built
> For those to dwell in, that are chosen his,
> His chosen people purged from sinful guilt
> With precious blood, which cruelly was spilt
> On cursed tree, of that unspotted Lamb,
> That for the sins of all the world was kilt:
> Now are they saints all in that city sam,
> More dear unto their God than younglings to their dam!'
> *Stanzas from Edmund Spenser: 'The Faerie Queene',*
> *Book 1: 'The Legend of the Knight*
> *of the Red Cross, or of Holiness'*

Two years later, after recovering from a severe bout of influenza, he wrote the poem *Palestine*, first actually printed in 1807. This text inspired the child prodigy William Crotch (1775 - 1847), who at the age of three had played before the King and Queen, to write the Oratorio *Palestine*. It was described as the first English Oratorio of real note for forty years. Crotch who was Professor of Music at Oxford at the age of 22 and the first Principal of the Royal Academy of Music, would not print the musical parts, but made them available with his own services as conductor for a fee of two hundred guineas. Its first performance in London's Hanover Square Concert Room was well received: Mr. François Cramer led the band. Walter Scott was enjoying breakfast with Heber at Brasenose while the poem was being written; and one suggestion was immediately incorporated into the text.

RECITATIVE

But who is He, the vast, the awful form!
Girt with the whirlwind, sandal'd with the storm;
A western cloud around His limbs is spread,
His crown a rainbow, and a sun His head?

AIR

To highest heav'n He lifts His Kingly hand,
And treads at once the ocean and the land!
And hark! His voice amid the thunder's roar,
His dreadful voice, that, *Time shall be no more.*

SESTETT

Lo! Cherub bands the golden courts prepare,
Lo! thrones are set, and ev'ry Saint is there!
Earth's utmost bounds confess their awful sway,
The mountains worship, and the isles obey.
Nor sun nor moon they need, nor day nor night,
God is their temple, and the Lamb their light.

RECITATIVE

And shall not Israel's sons exulting come,
Hail the glad beam and claim their ancient home!
On David's throne shall David's offspring reign,
And the dry bones be warm with life again.

. . . I have got into a habit of tolerably early rising, which I intend to adhere to; the plan is that another man, who has been my companion in the course of mathematics which I have gone through, has agreed to read with me every morning from six till chapel, by which scheme we gain two hours of the best part of the whole day. This system must, however, be altered, when chapel begins at six, which it does in summer.

Reginald Heber writing from Oxford to his friend John Thornton at Cambridge on 15th January 1801

– – – – –

I have been, through my Cheshire connexions and the long residence of my brother, introduced to a great many people; and this has, of course, produced very numerous parties, but, I assure you, I shall preserve my character for sobriety: no man is obliged to drink more than he pleases . . . You seem not much to like the concerts at Cambridge. I very much approve of ours here, both as it is a rational scholar-like amusement, and as it affords a retreat if necessary, from the bottle.

Reginald Heber writing from Oxford to his friend John Thornton, 1801

SOLO AND CHORUS

Hark! white rob'd crowds their loud Hosannas raise,
And the hoarse flood repeats the sound of praise;
Ten thousand harps attune the mystic song,
Ten thousand thousand Saints the strain prolong!
Worthy the Lamb, Omnipotent to save,
Who died, Who lives triumphant o'er the grave!

Hallelujah!

Amen

Passages selected by William Crotch from
Reginald Heber's 'Palestine' for his oratorio

In 1803, Heber spent the Long Vacation at Malpas helping his half-brother to raise a corps of volunteers against the threatened French invasion. One night his father called on him to write verses to be sung by the recruits the following morning. At this time he met Charlotte Dod, one of five daughters of his father's friend, the Squire of Edge. Over the years, Reginald and Charlotte carried on a remarkable correspondence: after his mother and his wife, she was to be a third woman in his life! Early in 1804, Reginald received the sad summons home to his father's death-bed. The following year he completed his formal education reciting *A Sense of Honour*, the University Bachelors' Prize Essay in the Theatre, Oxford.

> How slowly, clogg'd with doubt and fear,
> The months of absence melt away!
> Oh, when shall I those accents hear?
> Oh, when that blush, that smile survey?
> Yet still — to faithful memory dear —
> I bless my Charlotte's natal day.
>
> *Reginald Heber: Part of a poem sent to*
> *Charlotte Dod on a later birthday*

> For, a politician neither must nor can destroy the propensities he attempts to guide. He must take mankind as he finds them, a compound of violence and frailty; he must oppose vice to vice, and interest to interest; and, like the fabled Argonaut, accomplish his glorious purpose by the labour of those very monsters who were armed for his destruction.
>
> *'A Sense of Honour': a prize Essay recited in the Theatre, Oxford 26th June 1805*

With his friend John Thornton, the Grand Tour was begun but war prevented their following the traditional route. On 1st August 1805, the pair landed at Gothenburg in southern Sweden. Heber's journal shows his talent as a travel writer and his letters home are full of detail: a few selections provide the flavour of a fifteen month journey, begun in a two-horse carriage:

. . . were detained a couple of hours by the roguery of the Swedish Custom-house officer, who, on pretence of some informality in our papers, refused to let us proceed without paying a hundred and fifty rix-dollars; but when we threatened to complain of him to the government at Stockholm, and declared ourselves ready to go back, he altered his tone and begged for six rix-dollars, as the price of our passage across the river into Norway.

— — — — —

The neighbourhood of Friderickshall is certainly striking, but far inferior in beauty to the romantic descriptions and drawings which I have seen of it; and the people, who affect to despise the Swedes, fall far short of them both in civilisation and honesty.

— — — — —

At Christiania there is a small private theatre, in which, during the winter, the gentry of the place amuse themselves by acting Danish and sometimes French plays.

— — — — —

At Rörass, where are their principal copper-mines, no corn or garden-stuff will grow, and in winter quick-silver is frozen. We stayed here a day or two, and went a day's journey into the mountains in quest of a small tribe of Laplanders, or Finns, as the Danes call them, who have been, time immemorial, wanderers in this neighbourhood. In the valleys we had been tormented by heat, but in this inhospitable tract it snowed fast . . .

— — — —

I was surprised, at first, at the great apparent liberty of all classes; but soon found reason to attribute the mildness of their government to the weakness of the ruling nation, and the circumstance that every peasant in Norway is armed and disciplined.

— — — — —

At Upsala we passed two days, and saw every thing of note in this northern Athens. There is a very respectable library, and a noble building as a green-house and museum, built by Gustavus the Third, of which the principal portico is Doric, very remarkable for its proportion and beauty . . . The Cathedral is well-proportioned, and has been of the best style of Gothic in general; plain, and not very unlike Westminster Abbey . . . with large Doric cornices, and two bright blue things, like pepper-boxes, on the two towers, has so beautified it, that, if the bishop who founded it, and the mason who built it, were to return again, they would not know their own child in its present dashing uniform.

— — — — —

On our route from Louisa, the last frontier town in Sweden,

to Petersburg, nothing is more remarkable than the change which takes place in the appearance, dress, and apparent circumstances of the peasantry. In Swedish Finland the peasant has all the cleanliness, industry, and decency of a Swede; he is even more sober, but very inferior in honesty. In Russia you see an immediate deterioration in morals, cleanliness, wealth, and every thing but intelligence and cunning. The horses, which through the Swedish territories were uniformly good, became poor miserable hacks; and to the good roads, which we had enjoyed ever since we left Gottenburg, we now bade a long, very long adieu.

— — — — —

I could get no music either in Sweden or Norway; in Sweden they have none worth hearing; and in Norway, though they have many beautiful simple songs, they have none with the notes printed or written. I hope to get a good deal in Russia.

— — — — —

ST. PETERSBURG
Our time is passed pleasantly and, I hope, profitably, in learning German, improving in French, seeing sights, and listening to, not joining in, political discussions. These employments, with a few Greek books which I hope to borrow, will give us ample amusement for the time we intend to stay here . . .

— — — — —

. . . about the palaces here and in the neighbourhood, of which the Taurida is the only one that has quite answered my expectation . . . The great palace is a vast tasteless pile of plaistered brick, and the marble palace is tamely conceived, and its pilasters look like slices of potted beef or char.

— — — — —

The other ceremony I mentioned was the commencement of the month Ramadan, or Mahomedan Lent, and was chiefly remarkable for its novelty, and for the number of the followers of Mahomet among the lower classes in Petersburg. It must also be observed that they were the most decent, attentive congregation that I have seen since I left England.

— — — — —

The baths are, however, by no means sufficient to keep them

sweet; and to pass to leeward of a Russian peasant is really so terrible an event that I always avoid it if possible . . .

— — — — —

The chapel was crowded, and the singing the most beautiful I ever heard; no musical instruments are allowed by the Greek Church, and never was more delightful harmony voice produced . . .

> Virgin-born, we bow before Thee;
> Blessèd was the womb that bore Thee;
> Mary, Mother meek and mild
> Blessèd was she in her Child.
>
> Blessèd was the breast that fed Thee;
> Blessèd was the hand that led Thee;
> Blessèd was the parent's eye
> That watch'd Thy slumbering infancy.
>
> Blessèd she by all creation,
> Who brought forth the world's salvation,
> And blest they — for ever blest,
> Who love Thee most and serve Thee best.
> *The first stanza is then repeated*
>
> *Reginald Heber*
> *For the Third Sunday in Lent, tunes used*
> *include QUEM PASTORES LAUDAVERE,*
> *MON DIEU, PRÊTE-MOI L'OREILLE,*
> *URQUELL ALLER SELIGKEITEN*

MOSCOW

We now approach the holy gate of the Kremlin, which is separated from the city by a vast ditch and mound, crowned with a high brick rampart, which is garnished with very tall towers of a circular form, diminishing like pagodas, and surmounted with high spires. The breast-works of the wall are in a very singular style, and seem to be intended as an imitation of palisadoes. The whole has a perfectly eastern air. The holy gate is painted red, and most of the towers have green spires; beyond the whole building is a cluster of turrets, spires, and domes. The famous Church of St. Basil, built by Solarius, an Italian architect, for Ivan the Second, who put out the artist's eyes in consequence of a foolish boast, is on the left hand; a strange building of painted brick, clustered with seven spires rising like a crown one above another. On the right hand side is the great market; a fine range of shops under regular arcades and well disposed. You enter the holy gate by a long narrow bridge over the fosse; on the left hand is a noble view down to the river.

In all manufactories and all in-doors' employment the Russian peasant wears nothing but his shirt and drawers; the former is generally dyed red and embroidered with blue under the arms; it is made round and full like a tunic, and hangs over the drawers to the knee.

— — — — —

The police of Moscow is very good, and the prison in excellent order; it is a stone building, on a very convenient plan, consisting of four wings with a Chapel in the centre. The number of prisoners I do not remember; most of them were runaway slaves. One well-dressed man was imprisoned for forgery; and three young men in uniform, with their father, a venerable peasant of sixty or seventy years old with a long beard, were just found guilty of issuing false government notes; their punishment awaited the emperor's decision. Banishment to Siberia was expected to be the sentence.

— — — — —

. . . it is the only place since I left England where I have met with a really interesting female society . . .

— — — — —

The detour of the Crimea we are induced to take as a sort of substitute for Greece and Italy; and in this country travelling is so rapid that a small increase of distance would not induce, or even justify us, in relinquishing one of the most beautiful and interesting countries in the world, and where we need apprehend neither plague, nor French, nor banditti.

— — — — —

Count Alexis Orlof we have also been presented to, and have been at his ball . . . his daughter, a pleasing but not beautiful girl of about eighteen, who sings, plays, dances, rides, hunts, speaks French, English and German, all to perfection, is, for these accomplishments, as well as for the additional one of being heiress to about 400,000 roubles a year, the 'cynosure of Russian eyes'.

— — — — —

Madam Cashparof gave us several particulars respecting the Scotch missionaries at Georgiessk; they are to the number of thirty men and women . . . Brunton . . . possessing great

But though, in Russia, the murderer might be killed by the kindred of the deceased during the heat of blood, no other person had a right to take such vengeance on him; and the judge was contented with imposing a pecuniary fine. A robber, if found in the fact, might be killed on the spot; but if taken alive was to be brought to the judge uninjured.

— — — — —

On the ninth of May was a great festival, in which all the mares of their herds, and particularly those of a white colour, were brought together to be blessed by their magicians; and, on this occasion, the Mahomedan moullahs and the Nestorian monks were also obliged to attend. The Christians among them . . . all very ignorant, complying, without scruple, with the idolatrous and magical ceremonies of their masters, and placing almost the whole of religion in an abstinence from mares' milk and koumiss.

Extracts from Reginald Heber: 'History of the Cossacks'

power of acquiring languages . . . extraordinary progress in
the Russian and Circassian tongues . . . suffered greatly by
disease . . . The Circassians of the horde of Little Kabard are
allied with Russia, but those of the other tribes are mostly
hostile.

— — — — —

On Monday, then 'twenty adieus, my frozen Moscovites'
(though their climate is the only thing that we have found
frozen about them) . . .

— — — — —

POLAND

No part of Ancient Russia, that I have seen, except, perhaps,
some part of the province of Yaroslav, can at all compare
in fertility or beauty with her Polish acquisitions . . . The
difference which principally struck us was in the appearance
of the houses and towns, the paved and narrow streets, the
crucifixes by the roadside, the monasteries, the Latin
inscriptions, and the other marks of a different religion, and
habits more nearly approaching the rest of Europe . . .

— — — — —

BUDA

We afterwards went with Count Nittrai to the theatre where
we saw Blue-beard performed; it was divested of all the
miraculous part, and rendered very absurdly probable;
the key, instead of being stained with blood, was broken
in the lock, and the ghosts were all omitted.

— — — — —

. . . we had a considerable altercation with our landlord, who
brought us one of the most extravagant bills I ever saw; but
which we at last succeeded in prevailing on him to reduce.

— — — — —

Characters in the extract: FADALLAH (an old Turk)
SELIM (a young Turk)
AYESHA (Fadallah's younger daughter)

FADALLAH   Good neighbour, be quiet! my word is law —
I have said that my daughter shall wed the Bashaw!

SELIM   But, neighbour, your promise!

FADALLAH — My promise! go!
With *him* must I break it to keep it with *you?*

SELIM — You promised me first!

FADALLAH — But I promised him since!
And what saith the Koran? *Speak truth to thy prince!*

SELIM — You swore by the Prophet!

FADALLAH — I tell thee, forbear!
In abundance of words is abundance of care!
And again saith the Koran, in Surah the third
Confine not thy neighbour too close to his word!

SELIM — Would you yield to this monster your Fatima's life?
Why, he eats every night for his supper a wife!

FADALLAH — Mere libellous nonsense! I tell thee, Selim,
I know nothing less like a monster than him.

AYESHA — Oh, father! but think on his whiskers of blue!

FADALLAH — I tell you, the man is as rich as a Jew!
I wish I could find such a husband for you!

*Reginald Heber: Opening lines of 'Blue-beard',
a serio-comic Oriental romance, written several
years later for family celebrations at Christmas*

— — — — —

HUNGARY
The roads, indeed, are very like those of Shropshire or Cheshire; but the horses and inns are excellent; and the whole country displays a wealth and population far superior to all which we have yet seen out of England. The market towns and boroughs, with their town halls, whipping-posts, and gallows, things little known on the Continent, are exactly in the style of building which we see in Hogarth's prints. Like England, Hungary still shows everywhere the deep scars of her former civil disturbances. Every country town has its ruined walls; and the hills, particularly the Carpathian mountains, are full of castles, the ruins of which are sometimes very fine.

— — — — —

VIENNA
The French troops appear to have behaved with great moderation while in Vienna; but, though private property has

been respected, the state has been terribly plundered; and a season of great scarcity having accompanied the other misfortunes, the necessary purchase of corn has contributed still more to drain the country of treasure, which they seem to have but scanty means, at present, of replacing; their paper is at fifty per cent discount.

— — — — —

AUSTERLITZ
. . . the battle of Austerlitz. Except a few skeletons of horses, and a few trees which have been slivered by bullets, all wears its ancient appearance.

'As if these shades since time was born
Had only heard the shepherd's reed
Nor started at the bugle horn.'

— — — — —

. . . The loss of the battle is entirely attributable to the scandalous want of information of the Austrians, and to the extended line on which Kotusof made the attack . . . I drew three or four plans of the ground, and at last succeeded in making a very exact one. While I was thus employed I was taken for a French spy, and accosted by some farmers, who asked, with many apologies, for my passport. I told them I had none, and a very curious village council of war was held, which was terminated by the arrival of Thornton and the guide we had taken from Brünn.

— — — — —

So, after visiting Prague, Dresden, Leipzig, Halle, Wittenberg and Berlin, Heber and Thornton reached Hamburg, to make the sea trip to Yarmouth, landing on 14th October 1806.

Heber found his half-brother contesting the University seat of Oxford and threw himself into the election campaign: Richard was unsuccessful but was eventually elected to Parliament in 1821. Early in 1807, Heber and Thornton met William Wilberforce, congratulating him in the Palace Yard on the final triumph in Parliament in ending British support for the slave trade. So to Hodnet, named after the De Hodenets who once held the old manor on condition of keeping in good repair the fortress of Montgomery, and from whom it was eventually inherited by the Hebers. Here he was to serve as the local parson and squire for more than fifteen years and to write extensively.

. . . The Methodists in Hodnet are, thank God, not very numerous, and I hope to diminish them some more; they are, however, sufficiently numerous to serve as a spur to my emulation.
Reginald Heber writing from Hodnet on 7th August 1807

I have reason to believe that both my conduct and my sermons are well liked, but I do not think any great amendment takes place in my hearers. My congregations are very good, and the number of communicants increases. The principal faults of which I have to complain are occasional drunkeness and, after they have left church, a great disregard of Sunday . . . I have sometimes thought, and it has made me really uncomfortable, that since Rowland Hill's visit to the country my congregation was thinner. Perhaps it was only owing to the bad weather, as my numbers are now a little increasing again . . .

Reginald Heber in correspondence to Thornton, 1808

When Spring unlocks the flowers to paint the laughing soil;
When Summer's balmy showers reflect the mower's toil;
When Winter binds in frosty chains the fallow and the flood,
In God the earth rejoiceth still, and owns his Maker good.

The birds that wake the morning, and those that love the shade;
The winds that sweep the mountain or lull the drowsy glade;
The Sun that from his amber bower rejoiceth on his way,
The Moon and Stars, their Master's name in silent pomp display.

Shall Man, the lord of nature, expectant of the sky,
Shall Man, alone unthankful, his little praise deny?
No, let the year forsake his course, the seasons cease to be,
Thee, Master, must we always love, and Saviour, honour Thee.

The flowers of Spring may wither, the hope of Summer fade,
The Autumn droop in Winter, the birds forsake the shade;
The winds be lull'd — the Sun and Moon forget their old decree,
But we in Nature's latest hour, O Lord! will cling to Thee.

Reginald Heber: hymn for the Seventh Sunday after Trinity
It is sung sometimes to GOSTERWOOD

HEBER'S RECTORY, HODNET

Enough of vengeance! O'er th'ensanguin'd plain
I gaze, and seek their numerous host in vain;
Gone like the locust band, when whirlwinds bear
Their flimsy legions through the waste of air.
Enough of vengeance! — By the glorious dead,
Who bravely fell where youthful Lewis led;
By Blücher's sword in fiercest danger tried,
And the true heart that burst when Brunswick died;
By her whose charms the coldest zeal might warm,
The manliest firmness in the fairest form —
Save, Europe, save the remnant! — Yet remains
One glorious path to free the world from chains.
Why, when yon northern band in Eylau's wood
Retreating struck, and track'd their course with blood,
While one firm rock the floods of ruin stay'd,
Why, generous Austria, were thy wheels delay'd?

From 'Europe: Lines on the Present War' 1809

In April 1809, he married Amelia Shipley, daughter of the Dean of St. Asaph and grand-daughter of its Bishop. The Rectory at Hodnet was too unhealthy to occupy and the newly-weds lived a few miles distant at Moreton Say, while a new Rectory was planned by Heber himself. His many skills included architectural design! The Clive family, whose forebear Baron Robert had founded the British Empire in India, lived near Moreton Say, and Heber gained from them extensive information about that land. He contemplated introducing the *Olney Hymn Book* into his parish, reporting the psalm-singing was bad.

Over the years, Reginald Heber's literary work was extensive: his wife noted it was his practice to spend seven or eight hours each day with his books. Two major works were never completed. His trip to Russia inspired a History of the Cossacks: a Dictionary of the Bible occupied many hours.

> You may go where you please, as I am sure you will not exceed the limits of moderation, except to Sunday evening parties, to which I have a very serious objection.
>
> *Reginald Heber writing to his wife during her first visit to London, 1814*

God of the poor, the poor and friendless save!
Giver and Lord of freedom, help the slave! —
North, south, and west the sandy whirlwinds fly,
The circling horns of Egypt's chivalry.
On earth's last margin throng the weeping train:
Their cloudy guide moves on: — *And must we swim the main?*
'Mid the light spray their snorting camels stood,
Nor bath'd a fetlock in the nauseous flood —
He comes — their leader comes! — the man of God
O'er the wide waters lifts his mighty rod,
And onward treads — The circling waves retreat,
In hoarse deep murmurs, from his holy feet;
And the chas'd surges, inly roaring, show
The hard wet sand and coral hills below.

With limbs that falter, and with hearts that swell,
Down, down they pass — a steep and slippery dell.
Around them rise, in pristine chaos hurl'd,
The ancient rocks, the secrets of the world;
And flowers that blush beneath the ocean green,
And caves, the sea-calves low-roof'd haunt, are seen.
Down, safely down the narrow pass they tread;
The bustling western storm above their head;
While far behind retires the sinking day,
And fades on Edom's hills its latest ray.
        Reginald Heber: From 'The Passage of the Red Sea'

He wrote song lyrics and poems, contributed to the *Gentleman's Magazine* and the *Quarterly Review*; he wrote scripts for house celebrations at Christmas, including *The*

68

If gaily clothed and proudly fed,
In dangerous wealth we dwell;
Remind us of thy manger bed,
And lowly cottage cell!

*Christmas Day:
'O Saviour, whom this holy morn'*

He turned o'er the books of his Elders in sin
And found that with murder he first must begin
So the Vicar he slew, nor with Hell was he daunted
For who could fear Hell, who wished to be haunted —

He plucked off the wig with his homicide hands
And he muttered fell charms as he tore off his bands,
And he severed the head as the head of a Swine,
And dire was the snort of the groaning divine,
Then he soused the broad cheeks in a Caldron so hot
Till the Vicar-Broth bubbled and boiled in the Pot.

*From Reginald Heber's 'A Ballad — An Old and
Approved Receipt for Raising the Devil founded
on Tradition and now offered to the Public
by an Amateur of The Black Arte'*

Masque of Gwendolen, taken from Chaucer's *Wife of Bath's Tale* and material based on the Oriental Stories of *Il Bondocani*. An unusual text attributed to him when published many years after his death is entitled *A Ballad — An Old and Approved Receipt for Raising the Devil founded on Tradition and now offered to the Public by an Amateur of the Black Arte*. He edited all ten volumes of the works of Jeremy Taylor, the seventeenth century divine who, after deprivation of his living by the Puritans and imprisonment under the Commonwealth, was eventually appointed Bishop of Down in 1661. The edition includes a life of Taylor written by Heber and extensive notes.

When God sent the blessed Jesus into the world to perfect all righteousness, and to teach the world all his Father's will, it was said, and done, *I will give my laws in your hearts, and in your minds will I write them*; that is, 'you shall be governed by the law of natural and essential equity and reason, by that law which is put into every man's nature: and besides this, whatsoever else shall be superinduced, shall be written in your minds by the Spirit, who shall write all the laws of Christianity in the tables of your consciences. He shall make you to understand them, to perceive their relish, to remember them because you love them, and because you need them, and cannot be happy without them; he shall call them to your mind, and inspire new arguments and inducements to their observations, and make it all as natural to us, as what we were born with.'

Jeremy Taylor writing on 'Conscience in the Mind of a Man'

I am in a sort of half-way station, between a parson and a squire; condemned, in spite of myself, to attend to the duties of the latter, while yet I neither do nor can attend to them sufficiently; nor am I quite sure that even my literary habits are well suited to the situation of a country clergyman . . . I am occasionally disposed to fancy that a man cannot attend to two pursuits at once, and that it will be at length necessary to burn my books, like the early converts to Christianity . . .

Reginald Heber in a letter to John Thornton in May 1813

Heber was sometimes concerned that his literary activities and his duties as squire distracted from his responsibilities as a parson: but his combined literary, theological and pastoral work came together in writing hymns. The first of these were contributed in 1811 to *The Christian Observer*. Heber was one of the pioneers in producing a hymnbook for the use of an Anglican parish, with material for each Sunday in the Church calendar and a few other red letter days. He proceeded cautiously but by 1820, work was almost complete and he took the liberty of sounding out the Bishop of London concerning its publication for wider use. He sought permission to issue it in due time from the Archbishop of Canterbury, but this was refused. After his death, however, his wife was allowed to publish the volume and to dedicate it to the Archbishop.

. . . I began this work with the intention of using it in my own Church, a liberty which, I need not tell your Lordship, has been, for many years back, pretty generally taken by the clergy, and which, if custom alone were to be our guide, would seem almost sufficiently authorised. Thus the morning and evening hymn of Bishop Ken are, in country parishes, almost universally used. Hardly a collection is made for charitable purposes without a hymn for the occasion. Of the anthems used in our Cathedrals, many are taken from other sources than either the Scripture or the Liturgy. And, even in sacred oratorios, such songs as *Angels ever bright and fair*, etc, may be considered as admissions of the right to introduce into places of worship compositions not regularly authorised by the rubric. But the most remarkable instance of the kind which I have met with was during the installation of the Duke of Gloucester at Cambridge, when, during Divine Service in the University Church, and in the presence of her Reverend and Right Reverend heads, I heard a poem sung in the style of Darwin, in which the passion-flower was described as a virgin, devoting herself to religion, attended by as many youths as the plant had stamina.

I might, then, perhaps, without troubling your Lordship, have been content to transgress the rubric in so good company, and have taken the same licence with my neighbours, had I not, in looking over the popular collection from which I wished to glean for my own, been much shocked and scandalised at many things which I found, and which are detestable, not in taste only, but, to the highest degree, in doctrine and sentiment. The famous couplet —

> Come ragged and guilty,
> Come loathsome and bare . . .

is far more tolerable than many which I could instance; and, I own, I began to dislike a liberty, however conceded or assumed, which had been abused so shamefully.

— — — — —

. . . Nor I am without hope, if encouraged by your Lordship to proceed, of obtaining the powerful assistance of my friends Scott and Southey. By far the greater part, however, of my present collection are of my own making, a circumstance which, I trust,

The following hymns are part of an intended series, appropriate to the Sundays and principal holy days of the year, connected in some degree with their particular Collects and Gospels, and designed to be sung between the Nicene Creed and the sermon. The effect of an arrangement of this kind, though only partially adopted, is very striking in the Romish liturgy; and its place should seem to be imperfectly supplied by a few verses of the Psalms, entirely unconnected with the peculiar devotions of the day, and selected at the discretion of a clerk or organist . . .

In one respect, at least, he hopes the following poems will not be found reprehensible; no fulsome or indecorous language has been knowingly adopted; no erotic addresses to Him whom no unclean lips can approach; no allegory, ill understood and worse applied . . .

From Reginald Heber's preface to hymns published in the 'Christian Observer', 1812

I have been for some time engaged in correcting, collecting, and arranging all my hymns, which, now I have got them together, I begin to have some high Church scruples against using in public. Otherwise, I have a promise of many fine old tunes, not Scotch, as I once dreamed of having, but genuine Church melodies. This amusement, for I cannot call it business, together with the business which I cannot call amusement, of making two sermons weekly, has left me very little time either for my dictionary or the *Quarterly*. Yet the first goes on, however slowly; and for the latter, I am preparing an article on Kinneir's Travels, compared with Rennel's retreat of the ten thousand and another on Hunt's translation of Tasso.

From Reginald Heber's letter to Wilmot Horton

70

. . . Being accustomed to judge of metres rather by his fingers than by any other test, he is less tolerant than I could wish of anapaestics and trochaic lines. He was surprised, however, when I showed him that your *Chariot for Advent Sunday* rolled to the same time with the old 104th Psalm. In other respects his taste is exquisite; though, where my own lines were concerned, I thought him sometimes too severe and uncompromising a lover of simplicity. On the whole, however, we have passed his ordeal triumphantly. He encourages us to proceed, and even suggests the advantage of Psalms, two for each Sunday, from the different authorised versions enumerated by Todd, to be published in the same volume with our hymns. This we may talk over when we meet. At present a muse would hardly venture over the threshold of my study, though she were to come in the disguise of a parish clerk, and escorted by Thomas Sternhold Esq, Gentleman-Usher of the Black Rod.

Reginald Heber writing to Henry Hart Milman in December 1822

will not expose me to the imputation of vanity, when the difficulty is considered of finding unexceptional words suitable to the plan which I have adopted . . .

Under these circumstances, my Lord, I feel I am taking a great liberty, but one for which I hope I shall be pardoned, in requesting to know whether you think it possible or advisable for me to obtain the same kind of permission for the use of my hymns in Churches as was given to Tate? and if so, what is the channel through which I should apply? Or if, from the mediocrity of my work, or for any other reason, this would be improper or unattainable, whether I may conscientiously assume the same liberty that many of my neighbours do, and have a few copies printed, not for publication, but for the use of my own Church? This I should, on some accounts prefer, so far as I am myself concerned, to the more ambitious project, inasmuch as I am well aware that no great renown is to be expected by the publisher of religious poetry.

Reginald Heber writing about the hymnbook he has compiled to the Bishop of London in October 1820

It has seemed worth reproducing the contents list in full. It shows the majority of the work as his own writing, with some contributions from his friend Henry Hart Milman. There are a few from other writers, and some with authorship unacknowledged. Several remain in common use to-day. Even the first lines give us a feel of subject and language tested on that early nineteenth century congregation:

Advent Sunday — Hosanna to the living Lord! (R.H.) / Lord! come away! (Bishop Taylor)

Second Sunday in Advent — The Lord will come! the earth shall quake (R.H.) / The chariot! the chariot! its wheels roll on fire (H.H.M.) / In the sun and moon and stars (R.H.)

Third Sunday in Advent — Oh Saviour, is thy promise fled? (R.H.)

Fourth Sunday in Advent — The world is grown old, and her pleasures are past (R.H.)

Christmas Day — Oh Saviour, whom this holy morn (R.H.) / Hark! the herald Angels sing

St. Stephen's Day — The Son of God goes forth to war (R.H.)

St. John the Evangelist's Day — Oh God! who gav'st thy servant grace (R.H.)

Innocents' Day — Oh weep not o'er thy children's tomb (R.H.)

Sunday after Christmas, *or* Circumcision — Lord of mercy and of might! (R.H.)

Epiphany — Sons of men, behold from far (Anon.) / Brightest and best of the sons of the morning (R.H.)

First Sunday after Epiphany — Abash'd be all the boast of Age! (R.H.) / By cool Siloam's shady rill (R.H.)

Second Sunday after Epiphany	Oh hand of bounty, largely spread (R.H.)
	Incarnate Word, who, wont to dwell (R.H.)
	When on her Maker's bosom (R.H.)
Third Sunday after Epiphany	Lord! whose love, in power excelling (R.H.)
Fourth Sunday after Epiphany	Lord! Thou didst arise and say (H.H.M.)
	With reverence let the just appear (From Psalm 89)
	With glory clad, with might array'd (From Psalm 93)
	When through the torn sail the wild tempest is streaming (R.H.)
Fifth Sunday after Epiphany	The angel comes, he comes to reap (H.H.M.)
Sixth Sunday after Epiphany	Lo, He comes, in clouds descending
	The day of wrath! that dreadful day (Walter Scott)
Septuagesima	The God of Glory walks his round (R.H.)
Sexagesima	Oh God! by whom the seed is given (R.H.)
Quinquagesima	Lord of Mercy and of might (R.H.)
	Lord! we sit and cry to Thee (H.H.M.)
Ash Wesnesday *or* First Sunday in Lent	Oh merciful Creator! hear (Drummond)
Second Sunday in Lent	Oh help us Lord! each hour of need
Third Sunday in Lent	Virgin-born! we bow before Thee! (R.H.)
Fourth Sunday in Lent	Oh King of earth and air and sea! (R.H.)
Fifth Sunday in Lent	Oh Thou whom neither time nor space (R.H.)
Sixth Sunday in Lent	Ride on! ride on in majesty (H.H.M.)
	The Lord of might, from Sinai's brow (R.H.)
Good Friday	Bound upon th'accursed tree (H.H.M.)
	Cleft are the rocks, the earth doth quake (Anon.)
	Oh more than merciful! whose bounty gave (R.H.)
Easter Day	Jesus Christ is risen to-day, — Hallelujah!
	God is gone up with a merry noise (R.H.)
	The Sun of Righteousness appears (Anon.)
First Sunday after Easter	Behold the Mountain of the Lord (Logan)
Second Sunday after Easter	My shepherd is the living Lord (Psalm 23 Old V.)
	The Lord my pasture shall prepare (Addison)
Third Sunday after Easter	God moves in a mysterious way (Cowper)
Fourth Sunday after Easter	Greater Spirit! By whose aid (Dryden)
Fifth Sunday after Easter	Life nor Death shall us dissever (R.H.)
Ascension Day *and* Sunday after	*Sit Thou on my right hand, my Son!* saith the Lord (R.H.)
Whitsunday (Ordination Service)	Come, Holy Ghost! our souls inspire
Whitsunday	Spirit of Truth on this Thy day (R.H.)
Trinity Sunday	Holy, holy, holy, Lord God Almighty! (R.H.)
First Sunday after Trinity	Room for the Proud! Ye sons of clay (R.H.)
	The feeble pulse, the gasping breath (R.H.)
Second Sunday after Trinity	Forth from the dark and stormy sky (R.H.)
Third Sunday after Trinity	There was joy in Heaven! (R.H.)
Fourth Sunday after Trinity	I prais'd the Earth in beauty seen (R.H.)
Fifth Sunday after Trinity	Creator of the rolling flood! (R.H.)
Sixth Sunday after Trinity	Lord! have mercy when we strive (H.H.M.)
Seventh Sunday after Trinity	When Spring unlocks the flowers to paint the laughing soil (R.H.)
Eighth Sunday after Trinity	The man is bless'd that hath not lent (First Psalm, Old Version)
Ninth Sunday after Trinity	When rising from the bed of death (Addison)

Tenth Sunday after Trinity	Jerusalem, Jerusalem! enthroned once on high (R.H.)
Eleventh Sunday after Trinity	Oh Lord, turn not Thy face away from them that lowly lie (Sternhold)
Twelfth Sunday after Trinity	Hark! a glad voice the lonely desert cheers! (Pope)
Thirteenth Sunday after Trinity	Who yonder on the desert heath (R.H.)
Fourteenth Sunday after Trinity	Full of mercy, full of love (Bp. Taylor)
Fifteenth Sunday after Trinity	Lo the lilies of the field (R.H.)
Sixteenth Sunday after Trinity	Wake! not, oh mother! sounds of lamentation! (R.H.) When our heads are bow'd with woe (H.H.M.)
Seventeenth Sunday after Trinity	Great God of Hosts! come down in Thy glory (H.H.M.)
Eighteenth Sunday after Trinity	When God came down from Heav'n — the living God (H.H.M.)
Nineteenth Sunday after Trinity	The spacious firmament on high (Addison) Oh blest were the accents of early creation (R.H.)
Twentieth Sunday after Trinity	Lord, have mercy and remove us (H.H.M.)
Twenty-first Sunday after Trinity	The sound of war! In earth and air (R.H.)
Twenty-second Sunday after Trinity	Oh God! my sins are manifold, against my life they cry (R.H.)
Twenty-third Sunday after Trinity	From foes that would the land devour (R.H.)
Twenty-fourth Sunday after Trinity	To conquer and to save, the Son of God (R.H.)
St. James' Day	Though sorrows rise, and dangers roll (R.H.)
St. John the Baptist's Day	The last and greatest herald of Heaven's King (Drummond)
Michaelmas Day	To Thee oh Christ! thy Father's light (Drummond) Oh captain of God's host, whose dreadful might (R.H.)
A Day of Public Thanksgiving	Before Jehovah's aweful throne (Anon.) When all Thy mercies, oh my God (Addison)
In Times of Distress and Danger	Oh God that madest earth and sky, the darkness and the day (R.H.)
Before a Collection made for the Society for the Propagation of the Gospel	From Greenland's icy mountains (R.H.)
An Introit, to be sung between the Litany and Communion Service	Oh most merciful (R.H.)
Hymn after Sermon	Lord, now we part in thy blest name (Anon.)
Before the Sacrament	Bread of the world, in mercy broken! (R.H.)
Morning Hymn	Awake my soul, and with the sun (Bp. Ken)
Evening Hymn	Glory to Thee my God! this night (Bp. Ken) God that madest Earth and Heaven (R.H.)
At a Funeral	Beneath our feet and o'er our head (R.H.) Thou art gone to the Grave, but we will not deplore thee (R.H.)
On Recovery from Sickness	Oh Saviour of the faithful dead (R.H.)

... it is not only our duty to do our enemies no harm, we must go still farther; and, if they need our assistance, we must be ready to do them good. *If thine enemy hunger, feed him; if he thirst, give him drink.* And, strange as it may seem, this

Many of the sermons given in the Parish were preserved and later published by his wife. In 1813, he preached on behalf of the British and Foreign Bible Society directing the congregation's attention *to those mighty fields whose harvest has not yet sounded under the Christian reaping hook, to benighted Africa waiting for our illumination, and to those vast regions of India's ignorance which Providence has planted under our country's care.* In 1816, he gave the Bampton lecture in Oxford. In 1817 he was appointed Prebendary of St. Asaph. In 1818, he accepted the Preachership of Lincoln's Inn, which involved him and his wife spending three months each year in London. He took an initiative in the hope that competition might be avoided between competing bodies undertaking Missionary work.

. . . the one called Gehinnon, or Tophet, — the other Hades, or Sheol. Both these are called Hell in English; but, I think, improperly; as Gehinnon is that dreadful lake, burning with brimstone and fire, into which both the souls and bodies of the wicked will be thrown, after the general judgement and resurrection of the last day, and after this world, and all its elements, shall have melted away with fervent heat; while Hades is described as a hollow place below the earth, in which the souls of all men shall abide, while separated from their bodies, and while waiting for the day of judgement. Of this place, then, and of its different regions, a description is here given; and though the words of Christ are certainly not to be understood in a gross or bodily sense; yet, as we may be sure, that He would not, even in a parable, give us a false idea of the other world, we must learn hence, that, immediately after death, the soul of man does not, as some have fancied, sleep till the day of judgement; but that it is immediately carried, either to a place of pain, or to a place of pleasure, (such pain, and such pleasure, as spirits are capable of feeling) both which should appear to be situated under the earth; and to be divided by a mighty gulf from each other.

From Heber's sermon at Hodnet for the First Sunday after Trinity on Luke 16.22

In 1819, the Society for the Propagation of the Gospel raised £60,000 for missionary work in India, of which three-quarters came from a nationwide collection in both churches and chapels in England, an appeal authorised by royal letter. Heber's father-in-law, the Dean of St. Asaph and Vicar of Wrexham had invited his son-in-law to deliver a series of Sunday evening sermons at the latter. Consequently he was around the day before the appeal was to be made there and wrote at great speed *From Greenland's icy mountains,* sung now to many tunes including MISSIONARY, GREENLAND, HEBER, CRÜGER, AURELIA and MOFFAT (DUNKIRK).

is the wisest as well as the most Christian course which we can pursue. In the first place, by these acts of kindness, we make our own task easier of combating our resentment; and extinguishing every spark of malice in our hearts. If we accustom ourselves to view our enemies as objects of pity; if we practice kindness to them; and even force our inclinations to do them service, we shall find, ere long, the glow of returning good will; and shall feel all those malignant passions fading, which were the curse and torment of the heart which nourished them.

Sermon preached at Hodnet on the Third Sunday after Epiphany from the Epistle for the Day (Romans 12. 19, 20, 21)

May I hope your Lordship will pardon the liberty thus taken by a stranger, who would not have ventured to trespass on your valuable time if it were not on a subject which he conceives important to the peace of the Church and the propagation of the Gospel among the heathen . . . Why . . . should there be two societies for the same precise object? . . . since the charter of the Society for the Propagation of the Gospel in Foreign Parts forbids their joining us, why might not we, as a body, make an offer to transfer our subscriptions, our funds, and our missionary establishments to them . . .

Reginald Heber advocating to a Bishop that the Church Missionary Society should unite with its rival society in a letter written from Hodnet in October 1818

…

Heber's MS Hymn-book suggests
these tunes:

Brightest and best
Wandering Willie
**The God of glory walks
his round**
Banks of Doon
Forth from the dark
Rousseau's Dream
O Saviour, is Thy promise fled
Mary's Dream
**O God, that madest heaven
and earth**
Auld Robin Grey
When on her Maker's bosom
John Anderson, my Jo

From Greenland's icy mountains,
From India's coral strand,
Where Afric's sunny fountains
Roll down their golden sand;
From many an ancient river,
From many a palmy plain,
They call us to deliver
Their land from error's chain!

What though the spicy breezes
Blow soft o'er Java's isle,
Though every prospect pleases
And only man is vile:
In vain with lavish kindness
The gifts of God are strewn,
The Heathen, in his blindness,
Bows down to wood and stone!

Can we, whose souls are lighted
With Wisdom from on high,
Can we to men benighted
The lamp of life deny?
Salvation! oh Salvation!
The Gospel sound proclaim
Till each remotest nation
Has learn'd Messiah's name!

Waft waft ye winds his story,
And you ye waters roll,
Till like a sea of glory,
It spreads from pole to pole;
Till o'er our ransom'd Nature,
The Lamb for sinners slain,
Redeemer, King, Creator,
In bliss returns to reign!
As printed in Heber's hymnbook

He also wrote to Charlotte Dod explaining where he took issue with the Shrewsbury Methodist preacher, Thomas Scott.

In one respect there has, indeed, been a difference in our system of inquiry, inasmuch as, though I have always prayed God for the aid of His spirit to guide me *generally* into all truth, and more *especially* into the knowledge of whatever truth was necessary or profitable to my salvation and the salvation of others, yet I have not ventured to ask or hope that the Holy Ghost would secure me from *all* error, or enable me to decide on topics so abstruse as those of free will and the final perseverance of the elect. You will, therefore, take my notions on these and suchlike points as the opinion of one sufficiently weak and fallible, and who, though he believes himself right in his conclusions, has looked for no other aid in forming them than (what I really trust I have received in answer to my worthless prayers) a teachable mind, and grace to use diligently the means of information offered to me.

That Mr. Scott has expected more than this seems to me the lurking root of the errors into which he has fallen.

. . . *secret things belong to the Lord our God*: but on the necessity of an atonement, on justification by faith, and on the obligation which lies on us to work out, with fear and trembling, the salvation thus begun in us, no real difficulties exist, and by these, on every system, our entrance to heaven is to be secured.

Reginal Heber writing to Charlotte Dod of the
Shrewsbury Methodist Preacher, Thomas Scott
and his book, 'Force of Truth', 1819

In 1820, he visited Elizabeth Fry at Newgate Prison.

. . . we went over the female side of the prison — a number of long, narrow, dismal rooms, with paper instead of glass in the windows, crowded with little iron bedsteads, and every vacant space occupied by implements of work etc. A large Bible lay in every room, and all was very clean, considering the crowded state of the prison. A great difference might be observed between the new-comers to prison and those who had been some time there and experienced the good effects of Mrs. Fry's discipline. The latter were all clean, humble, and quiet-looking, and sate with their eyes cast down and every appearance of penitence and modesty, their clothes too, though chiefly very poor, were not ragged. The former were wild, staring, half-starved, and more than half-naked creatures, with misery and wickedness marked in every line of their countenances. Among these last were two girls, one twelve, the other nine years old, the bones of their naked shoulders standing out almost through the skin; pale as ashes, but the elder with an affected simper which was quite ghastly. These were pickpockets. Most of the rest were for passing forged notes . . .

. . . there are a set of men who cannot bear that anybody should do good in a new way, who absolutely *hate* Mrs. Fry, and when I was in Oxford I had to fight her battles repeatedly with persons whom that arch bigot Sir Wm. Scott had been filling with all possible prejudices against her.

Extracts from Reginald Heber's letter
to Charlotte Dod describing a visit to
Mrs. Elizabeth Fry at Newgate Prison in 1820

Every morning brings fresh accounts of the attempts made by the mob to bring the soldiery over to them, and the allegiance of the latter is believed to be badly shaken. I can hardly conceive in any country the existence of stronger symptoms of a probable revolution, and, what is worse, I find almost everybody of nearly the same opinion.

From Reginald Heber's letter to Charlotte Dod in June 1820

If we are forbidden to see our neighbour suffer hunger, disease, or nakedness without, to the best of our power, endeavouring to relieve his sufferings; if it be a crime to suffer our enemy's beast of burthen to fall beneath its load without rendering it our assistance, of what punishment must he be worthy who looks on with dry eyes and without an effort to abate the evil on millions stretched out in deadly darkness of idolatry and superstition; on millions more surrounded with light, yet, by some strange fatality, continuing to work the works of darkness; on millions as yet incapable of good or evil, whose happiness or misery, both in this world and the world to come, must depend on the sort of education which is given them?

Reginald Heber preaching at Whittington in 1820 on behalf of the Church Missionary Society

A sermon preached that year at Whittington on behalf of the Church Missionary Society shows something of the theology which gave urgency to the missionary endeavour of the period. The pulpit was one to be occupied later by hymnwriter William Walsham How, author of *Summer suns are glowing*, who served as incumbent in the second half of the century. Heber was also concerned at this time about the possibility of serious civil unrest in England, with perhaps the troops siding with the people against authority. The same year a throat virus laid many Hodnet cottagers low and Heber without thought for himself visited them with medicine and nourishment. He finally succcumbed and was seriously ill himself.

In 1822, *Palestine* was translated into Welsh; whilst he wrote *Hawarden Castle* for the Royal British Bowmen.

Smile, smile, ye dear hills, 'mid your woods and your flowers,
Whose heather lies dark in the morn's dewy glow!
A time must await you of tempest and showers,
An autumn of mist, and a winter of snow!
For me, though the whirlwind has shiver'd and cleft me,
Of wealth and of empire the stranger bereft me,
Yet Saxon, – proud Saxon, – thy fury has left me
Worth, valour, and beauty, the harp and the bow!

Reginald Heber: From 'Hawarden Castle', a song of the bow written for a meeting of Royal British Bowmen.

The Hodnet years had not been without sadness. In 1816, Heber's younger brother Thomas died and in 1818 the Hebers lost an infant daughter. The birth of Emily in 1821 was a long awaited delight.

It took five months for the news of the death of the first Bishop of Calcutta to reach England. The responsibility for suggesting possible successors fell to Heber's associate of college days, the Rt. Hon. C. W. Williams Wynn, then President of the Board of Commissioners for the Affairs of India. When Heber was sounded about taking on the see his first response was negative. He was swayed by medical opinion that his daughter Emily would not be strong enough to live in India on a permanent basis; whilst his mother urged he must do what was right, her counsel was accompanied with a flood of tears as she considered such a posting would mean that she would not, on account of her age, be likely to see her son again before her death. A fortnight later, after a Bengal medical expert gave a more favourable opinion on the effect India might have on Emily, Heber intimated: *The sacrifice which I would not make for the sake of wealth and dignity, both my wife and myself will cheerfully make in order to prevent any serious inconvenience to a cause of so much importance.*

In the early months of 1823, the University of Oxford conferred on him by diploma the degree of Doctor of Divinity; the Fellows of All Souls desired him to sit for a portrait. He paid a farewell visit to Charlotte Dod. During Lent, Crotch's oratorio based on Heber's *Palestine* was revived at London's Drury Lane Theatre. On 22nd April, the Hebers left Hodnet. On 1st June, Reginald was consecrated Bishop in the chapel of Lambeth Palace in London. In the succeeding few days, he had an audience of King George; he *dined with the East India Directors at a monstrous table covered with turtle and French wines*, and was reluctantly obliged to make *a speech to thank them for their kindness in giving me a house and shortening my term of residence.* He preached a sermon for the benefit of the London Charity School in St. Paul's Cathedral and had dinner with the Duke of Gloucester and the Lord Mayor of London. Between these engagements, he set to learning Hindostani.

Again, his gift as a travel writer and correspondent provides us with detailed accounts of the voyage to India. His letter of 12th July, from Lat.14.1 North, Long.27.40 West to Charlotte Dod includes many word pictures:

. . . I rise between six and seven. The men all assemble to breakfast in the common cabin at half-past eight. After breakfast and reading the Psalms and Lessons to Emily, I write my journal or prepare my Hindostani or Persian lessons till twelve, from which time till half-past two we are construing, etc., with one of the cadets, a very clever lad, who was introduced to us by Dr. Gilchrist in London, and who both there and during our voyage has performed the part of our tutor. At three we sit down, closely wedged, to dinner, and after a plentiful and handsome, though not very elegantly dressed meal, walk on deck till tea-time (six). Tea is followed by prayers, which I found not the least difficulty in introducing, and the rest of the evening is passed on deck and in conversation, either walking or seated, till about half-past nine, when Captain Manning hints to us that it is bed-time . . .

— — — — —

I have of late, indeed, once or twice ventured to fence with one of the cadets; but, as this may be objected to as not altogether an Episcopal amusement, I do not care to do it too often or too long together . . .

The dome and broad aisle of the church was crowded with well-dressed folks (no fewer than 7000 in number, as one of the stewards informed me); an immense orchestra in front of the organ filled with the choir singers (the best Protestant singers in London) in surplices, and above 5000 boys and girls ranged in an amphitheatre all round, in uniform dresses, and packed so close, and ranged on so steep a declivity, that the whole looked like a tapestry of faces and clothes. Whenever they sat down or stood up the rustle was actually like very distant thunder. And their singing! I never felt anything of the kind so strangely and awfully impressive. It was not like singing, but like the sound of winds, waters, birds and instrumental music all blended; and yet one distinguished the words with the exception of the coronation anthem, in which their Hallelujah was very magnificent.
Reginald Calcutta, describing to Charlotte Dod the scene, when he was appointed to preach at London's St. Paul's Cathedral on 8th June 1823

We have had visits from grampuses, sharks, and whales, and shoals or flights (call them which you will) of flying fish are continually skimming round us, the sun shining from their white and blue scales, and at a distance and at first sight not unlike flocks of swallows. What has most struck me, however, is the deep and beautiful blue of the sea, so unlike the cold green glass which girds in the shores of Wales and Cheshire. This, where the breeze curls it, is like lapis-lazuli streaked with silver, and in the vessel's wake, when agitated by the motion of the rudder, it assumed all tints, from light green to the glossy purple of a peacock's neck.

— — — — —

The next day, the Bishop, who had taken the local black-smith to task at Hodnet over the use of Sunday, recorded in his journal:

A large shoal of dolphins were playing round the ship, and I thought it right to interfere to check the harpoons and fishing-hooks of some of the crew. I am not strict in my notions of what is called the Christian Sabbath: but the wanton destruction of animal life seems to be precisely one of those *works* by which the sanctity and charity of our weekly feast would be profaned.

On 16th August, he was delighted that *dear little Emily* was able to repeat in his hearing *a part of the Lord's Prayer* which her mother had been teaching her on board ship. A month later, Heber's journal describes a magnificent sunset:

This evening we had a most beautiful sunset . . . and I think the most magnificent spectacle I ever saw. Besides the usual beautiful tints of crimson, flame-colour etc., which the clouds displayed, and which were strangely contrasted with the deep blue of the sea, and the lighter, but equally beautiful blue of the sky, there were in the immediate neighbourhood of the sinking sun, and for some time after his disc had disappeared, large tracts of a pale translucent green, such as I had never seen before except in a prism, and surpassing every effect of paint, or glass, or gem. Every body on board was touched and awed by the glory of the scene . . .

Not all the journey was smooth. His wife did not prove to be a good sea-traveller and suffered much sickness, aggravated perhaps by her pregnancy. In times of storm, Heber doubtless recalled his hymn for those at sea. Both he, and perhaps more especially his wife must have been glad when on 23rd October, their voyage was accomplished.

When through the torn sail the wild tempest is streaming,
When o'er the dark wave the red lightening is gleaming,
Nor hope lends a ray the poor seaman to cherish
We fly to our Maker – *Help, Lord! or we perish!*

Opening verse of a hymn for those at sea, which
also has a verse about the whirlwind of passion

Reginald Heber became one of the seven chief British missionaries of the age to India. His story stands alongside those of Charles Grant, Presbyterian and then Anglican layman, of Baptist William Carey, Henry Martyn, an Anglican; and of three Presbyterians, John Wilson, Alexander Duff and Stephen Hislop. Their charter forced on the directors of the East India Company the bare toleration of Christianity and the provision of Anglican and Presbyterian pastors for the expatriates. This had begun to bear some fruit in proclaiming the Christian gospel to the native population; Swiss and German missionaries were also active. But when Heber arrived, no ordained missionary of the Church of England was at work teaching or preaching to India's peoples in their own tongue and no native had been episcopally ordained.

Three months before the Hebers sailed from England, Lord Amherst had set out as the newly-appointed Governor-General. His previous experience did little to fit him for the role or the decisions he would have to take in the years ahead. Heber described Government House in Calcutta as a building *which narrowly missed being a noble structure.* The architect in him reported that *it consists of two semicircular galleries, placed back to back, uniting in the centre in a large hall, and connecting four splendid suites of apartments. Its columns are, however, in a paltry style, and instead of having, as it might have had, two noble stories and a basement, it has three stories, all too low, and is too much pierced with windows on every side . . .*

His journal describes the cathedral thus:
. . . a very pretty building, all but the spire, which is short and clumsy. The whole composition, indeed, of the Church, is full of architectural blunders, but still it is in other respects handsome. The inside is elegant, paved with marble, and furnished with very large and handsome glass chandeliers . . . with a light pulpit, with chairs on one side of the chancel for the Governor-General and his family, and on the other for the Bishop and Archdeacon.

In December, a graphic letter to Charlotte Dod gives many impressions of what Reginald Heber found in his new see:

Accept, O blessed Lord, my hearty thanks for the protection which Thou hast vouchsafed to me and mine during a long and dangerous voyage and through many strange and unwholesome climates. Extend to us, I beseech Thee, Thy fatherly protection and love in the land where we now dwell, and among the perils to which we are now liable. Give us health, strength, and peace of mind; give us friends in a strange land, and favour in the eyes of those around us; give us so much of this world's good as Thou knowest to be good for us; and be pleased to give us grace to love Thee truly, and constantly to praise and bless Thee, through Thy dear Son Jesus Christ, our Saviour. Amen.

The Bishop's prayer on entering his episcopate

Of the natural amiability of the man it is impossible to convey an adequate idea . . . His conversation is very lively, and, from his large acquaintance with books and men, very instructive, while he industriously seeks opportunities of public worship, Sunday and week day, and urges on all the importance of attending on the means of grace. Surely this land has cause of praise to God that such an one has been placed at the head of affairs here.

The Senior Chaplain, Mr. Corrie who had 'stood in as far as possible' while waiting for Heber to arrive, describes the new Bishop

. . . all Bengal is described to us as like those parts which we have seen — a vast alluvial plain, intersected by the innumerable arms of the Ganges, overflowed once a year, but now covered with rice-fields, divided by groves of tall fruit-trees, with villages under their shelter, swarming with a population beyond anything which Europe can show and scarcely to be paralleled in China . . .

— — — — —

. . . a crowd of people in the streets beyond anything to be seen even in London, some dressed in tawdry silks and brocades, more in white cotton garments; and most of all black and naked, except a scanty covering round the waist; hideous figures of religious mendicants with no clothing but their long hair and beards in elf locks, their faces painted white or yellow, their beads in one ghastly lean hand, and the other stretched out like a bird's claw to receive donations: marriage processions, with the bride in a covered chair, the bridegroom on horseback, and so swathed round with garlands as hardly to be seen: tradesmen sitting on the ground in the midst of their different commodities, and old men, lookers-on, perched naked as monkeys, smoking on the flat roofs of the houses; carts drawn by oxen, and driven by wild-looking men with thick sticks, so unmercifully used as perfectly to undeceive all our notions of Brahminical humanity; attendants with silver maces peeping through the crowd before the carriage of some great man or other; no women seen except of the lowest class, yet even these with heavy silver ornaments on their dusky arms and ankles; while coaches, covered up close with red cloth, are seen conveying the inmates of the neighbouring seraglios to take what is called *the air*; a constant creaking of cart wheels, which are never greased in India; a constant clamour of voices and an almost constant thumping and jingling of drums, cymbals, etc., in honour of some one or other of their deities; and add to all a villainous smell of garlic, rancid coconut oil, sour butter, and stagnant ditches, and you will understand the sights, sounds and smells of what is called *the Black Town* of Calcutta . . .

— — — — —

. . . the Governor General . . . has most of the usual appendages of a sovereign . . . bodyguards, gold sticks, spearmen, peacocks' plumes, state carriage, state barge and elephants . . .

— — — — —

First Sunday after Trinity

The feeble pulse, the gasping breath,
The clenched teeth, the glazed eye,
Are these thy sting, thou dreadful Death?
O Grave, are these thy victory!

The mourners by our parting bed,
The wife, the children weeping nigh,
The dismal pageant of the dead, –
These, these are not thy victory!

But, from the much-loved worlds to part,
Our lust untamed, our spirit high,
All nature struggling at the heart,
Which, dying, feels it dare not die!

To dream through life a gaudy dream
Of pride and pomp and luxury,
Till waken'd by the nearer gleam
Of burning, boundless agony;

To meet o'er soon our angry king,
Whose love we past unheeded by;
Lo this, O Death, thy deadliest sting!
O Grave, and this thy victory!

O Searcher of the secret heart,
Who deign'd for sinful man to die!
Restore us ere the spirit part
Nor give to Hell the victory!

Heber's Hymn for the
'First Sunday after Trinity'

. . . Two years ago no woman in India could either read or write; now, in Calcutta and the neighbourhood, there are twenty-three female schools . . .

– – – – –

. . . Do we encounter no opposition? Unfortunately we do. An apostate Brahmin, Rammohun Roy, who was once half-Christian, but now wants to found a sect of his own, has written some mischievous pamphlets against us . . . the Dissenters . . . putting down their schools in rivalry whenever our schools are fairly established . . . the Lancasterian British and Foreign School Society . . . have pledged themselves not to teach Christianity in Bengal, and therefore have excluded the Scriptures from their school-books . . .

. . . Our stay in Calcutta must, of course, depend on my child's health and my wife's recovery . . . If all goes on well, my present plan is to set out with tents and elephants to march up the country in February. Two months will bring us to the neighbourhood of Benares, where we must halt for the hot winds. We should then go by water to Cawnpore and again by land to Meerut. The following cold season will be spent in our return through Lucknow, Moorshedabad, etc. I shall then have seen one-third of my immense diocese in a journey of 2500 miles, during the greater part of which we should sojourn like the ancient patriarchs. God grant that, like them, we may look from our tabernacles to an eternal city.

His journal and correspondence also allow him to tell in his own words something of the early months of 1824:

. . . a stage had been constructed of bamboos about eighteen inches or two feet above the ground, *on* which the dead body had been laid, and *under* which, as my native servants told me, the unhappy widow had been stretched out, surrounded with combustibles. Only a heap of glowing embers was now seen here, besides two long bamboos, which seemed intended to keep down any struggles which nature might force from her. *On* the stage was what seemed a large bundle of coarse cotton cloth, smoking, and partially blackened, emitting a very offensive smell. This my servants said was the husband's body. The woman they expressly affirmed had been laid *below* it, and ghee poured over her to hasten her end, and they also said the bamboos had been laid *across* her . . . I felt very sick at heart, and regretted I had not been half an hour sooner, though probably my attempts at persuasion would have had no chance of success. I would at least have tried to reconcile her to life. There were perhaps twenty or thirty people present, with about the same degree of interest, though certainly not the same merriment, as would have been called forth by a bonfire in England. I saw no weeping, and heard no lamentations. But when the boat drew near, a sort of shout was raised, I believe in honour of Brahma, which was met by a similar outcry from my boatmen.

— — — — —

Accordingly, though the general sobriety of the Hindoos (a virtue which they possess in common with most inhabitants of warm climates) affords a very great facility to the maintenance of public order and decorum, I really never have met with a race of men whose standard of morality is so low, who feel so little apparent shame on being

detected in a falsehood, or so little interest in the suffering
of a neighbour, not being of their own caste or family: whose
ordinary and familiar conversation is so licenctious; or, in
the wilder and more lawless districts, who shed blood with so
little repugnance.

— — — — —

BENGALI PEASANTRY

. . . the appearance and condition of some forty millions of
peasantry subject to British rule — very poor, as their
appearance sufficiently indicates (at least in those points
wherein an Englishman places his ideas of comfort and
prosperity), yet not *so* poor, and not by any means so rude
and wild as their scanty dress and simple habitations would
at first lead an Englishman to imagine. The silver ornaments
which the young woman wears on her ankles, arms, forehead,
and in her nose, joined to the similar decorations on her
children's arms, would more than buy all the clothes and
finery of the smartest servant-girl in the rows of Chester . . .

— — — — —

Did I tell you . . . that the other day I met with one of my
hymns *(From Greenland's icy mountains)* translated into
Bengali?

— — — — —

I have been unwell during a considerable part of this year.
It began by a fall from my horse, in itself of little
consequence, but the cut on my leg, in this inflammatory
climate, was followed by a succession of boils, a very

common disease here, and I am told reckoned rather beneficial than otherwise to the general health. They were, however, very painful and troublesome, and were, in my case, aggravated, as I am told, by too great abstinence. Certain it is I have been much better since I have eaten meat regularly and drunk wine, though in both I am still more moderate than most of my neighbours. This is also in strict confidence, and not to be repeated. I am very anxious my poor mother should not know of my having been unwell. From you I will not conceal it, and I know you will believe me when I say that I am now almost as well as ever I was, and I have every reason to think the climate will agree with me. I wish I could be equally confident respecting my poor wife and children. The baby is, however, as fine and fat a child as can be, and little Emily, though thin and delicate, is very much better than she has been. My poor wife is by no means well . . . we are established in a house so large as quite to exceed all our ideas of comfort. I feel almost lost in a dining-room sixty-seven feet long, a drawing-room of the same dimensions, a study supported by arcades, and though low in proportion to its size, forty-five feet square.

— — — — —

SHIVA PAGODAS BESIDE HEBER'S HOUSE, TITAGHUR

The Hebers' second daughter Harriet was christened on her father's birthday. They had a great dinner and evening party inviting also some of the wealthy natives. Three days later Heber reported the *Cholera Morbus* was *making great ravages* though few Europeans had yet died. It is *sufficiently near to remind us of our utter dependance on God's mercy, and how near we are in the midst of life to death!* So Heber was still in Calcutta to preach in the cathedral on Ascension Day. His sermon showed his reservations about Roman Catholic missionary work. Whilst the Romish faith was on a higher level than the Brahmanical, it was nevertheless a corrupt form of Christianity. Though he rejoices at every conquest made among the heathen, he would not wish to emulate Xavier teaching tens of thousands to patter their rosary in Latin instead of Sanskrit, and to transfer to the Saints the honour which they had paid to the Devtas.

On 15th June, Heber began his trip from Calcutta to Bombay. Heber had not applied for the services of an Assistant Surgeon for the trip, not feeling it right to deplete the medical resources available to go with a military expedition to Rangoon. Without a doctor, he felt he must leave wife and children behind. The party consisted of one Englishman besides himself, and over forty natives. Mr. Corrie and his family set out in a budgerow simultaneously and for the first few days of the river trip, they sailed together, thereafter taking different routes to meet up on 10th August at Boglipoor. Just a sentence taken from Heber's journal for each day relates some of his adventures:

15th June: Accompanied by my domestic Chaplain, Mr. Stow, I embarked on board a fine 16 oared pinnace for Dacca . . .

'PANCHWAY' – BOAT FOR THE BISHOP'S SERVANTS

16th June: Between Barrackpoor and Chandernagore are some large and handsome pagodas . . .

17th June: I have never heard louder thunder, or seen so vivid and formidable lightening . . .

18th June: . . . we were received by the Raja Omichund, a fat shortish man, of about 45, of rather fair complexion, but with no other clothes than his waistcloth and Brahminical string, and only distinguished from his vassals by having his forehead marked all over with alternate stripes of chalk, vermilion, and gold leaf.

19th June: One of the greatest plagues we have as yet met with in this journey is that of the winged bugs . . .

20th June: . . . some fishermen brought a very noble fish alongside us for sale, of exactly the shape and appearance of a chub, but weighing at least 20 or 25 pounds . . . the fish was very good, exceedingly firm and white, like a jack . . .

21st June: Holland itself could not have furnished a thicker or more stinking fog than hung over the banks of the river early this morning . . .

22nd June: At the more difficult of these places we generally found a Musselman fakir or two established, who came, or sometimes swam, to beg alms, pleading the efficacy of their prayers in getting us past the dangers . . .

23rd June: The jackalls were very noisy this night . . .

24th June: A large tree bearing a small and not ill-tasted fig, attracted my attention from the strange manner in which its fruit grew, attached to the bark both of boughs and stems, like a gall-nut, oak apple, or similar excrescence. Its name is Goolun . . .

25th June: We stopped for the night at a beautiful village with splendid banian and peepul trees, and surrounded by natural meadows and hedge-rows, so like English, that, but for the cocos, we could have supposed ourselves there . . .

26th June: We saw an ingenious water-pump, worked by 12 men, and intended, as I conceive, to irrigate a piece of cane-ground . . .

27th June: We passed to my surprise a row of no less than nine or ten large and very beautiful otters, tethered with straw collars, and long strings to bamboo stakes on the bank . . . I was told that most of the fishermen in this neighbourhood kept one or more of these animals, who were almost as tame as dogs, and of great use in fishing . . .

28th June: The betel is a beautiful tree, the tallest and slenderest of the palm kind, with a very smooth white bark. Nothing can be more graceful than its high slender pillars, when backed by the dark shade of bamboos and other similar foliage . . .

29th June: A poor miserable-looking man came along-side, and with joined hands, and in accents of deep distress, asked for medicine . . . he and eight others, a boat's crew, were all lying within a few yards, so ill and weak . . . Our serang said it was the Sunderland disease, in fact a marsh fever. Stow immediately fell to work to make some pills of calomel and colocynth . . .

God that madest Earth and Heaven,
Darkness and light!
Who the day for toil hast given,
For rest the night!
May Thine Angel guards defend us,
Slumber sweet Thy mercy send us,
Holy dreams and hopes attend us,
This livelong night!

Reginald Heber's single-stanza 'Evening Hymn'
It is often sung with a second verse added by
Richard Whately, an Archbishop of Dublin.
Tunes used include AR HYD Y NOS,
NUTFIELD and EAST ACKLAM

30th June: The only interesting occurrence was the capture of a very large and beautiful iguana, or lizard, 2 feet 9 inches long, with five toes on each foot, and a forked tongue, beautifully marked with tyger-like stripes of yellow and black . . .

1st July: I had the delight to-day of hearing again from my wife, and this is worth all the fine scenery in the world . . .

2nd July: We passed a considerable indigo factory, with a very pretty house attached to it . . . the appearance of the workmen, whose naked limbs and bodies were covered with the blue dye, was very singular . . .

3rd July: . . . with such a wind, it was impossible for the pinnace to reach Dacca by Church-time next day, I determined on going thither in the jolly-boat, leaving Stow, whose health would not admit of his joining such an expedition, behind. I accordingly embarked, taking with me, besides my clothes, a pocket-compass, and a common Bengalee umbrella, which being of straw, I thought would keep off the sun more effectually than my own . . .

4th July: I preached to a small congregation, in a very small but pretty Gothic Church . . .

5th July: Dacca, as Abdullah truly said is *much place for elephant*. The Company have a stud of from 2 to 300 . . .

At Dacca, Heber's chaplain became critically ill and died, making Heber's round of duties burdened with grief. In eighteen days, he met with civil and military dignitaries; received the Archbishop of Echmiazin twice, visited the Nawab, inspected the prison, and presided at a Confirmation Service, besides generally getting to know the Anglican community. On 22nd July he set out for Boglipoor and arrived there on 10th August.

23rd July: . . . No sooner, however, were the messengers seen, approaching, than half the village, fearing that it was some Government duty which was required, were seen running away to hide themselves . . .

24th July: I had left Dacca cheered with the hope that my wife . . . would be able to join me with our children at Boglipoor; but I received a letter from her . . . which made me see that this would be impossible. This news, added to the uncomfortable state of my mind and feelings, kept me awake great part of the night, and I arose ill and unrefreshed.

25th July: My health, which had been for some time a good deal deranged, appeared renovated . . . A beautiful and fragrant purple flower was shown me as the jalap plant.

26th July: . . . partly in looking over a curious document . . . his Gaol Calendar . . . in all 91 prisoners for trial . . . the nature of the defence usually set up, which, I observed, was

If thou wert by my side, my love,
How fast would evening fail,
In green Bengala's palmy grove,
Listening the nightingale!

If thou, my love, wert by my side,
My babies at my knee,
How gaily would our pinnace glide
O'er Gunga's mimic sea!

I miss thee at the dawning day,
When, on the deck reclined,
In careless ease my limbs I lay,
And woo the cooler wind.

I miss thee, when by Gunga's stream
My twilight steps I guide;
But most beneath the lamp's pale beam
I miss thee from my side.

I spread my books, my pencil try,
The lingering noon to clear;
But miss the kind approving eye,
Thy meek attentive ear.

But when of morn and eve the star
Beholds me on my knee,
I feel, though thou art distant far,
Thy prayers ascend for me.

Then on! Then on! where duty leads.
My course be onward still;
O'er broad Hindoostan's sultry meads,
O'er black Almora's hill.

That course nor Delhi's kingly gates,
Nor wild Malwa detain;
For sweet the bliss that me awaits
By yonder western main.

Thy towers, Bombay, gleam bright, they say,
Across the dark blue sea:
But ne'er were hearts so light and gay
As then shall meet in thee.

Bishop Heber's 'Verses to his Wife'
written from off Bogwangola, July 1824

in nine cases out of ten, an alibi, being the easiest of all others to obtain by the aid of false-witnesses. Perjury is dreadfully common and very little thought of.

28th July: . . . I received a letter from my poor wife, with an account of the severe illness of both our babies, and of the merciful deliverance which our beloved little Emily had received from God . . .

29th July: We passed, this evening, the first crocodile I have seen.

31st July: . . . I saw an ape in a state of liberty, but as tame as possible, the favourite, perhaps the deity, certainly the sacred animal of the villagers . . . He was about the size of a large spaniel, enormously fat, covered with long silky hair generally of a rusty red colour, but on his breast a fine *shot* blue, and about his buttocks and thighs gradually waving into a deep orange . . .

1st August: I cannot help admiring in the Mussulmans the manner in which their religion apparently mixes with every action of their lives . . .

2nd August: We arrived at Bogwangola . . . The common was covered with children and cattle, a considerable number of boats were on the beach, different musical instruments were strumming, thumping, squealing, and rattling from some of the open sheds . . .

3rd August: . . . we found fine dry fields of cotton and silkmulberries . . .

4th August: . . . a boat with four dervises, sturdy beggars enough, came after us, singing. I asked why they did not work, and was told by Abdullah, that it was one of the miseries of the country, that they were all a caste of beggars from father to son, trained to no labour, and even if they desired it, not likely to be employed by any body . . .

5th August: . . . I could almost have fancied myself at one moment on the estuary of the Dee, with my back turned toward the Welsh mountains, and looking across the plain of Chester up to

Beeston and the Stannaries.

7th August: The people of these mountains . . . are a race distinct from those of the plain in features, language, civilization, and religion. They have no castes, care nothing for the Hindoo deities, and are even said to have no idols . . .

8th August: I asked if they knew any thing about the cave on the other side of the hill, on which the old gossain, with an air of much importance, said, that nobody had ever seen its end; that 2000 years ago a certain Raja had desired to explore it, and set out with 10,000 men, 100,000 torches, and 100,000 measures of oil, but that he could not succeed; and, if I understood him rightly, neither he nor his army ever found their way back again!

9th August: The peasants here all walk with sticks as tall as themselves, and wear black, rough-looking blankets, thrown over their heads and shoulders . . .

10th August: I arrived at Boglipoor, or Bhaugulpoor . . . and found, to my great joy, my friends the Corries still there.

The journey to Bombay took until 26th April 1825, when he was at last to meet his wife and elder daughter whose sea-journey had been tedious and distressing, both from weather and sickness. Heber's journey, first again by river and then overland took him by way of Monghyr, Buxar, Benares, Allahabad, Cawnpore, Lucknow, Bareilly, Almora, Meerut, Delhi, Agra, Jyepoor, Ajmer, Neemuch and Baroda; a trip full of incidents, of which Heber's record of a few must suffice.

(August)
We passed a high building shaped something like a glass-house, with a stair winding round its outside up to the top, like the old prints of the Tower of Babel. It was built as a granary for the district,

There was joy in heav'n,
There was joy in heav'n,
When the billows heaving dark
Sank around the stranded ark,
And the rainbow's watery span
Spoke of mercy, hope to man,
And peace with God in heav'n.

*The second stanza of Heber's hymn
for the Third Sunday after Trinity
sung to GAUDIUM CELESTE*

Our bark has found its harbour now.
With furled sail, and painted side,
Behold the tiny frigate ride.
Upon her deck, 'mid charcoal gleams,
The Moslems' savoury supper steams,
While all apart, beneath the wood,
The Hindoo cooks his simpler food.

— — — — —

Yet mark! as fade the upper skies,
Each thicket opes ten thousand eyes.
Before, beside us, and above,
The fire-fly lights his lamp of love,
Retreating, chasing, sinking, soaring,
The darkness of the copse exploring;
While to this cooler air confest.
The broad Dhatura bares her breast,
Of fragrant scent, and virgin white,
A pearl around the locks of night!
Still as we pass in softened hum,
Along the breezy alleys come
The village song, the horn, the drum.

From 'An Evening Walk in Bengal'

Oh King of earth and air and sea!
The hungry ravens cry to Thee;
To Thee the scaly tribes that sweep
The bosom of the boundless deep;

To Thee the lions roaring call,
The common Father, kind to all;
Then grant Thy servants, Lord! we pray,
Our daily bread from day to day!

*Opening verses of Reginald Heber's
hymn for the Fourth Sunday in Lent*

in pursuance of a plan adopted about 35 years ago by Government, after a great famine, as a means of keeping down the price of grain, but abandoned on a supposed discovery of its inefficacy, since no means in their hands, nor any buildings which they could construct, without laying on fresh taxes, would have been sufficient to collect or contain more than one day's provision from the vast population of their territories.

— — — — —

(September)
During my progress through the holy places I had received garlands of flowers in considerable numbers, which I was told it was uncivil to throw away, particularly those which were hung round my neck. I now, in consequence, looked more like a sacrifice than a priest . . .

— — — — —

(September)
The case of one of these men had occasioned me some perplexity the day before, when Mr. Morris stated it to me; but I have now made up my mind. He was a convert of Mr. Corrie's, and six years ago married a woman who then professed herself a Christian, but soon afterwards ran away from him and turned Musalman, in which profession she was now living with another man. The husband had applied to the magistrate to recover her, but, on the woman declaring she was no Christian, and did not choose to be the wife of one, he said he could not compel her. The husband, in consequence, about two years ago, applied to Mr. Frazer to marry him to another woman. Mr. Frazer declined doing so, as no divorce had taken place, on which he took the woman without marriage, and had now two children by her. For this he had been repelled from the communion by Mr. Morris, but still continued to frequent the church, and was now very anxious for confirmation. After some thought, I came to the conclusion that the man should be reproved for the precipitancy with which he had formed his first connection, and the scandal which he had since occasioned, but that he might be admitted both to confirmation and the communion, and might be married to the woman who now held the place of a wife to him. It seemed a case to which St. Paul's rule applied, that if an unbelieving husband or wife chose to depart, on religious grounds, from their believing partner, this latter was, in consequence, free. At all events, as the runaway woman was, if a wife, living in open adultery, it was plain that he had a right to 'put

her away'. Though the laws of the country provided him no remedy, yet, as a matter of conscience, this right might be fitly determined by his religious guides, and I conceived myself warranted to declare him divorced and at liberty to marry again. My determination, I found, gave great satisfaction to Mr. Frazer and Mr. Morris . . .

— — — — —

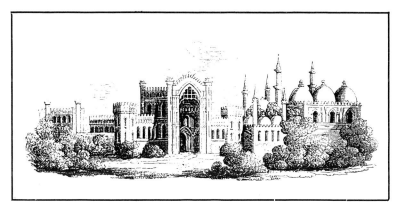

ROUMI DURWAZA AND IMAMBARA, LUCKNOW

(October)
. . . the language of Bengal, which is quite different from Hindoostanee, is soft and liquid. The common people are all fond of singing, and some of the airs which I used to hear from the boatmen and children in the villages, reminded me of Scotch melodies. I heard more than once *My boy, Tammy* and *Here's a health to those far away*, during some of those twilight walks, after my boat was moored, which wanted only society to make them delightful, when amid the scent and glow of night-blowing flowers, the soft whisper of waving palms, and the warbling of the nightingale, watching the innumerable fire-flies, like airy glow-worms, floating, rising, and sinking, in the gloom of the bamboo woods, and gazing on the mighty river with the unclouded breath of a tropical moon sleeping on its surface, I felt in my heart it is good to be here.

— — — — —

(November)
A strange receipt was suggested . . . for the benefit of Cabul's health, whose beauty attracts general notice, as well as his docility and fondness for me. It was a boiled sheep's head once in fourteen days! and the object was to make him strong and help his digestion. I asked Abdullah if he had ever

heard of such a *messala* or mess before? He answered, it was sometimes recommended, and he had tried it himself to his sorrow, since the horse never lived to have the dose repeated.

— — — — —

Oh, Saviour! with protecting care,
Return to this thy house of prayer!
Assembled in thy sacred name,
Where we thy parting promise claim!
Hosanna! Lord! Hosanna in the highest!

First Sunday in Advent: From 'Hosanna to the living Lord' Tunes used include PRAISES and HOSANNA

The Lord will come! a dreadful form,
With wreath of flame, and robe of storm,
On cherub wings, and wings of wind,
Annointed Judge of human-kind!

Second Sunday in Advent: 'The Lord will come! the earth shall quake'

Come, Jesus! come! and, as of yore
The prophet went to clear thy way,
A harbinger thy feet before,
A dawning to thy brighter day:

So now may grace with heavenly shower
Our stony hearts for truth prepare;
Sow in our souls the seed of power,
Then come and reap thy harvest there!

Third Sunday in Advent: 'Oh Saviour, is thy promise fled?'

Cold on his cradle the dew-drops are shining,
Low lies his head with the beasts of the stall,
Angels adore him in slumber reclining,
Maker and Monarch and Saviour of all!

Epiphany: From 'Brightest and best of the sons of the morning!' Amongst the tunes to which the hymn is sung are EPIPHANY HYMN, LIEBSTER, LIME STREET, JESMIAN and BEDE

(November)
'We are close upon him', said Mr. Boulderson; 'fire where you see the long grass shake, if he rises before you.' Just at that moment my elephant stamped again violently. 'There, there' cried the mohout, 'I saw his head!' A short roar, or rather loud growl, followed, and I saw immediately before my elephant's head the motion of some large animal stealing away through the grass. I fired as directed, and, a moment after, seeing the motion still more plainly, fired the second barrel. Another short growl followed, the motion was immediately quickened, and was soon lost in the more distant jungle. Mr. Boulderson said 'I should not wonder if you hit him that last time; at any rate we shall drive him out of the cover, and then I will take care of him.' In fact, at that moment, the crowd of horse and foot spectators at the jungle side began to run off in all directions. We went on to the place, but found it was a false alarm, and, in fact, we had seen all we were to see of him, and went twice more through the jungle in vain.

— — — — —

(November)
I had the gratification of having my own hymns *Brightest and best* and that for St. Stephen's day, sung better than I ever heard them in a church before.

— — — — —

(January)
. . . the Maha-Rannee . . . (lady mother)
. . . sent us some specimens of Hindoo

cookery, abundant in ghee, spice, and sugar, but without the garlic which forms so essential a part of Mussulman luxury. I tasted one of the messes, which was of rice, raisins, and some green sweetmeat, strongly scented with rose-water and seasoned with cinnamon, and thought it very good. The others were, apparently, kid or mutton minced small with rice and covered with a very rich brown sauce, *a thing to dream of, not to tell,* and which if eaten at night one should scarcely fail to dream of.

A noble army, men and boys,
The matron and the maid,
Around the Saviour's throne rejoice
In robes of light array'd.

They climb'd the steep ascent of Heaven,
Through peril, toil, and pain!
Oh God! to us may grace be given
To follow in their train!

St. Stephen's Day: From 'The Son of God goes forth to war.' The hymn is sung to ELLACOMBE, OLD 81st, ST. ANNE, FIGHT OF FAITH and OLD 137th

— — — — —

(February)
We marched to Ajmer, about seventeen miles. The country was as barren as ever, but more hilly, and saved from a wearisome uniformity by clusters of thorny trees and thickets of the cactus . . .

(February)
During my stay at Nusseerabad I was the guest of Brigadier Knox, the oldest cavalry officer now in India, and who has not seen England since he was a boy. His house had as yet been the only place for divine service, but was not nearly large enough for the station. There is a ball-room of sufficient size, but objections had been made to using this as a Church also, which I soon obviated, and the place was directed to be got ready for Sunday.

— — — — —

(March)
. . . I was glad to see that the people were at work in their poppy-grounds, and that the frost, to all appearance, had not extended far in this direction. The opium is collected by making two or three superficial incisions in the seed-vessel of the poppy, whence a milky juice exudes, which is carefully collected. The time of cutting them seems to be as soon as the petals of the flower fall off . . .

— — — — —

(March)
. . . there were a great many mhowah-trees, not yet in blossom, though they would be so we were told, in a fortnight or three weeks. They nearly resemble the oak in

size, form of the branches, and colour of the leaves . . . Its
flower, besides the intoxicating liquor obtained from it by
fermentation, when dried, resembles a small raisin both in
appearance and flavour. Its fruit, and the small pistachio nut
which grows wild among these hills in great abundance, are
the principal food of the wilder tribes of Bheels. The latter
are said to be deleterious till roasted, or at all events they
contain an oil so astringent as not to be eatable.

— — — — —

(April)
At Broach is one of those remarkable institutions which
have made a good deal of noise in Europe as instances of
Hindoo benevolence to inferior animals. I mean hospitals for
sick and infirm beasts, birds, and insects . . . Mr. Corsellis
described it as a very dirty and neglected place . . . several
different kinds there, not only those which are accounted
sacred by the Hindoos, as monkeys, peacocks etc., but
horses, dogs and cats, and they have also, in little boxes, an
assortment of lice and fleas. It is not true, however, that
they feed those pensioners on the flesh of beggars hired
for the purpose.

— — — — —

KUMAON SIKH, WITH ATTENDANT

So to Bombay . . . *nor is there any sea in the world more
beautifully blue, bordered by more woody and picturesque
mountains, and peopled with more picturesque boats and
fishermen* . . . Apart from the round of Church business and
courtesy calls, the Hebers visited Salsette and Poonah,
providing a short holiday. They set sail from Calcutta

on 15th August 1825, to break their journey home with an episcopal visit to Ceylon. Four incidents carry our story forward:

This morning, at three o'clock, we were roused by beat of drum to prepare for our march to Colombo; we formed a long cavalcade of palanquins and gigs, preceded by an escort of spearmen and noisy inharmonious music, and attended by some of Mr. Sansoni's lascarines, who answer in some respect to our peons in Calcutta; they wear rather a pretty uniform of white, red, and black, and a conical red cap, with an upright white feather in it. Instead of the chattah used with us, these men carry large fans made of the talipot palm, which is peculiar to Ceylon, from six to nine feet in length, over the heads of Europeans and rich natives, to guard them from the sun. The road was decorated the whole way as for a festival, with long strips of palm-branches hung upon strings on either side; and wherever we stopped we found the ground spread with white cloth, and awnings erected, beautifully decorated with flowers and fruits, and festooned with palm-branches. These remnants of the ancient custom mentioned in the Bible, of strewing the road with palm-branches and garments, are curious and interesting.

> Holy! Holy! Holy! Lord God Almighty!
> Early in the morning our song shall rise to Thee:
> Holy, Holy, Holy! Merciful and Mighty!
> God in Three Persons, Blessed Trinity.
> *Sung to NICAEA and BROMLEY COMMON*

We were on our guard against scorpions and centipedes, of which the tavern keeper told us that he had killed many within the last few days, but I was a little startled, while passing through a low door-way, to feel something unusual on my shoulder, and on turning my face round to see the head of a snake pointed towards my cheek . . . I had good reason to be thankful to Providence that he did not bite me; for besides the necessity, under the uncertainty of his poisonous nature, of using painful remedies, I should have had to bear many hours of suspense between life and death . . .
Heber's Journal, 5th July 1825, leaving Poonah

— — — — —

The new road from Colombo to Candy has been recently opened . . . it was a work of six or seven days to go from Colombo to Candy; it may now be done with ease, having relays of horses, in one, and the danger of sleeping by the way is avoided . . .

— — — — —

This man was very handsomely dressed, but his costume certainly the most extraordinary I ever saw; his turban, for here men begin to cover their heads, was richly ornamented with gold, intended to resemble a crown, but far more like an old toilette pincushion, a white muslin body, with immense sleeves, like wings, ornamented with gold buttons, a drapery of gold-flowered muslin, a broad gold band round his waist, and, as rank here is marked by the quantity as well as quality of their dress, he wore the finest muslin, swelled out round the hips by six or seven topettees, put on one above the other, which increased them to an immense circumference, while his hands were covered with rings of

96

rubies, set in a circle of more than two inches in diameter . . .

— — — — —

The horrible practice of female infanticide still prevails in some districts on the island . . .

— — — — —

Nothing can be more foolish, or in its effects more pernicious, than the manner in which spirits are distributed to European troops in India. Early every morning a pint of fiery, coarse, undiluted rum is given to every man, and half that quantity to every woman . . .

Heber's Journal: February 1826

Then came the sea trip from Ceylon back to Calcutta, to dock there on 21st October. While away, the authorities in England had added Australasia to his episcopate. Before the end of January, he set out again to visit Madras and the Southern Provinces. He was sad to leave his family so soon. Again his programme was hectic, but he found time to dictate notes of a scheme for the re-organisation of the Church of England in India through village evangelism using native ministers. His programme for 27th February began with breakfast with the Governor, a visit to Sir Ralph Palmer, an 'at home' session to receive visitors, conversation with his old friend the Chief Justice and a visit to the Female Asylum. His text for a sermon in St. George's Cathedral was *To die is gain*. By mid-March he was very tired, though observant still to notice Vepery Church as the finest Gothic ecclesiastical building in India.

VEPERY CHURCH, MADRAS

Some fifty-six miles west of the Bay of Bengal, isolated masses of crystalline gneiss rise from the plain. One of these, the Rock of the Three-headed Giant had for centuries been the centre of Davidic Brahmanism, and the precipice had been fortified and named Trichinopoly. British military might ensured that at the end of March in 1826 the flag of a *Christian* nation waved from the hill-top above the shrines of Ganesa, Siva and Vishnu. Yet, as Heber bemoaned in the very last letter he was to write to his wife, that *while the Raja kept his dominions, Christians were eligible to all the different offices of State, while now there is an order of Government against their being admitted to any employment!*

At midnight on 31st March, Reginald Calcutta arrived at Trichinopoly; in his party were two staff he intended to station there and a sick Bishop's chaplain. The surgeon had been left behind at Tanjor, dying of an abscess in the liver. Before eight next morning, Heber was at work receiving reports of the spiritual health of the military garrison and civil servants, of the five hundred native Christians converted by earlier missionary enterprise, and of the schools which had been set up, wrestling with ways of meeting the children's future needs on an infinitesimally small budget. Before retiring, there was a sermon to prepare, with confirmation addresses in English and Tamil, letters of thanks to write to the Resident at Tanjor, both in personal terms and in the question of the education of Prince Sewajee, a long letter to his friend, cousin of Lord Byron, the Under Secretary of State for the Colonies, Wilmot Horton, and a note to his wife. Next morning, he preached in extreme heat and with difficult acoustics at St. John's Church, confirming forty-two Christians, feeling afterwards a little under the weather. He was persuaded against preaching again to the Tamil congregation in the evening but found the energy to write to the Church Missionary Society about disputes in the Syrian Church. He and his chaplain, still unwell, discussed the blessedness of heaven, with Heber quoting from Charles Wesley's hymn *Head of Thy Church triumphant*, which he especially loved.

Head of Thy Church triumphant,
We joyfully adore Thee;
Till Thou appear
Thy members here
Shall sing like those in glory.
We lift our hearts and voices
With blest anticipation,
And cry aloud
And give to God
The praise of our salvation.

While in affliction's furnace
And passing through the fire,
Thy love we praise,
Which knows our days,
And ever brings us nigher.
We clap our hands exulting
In Thine almighty favour;
The love divine
Which made us Thine
Shall keep us Thine for ever.

It is, indeed intensely hot, often from 98 to 100 in the shade; but I could not defer it to another year, and I, thank God, continue quite well, though some of my companions have suffered, and I have been compelled to leave my surgeon behind sick at Tanjor. My chaplain I feared, yesterday, must have remained there also, but he has now rallied. I am compelled to pass on in order to get to Travancore, where I have much curious discussion before me with the Syrian Christians, before the monsoon renders that country impassable.
From Reginald Calcutta's letter to the Secretary of State to the Colonies the Saturday before his death

. . . What now remains but a constant and earnest recollection that the privileges and the duties of a Christian go always hand in hand; that the greater the mercies received the more need there is of showing forth our thankfulness: that we do not cease to be servants of God when we are admitted to the privileges of His children, but that from these last, on the other hand, a more illustrious obedience is expected . . .

. . . Let me entreat you to remember sometimes in your prayers those ministers of Christ who now have laboured for your instruction, that we who have preached to you may not ourselves be cast away, but that it may be given to us also to walk in this life present according to the words of the Gospel which we have received of our Lord, and to rejoice hereafter with you, the children of our care, in that land where the weary shall find repose and the wicked cease from troubling; where we shall behold God as He is, and be ourselves made like unto God in innocence, and happiness, and immortality!
From Bishop Heber's last sermon at Trichinopoly, 2nd April 1826

Thou dost conduct Thy people
Through torrents of temptation,
Nor will we fear,
While Thou art near,
The fire of tribulation.
The world with sin and Satan
In vain our march opposes,
Through Thee we shall
Break through them all,
And sing the song of Moses.

By faith we see the glory
To which Thou shalt restore us,
The Cross despise
For that high prize
Which Thou hast set before us.
And if Thou count us worthy,
We each, as dying Stephen,
Shall see Thee stand
At God's right hand
To take us up to heaven.

Wesley's hymn studied
by Bishop Heber the
day before his death

At daybreak on Monday, 3rd April, the Bishop drove to the Tamil church, confirming young Christians, using their mother tongue, and went on to the local schools and Mission-house. He dropped in on his sick chaplain before visiting the swimming bath at the home of his host, the Circuit Judge. He had enjoyed its refreshment on the two previous days. Here his family and his diocese were bereaved: his lifeless body was found in the water by his servant.

A salute of forty-three guns, corresponding with the Bishop's age was fired at his funeral next day. Four months later, the news reached England. A memorial was placed by public subscription in London's St. Paul's Cathedral as well as at Hodnet, and later at St. Oswald's, Malpas, the church of his boyhood.

How well I remember the day I first met thee!
'Twas in scenes long forsaken, in moments long fled,
Then little thought I that a *world* would regret thee!
And Europe and Asia *both* mourn for thee dead.

Ah! little I thought, in those gay social hours,
That round thy young head e'en the laurel would twine,
Still less that a crown of the amaranth's flowers,
Enwreathed with the *palm*, would, O Heber! be thine.

We met in the world, and the light that shone round thee
Was the dangerous blaze of wit's meteor ray,
But e'en then, though unseen, mercy's angel had found thee,
And the bright star of Bethlehem was marking thy way.

Amelia Opie. Opening stanzas of 'To the Memory
of Reginald Heber, Bishop of Calcutta'

Heber had often been concerned in India about the health of his wife and children. Amelia set towards publishing her husband's work. She gained the consent of the Archbishop of Canterbury, to whom she dedicated the book, to publish *Hymns, written and adapted to the Weekly Church Service of the Year*, the book about which Heber had been corresponding before his call to Calcutta. In seven years, it ran to ten editions. She also edited his papers to publish in 1828 *Narrative of a Journey through the Upper Provinces of India, with Notes upon Ceylon*. The following year *A Series of Engravings from the Drawings of Reginald Heber* were issued: by the end of 1829, the *Narrative* had reached four editions. Amelia eventually re-married and lived until 1870. Emily, whose health gave her father such concern, was to have five sons and six daughters and to live to a good age. She married episcopal links! Her husband's father was a Bishop of Carlisle and his mother, a daughter of an Archbishop of Canterbury. Harriet married the son of Reginald Heber's greatest friend John Thornton, who became Vicar of Ewell on the southern outskirts of London. She lived until 1888.

> How shall we mourn thee? — With a lofty trust,
> Our life's immortal birthright from above!
> With a glad faith, whose eye, to track the just,
> Through shades and mysteries lifts a glance of love,
> And yet can weep! for Nature so deplores
> The friend that leaves us, though for happier shores.
>
> *Felicia Hemans. From 'A Tribute to the Memory of Bishop Heber' 1828*

Robert Southey wrote a poem *On the Portrait of Reginald Heber*. He begins by telling of England's role in military conquest in India. *Late only hast thou set that standard up on pagan shores in peace*. That standard proclaiming peace was carried by Reginald Heber.

> ... Thither, devoted to the work, he went,
> There spent his precious life,
> There left his holy dust.
>
> *From Robert Southey: 'On the Portrait of Reginald Heber'*

SPRINGTIME

Arranged by Arthur Sullivan

1 For all Thy love and goodness, so bounti - ful and free, Thy Name, Lord, be a - dored!

(Last verse) Slower.

On the wings of joyous praise our hearts soar up to Thee: Glo - ry to the Lord! Al - le - lu - ia. A - men.

1 For all Thy love and goodness, so bounti|ful and free,
  Thy Name, Lord, be adored!
  On the wings of joyous praise our hearts soar|up to Thee;
  Glory to the Lord:

2 The Springtime breaks all round about, waking from|winter's night:
  Thy Name, Lord, be adored!
  The sunshine, like God's love, pours down in floods of |golden light:
  Glory to the Lord!

3 A voice of joy is in all the earth, a voice is in|all the air:
  Thy Name, Lord, be adored!
  All nature singeth aloud to God; there is gladness |everywhere:
  Glory to the Lord!

4 The flowers are strewn in field and copse, on the hill and |on the plain:
  Thy Name, Lord, be adored!
  The soft air stirs in the tender leaves that clothe the |trees again:
  Glory to the Lord!

5 The works of Thy hands are very fair; and for all Thy|bounteous love
  Thy Name, Lord, be adored!
  Better what, if this world is so fair, is the Better|Land above?
  Glory to the Lord!

6 Oh, to awake from death's short sleep, like the flowers from their|wintry grave!
  Thy Name, Lord, be adored!
  And to rise all glorious in the day when Christ shall|come to save!
  Glory to the Lord!

7 Oh, to dwell in that happy land, where the heart cannot|choose but sing!
  Thy Name, Lord, be adored!
  And where the life of the blessed ones is a beautiful|endless Spring!
  Glory to the Lord! Alleluia.

A - men.

Frances Jane Douglas, 1848, and William Walsham How, 1871

William Walsham How

William Walsham How, author of *For all the saints who from their labours rest*, might be described with affection as a workaholic saint. The elder son of a solicitor, he was born in Shrewsbury on 13th December 1823. His mother died before his third birthday: but his father, William Wyberg How married again in 1828. Walsham's step-mother was successful in nurturing the whole family into a close-knit unit: there were two daughters of the second marriage of whom William and his brother Thomas grew very fond. The death of Margaret at the age of seven was a great blow to them all.

Walsham's education was supplemented by private lessons with a local curate followed by attendance at Shrewsbury School. But throughout childhood and adolescence, his father played a significant educational role. He was a practising Christian, with high regard for the religious, yet possessing a great sense of fun. He had a gift for writing verse, at which skill he persuaded Walsham to try his pen at a young age. He loved gardening and passed on his green-fingered expertise. Shrewsbury is set on the River Severn: beyond the rich meadows, the Shropshire and Welsh Hills rise in the distance: on long walks, father introduced his son to the rich diversity of wild flowers in that varied countryside.

Walsham had a way with animals. He was rarely without a pet dog in later life. He was good, too, with horses, and whilst still in his teens, chased with the local staghounds. He was to give up hunting; but he found recreation in fishing throughout his life. He inherited two other valuable talents from his father, good money-management and orderliness of method in handling papers. At Oxford, however, good work-organisation was not in evidence. Perhaps at seventeen, there was too much to distract him. He loved dancing and sports. Though certainly no Holy Joe, he soon determined that his calling was to be that of a clergyman rather than a solicitor.

In the Long Vacation of 1842, he visited Ireland with the poet Arthur Hugh Clough and other friends. One of the party, so How recounts, was *exceedingly fastidious and nice about food, diet, water, beds &c*: Clough managed to drive *a flock of geese out of the road into his*

Ah yet, when all is thought and said,
The heart still overrules the head:
Still what we hope we must believe,
And what is given us receive;

Must still believe, for still we hope
That in a world of larger scope,
What here is faithfully begun
Will be completed, not undone.

My child, we still must think, when we
That ampler life together see,
Some true result will yet appear
Of what we are, together, here.

Arthur Hugh Clough
From 'What we, when face to face we see'

bedroom! They made a terrible mess. What a trick for a tutor! What a contrast we find in How and Clough! The first gave a life of service to the Established Church: his college friend Clough's gift for satire and verse asked searching questions and the Church of his day could not answer them satisfactorily for him. Perhaps Clough pointed a way to God for those whom How would not reach.

Thou shalt have one God only; who
Would be at the expense of two?
No graven images may be
Worshipped, except the currency;
Swear not at all; for, for thy curse
Thine enemy is none the worse:
At church on Sunday to attend
Will serve to keep the world thy friend:
Honour thy parents; that is, all
From whom advancement may befall;
Thou shalt not kill; but need'st not strive
Officiously to keep alive:
Do not adultery commit;
Advantage rarely comes of it:
Thou shalt not steal; an empty feat,
When it's so lucrative to cheat:
Bear not false witness; let the lie
Have time on its own wings to fly.
Thou shalt not covet, but tradition
Approves all forms of competition.

The sum of all is, thou shalt love,
If any body, God above:
At any rate shall never labour
More than thyself to love thy neighbour.

*Arthur Hugh Clough:
'The Latest Decalogue'*

. . . If one could but read two hours together without raising one's eyes or taking off one's thoughts, and then begin again and do two hours more . . .
*William Walsham How
writing from Oxford*

Walsham found concentrated reading far from easy. He was not surprised when eventually he received only a third class degree: being too young for ordination, he proceeded to Durham to read theology for a year. While at Oxford, he came under the influence of Richard Congreve, an advocate of the ideas of the French philosopher Auguste Comte. His system, known as Positivism, involved the *Religion of Humanity* in which the object of adoration was the Great Being or the personification of humanity as a whole. He was also under the influence of the Tractarian Movement, with its emphasis on the importance of ritual. He was to end up with a middle-of-the-road churchmanship, in which souls took precedence over ritual, but where all was done in a fitting, methodical and ordered manner.

In his college years, he maintained contact with his family, travelling in Belgium and Germany with his father. Some of the correspondence with his sister has survived: and there were shared activities with his brother Thomas, with whom he was to maintain contact throughout his life. His first curacy was at Kidderminster under the guidance of Reverend T. L. Claughton, later Bishop of St. Albans, who was to address him when congratulating his appointment as Bishop of Wakefield as *my very dear old friend*. As a young curate, How wrote to his brother about Fridays and fasting. When, many years later he and John Ellerton co-edited *Church Hymns*, they determined to include a hymn for every day of the week. For Friday, How contributed *O Jesu, crucified for man*: the music editor, Arthur Sullivan, chose as appropriate Edward Miller's ROCKINGHAM, widely sung to Isaac Watts' Friday hymn *When I survey the wondrous Cross*. How's hymn is also sung to INTERCESSION, a tune first published in *Easy Music for Church Choirs* in 1853.

My aim and object is just to hit the nail on the head, to make as plain as possible the subject I have chosen, and keep as well as possible out of all others . . .
William Walsham How writing to his sister about preparing sermons. February 1847

. . . I have earnestly wished Friday were properly observed as a day of mourning, as Sunday is a day of rejoicing and happiness (both being necessary for man's soul) . . .
William Walsham How writing to his brother

O Jesu, crucified for man,
O Lamb, all glorious on Thy throne,
Teach Thou our wondering souls to scan
The mystery of Thy love unknown.

We pray Thee, grant us strength to take
Our daily cross, what'er it be,
And gladly, for Thine own dear sake
In paths of pain to follow Thee.

As on our daily way we go,
Through light or shade, in calm or strife,
Oh, may we bear Thy marks below
In conquered sin and chastened life.

And week by week this day we ask
That holy memories of Thy Cross
May sanctify each common task,
And turn to gain each earthly loss.

Grant us, dear Lord, our cross to bear
Till at Thy feet we lay it down,
Win through Thy Blood our pardon there,
And through the cross attain the crown.

One of Walsham's fellow-curates at Kidderminster was William Douglas, who introduced him to his sister Frances, the eldest daughter of the Reverend Henry Douglas, Rector of Salwarpe and Canon of Durham. How was very happy in his job and reluctant to move; but in the autumn of 1848 his step-mother died, and he returned home to support his father and sister. In Shrewsbury, he served for nearly three years in the Parish of Holy Cross, whilst waiting for the living of Whittington, of which his father had purchased the next presentation, to become vacant. In 1849 Walsham married Frances Douglas. That same year, he began work on *Plain Words*, the written sermons which were to make him known as an author. They were to run to hundreds over the years.

WHITTINGTON PARISH CHURCH

Now, as our senses put us into connection with the world of matter, so does Faith with the world of spirit. Faith is to the spiritual world what sense is to the material. Thus Faith is often called the eye of the soul. But, in truth, Faith is not only the eye of the soul, which sees that which the bodily eye cannot see; it is also the ear of the soul, which hears that which the bodily ear cannot hear; the hand of the soul, which touches that which the bodily hand cannot touch. Our senses *realise* the world of matter — make it real, substantial, evident, to us. The work of Faith is to *realise* the world of spirit, to make that real, substantial, evident to us.
William Walsham How: From 'Plain Words on Prayer' (the fourth book in the series)

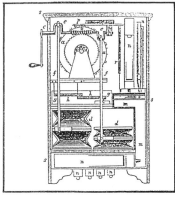

Earth's axis thou placed
    in position inclined,
Thus the seasons contrived
    with benevolent mind.
Text by the previous incumbent in 'The Christian Hymnbook'

On 23rd September 1851, Whittington, about seventeen miles north of Shrewsbury and near the English-Welsh border, welcomed its new rector and his young wife. He was to serve there for twenty-eight years. Its previous incumbent had served for forty: he was a strong adherent of the old Evangelical School: scriptural texts were not only painted in large white letters on the outside of the church but also on several of the cottages in the village. How described the church, built in 1804, as a curiously ugly brick building, with large round-headed windows. For music, there was a barrel-organ. If hymns were used at all in Anglican churches of the period, they were often the lyrics of the local Rector. How's predecessor had made his own *Christian Hymn Book*, delightfully prefaced with a note: *Many hymn writers have fallen into the mistaken notion that man is formed of clay, or have taught it for the convenience of rhyming. It is, however, quite false that man is made either in whole or in part of clay!* The fashion of Anglican worship in the Diocese of St. Asaph in 1851 meant that forms and ceremonies were considered of little importance, whilst orders and sacraments were also of small account. It was also the heyday of Nonconformity. It must have been hard for the new rector not to rush in with alterations to the pattern of worship so it might show some of the quality experienced at Kidderminster, but How patiently accepted his Bishop's guidance and made no changes in the first year. He and his bride also inherited a rectory which was far from a *desirable residence*, and whilst changes were made, the pair lived in the village. The rectory garden was transformed from wilderness by the incumbent's hard work and green fingers.

In 1852, the Bishop appointed How as one of the voluntary inspectors of schools, a work he carried through until the *Elementary Education Act* appointing statutory inspectors became effective in 1870. All How's diaries from 1853 onwards recorded the varied tasks he undertook, in taking church services, in visiting day schools, and in writing. They also list attendances at night school, choir and cricket practices, and fishing excursions, with the number of fish caught duly noted. The parish was seven miles from point to point: the Rector was a familiar figure riding his cob as he visited outlying parishioners. His wife was an active help-mate: not only did she carry on the usual mothers' meetings and clothing clubs; she was tireless in helping care for the sick, especially children who were ill.

William Walsham How began writing hymns when he was himself a child. If the siblings were unable to go to church, they would plan their own service at home, with Walsham writing a hymn. An early text compared the butterfly's life cycle to the Resurrection. How had a talent for music as well as for words: at Whittington, he trained his first choir, conducting their practices whilst playing the flute. Clearly there was a need for something to supersede his predecessor's *Christian Hymn Book*. By 1854 he had collaborated with Reverend Thomas Baker Morrell of High Wycombe, later Coadjutor Bishop of Edinburgh, in publishing a new words-only hymn book. *Most gladly would I see our new book, and all others, supplanted by a well-made collection authorised by the Church in Convocation.* Several editions and supplements were published. By 1860, the book had 121 hymn texts and 44 metrical psalms. In that edition the editors noted: *In compiling 'Hymns for the Public Worship of Almighty God', it appears a higher duty to make them as perfect and appropriate as possible than to adhere always to the exact words of the Author, especially in the case of Hymns not written expressly for Public Worship or for*

The following are in this parish generally approved and seriously recommended remedies for the whooping-cough, popularly called the *chin-cough*: To be swung nine times under a donkey. To pass the patient three times under and over a briar growing from a hedge, saying *Over the briar and under the briar, and leave the chin-cough behind.* Anything recommended by a seventh son. (One woman cured several people, she tells me, by sending them to meet a boatman who is a seventh son, and to ask him what would cure them.) Anything recommended by a man on a piebald horse. (I have been told of cures being thus effected by gin, honey, cold water, and an ounce of tea taken wholly.)

William Walsham How: 'Lighter Moments'

Stream alteration. Altogether it is a great improvement to the garden, especially to a botanist with a mighty love of ferns, of which I hope now to grow many of the rarer sorts, and do not despair of inducing the Hymenophylla to take up their abode on the spray-bespattered stones. If my successor is no fern-fancier, let him at least bring some one who is so, to see what is there before he lays violent hands on any of my nurselings.

I have just returned from a visit to the Lakes, and have brought back with me, and planted in the new rockwork by the water, roots of the following ferns: Allosorus (parsley fern), beech fern, oak fern, brittle fern, forked spleenwort and green, Wilson's filmy fern and mountain fern. I have already put in Osmunda regalis and Lastrea thelypteris and christata, with several of the common ferns.

Notes by William Walsham How in the Whittington Parish Papers

Church-people. The Organist and Choirmaster of the Parish Church at Henley-on-Thames provided a tunes book, providing twelve long metre and twenty-four common metre tunes, with a selection for the other measures from which to use. By 1872 the book had been enlarged to 258 hymns with a reduction of metrical psalms to 26. This time, there was full acknowledgement of authors' copyrights: the content reflected the explosion in new writing and translating of the previous decade. Of several original texts of How's published in the book he co-edited, *We give Thee but Thine own* reveals his parallel concerns for the saving of souls and the care of the needy. This hymn of Christian stewardship to be sung at the Offertory, has been set to CARLSRUHE, ST. GEORGE, WINDERMERE, IN MEMORIAM, BETHLEHEM, ST. MICHAEL and WE GIVE THEE BUT THINE OWN.

> Oh! hearts are bruised and dead;
> And homes are bare and cold;
> And lambs for whom the Shepherd bled
> Are straying from the fold!
>
> To comfort and to bless,
> To find a balm for woe,
> To tend the lone and fatherless,
> Is Angels' work below.
>
> *Verses from 'We give Thee but Thine own'*

The hymnwriter Dr. George Matheson, author of *O Love that wilt not let me go* wrote that this hymn *sounds the real humanitarian note to the fatherless and widows. Hymnology is feeble and ineffective when it ignores the humanitarian side of religion.* The opening lines of a contribution to the 1863 supplement remind us of Charles Wesley's *Soldiers of Christ arise.* Whilst Wesley, aware of the powers of darkness emphasises the strength of the armoury, How's *Soldiers of the Cross, arise!* concentrates in some measure on the might of the enemy but nevertheless sees the action ended when *the kingdoms of the world are the Kingdom of the Lord.* Tunes include INNOCENTS, CRUCES MILITES, MÜLLER, DENT DALE, UNIVERSITY COLLEGE and GOTT SEI DANK. Other original texts include one on Sunday and another on the Person of Jesus. By 1866, sales of How and Morrell's *Psalms and Hymns* had reached 200,000.

In 1854 the Bishop offered How the Rural Deanery of Oswestry, an office he was to hold for twenty-five years. The family holiday that year at the seaside resort of Barmouth in West Wales was marked by the illness of little Maynard. He died there and was buried in a tiny grave at Llanber, overlooking the waves. Walsham and Frances went often to the place where their first-born was laid to rest. They returned to Whittington with a great sense of loss but the solace of Maynard's young sister. The Hows were to have further children and family gatherings for holidays were arranged on many occasions through the years.

Soldiers of the Cross, arise!
Gird you with your armour bright;
Mighty are your enemies,
Hard the battle ye must fight.

O'er a faithless fallen world
Raise your banner in the sky;
Let it float there wide unfurled;
Bear it onward: lift it high.

'Mid the homes of want and woe,
Strangers to the living word,
Let the Saviour's herald go,
Let the voice of hope be heard.

Where the shadows deepest lie,
Carry truth's unsullied ray;
Where are crimes of blackest dye,
There the saving sign display.

To the weary and the worn
Tell of realms where sorrows cease;
To the outcast and forlorn
Speak of mercy and of peace.

Guard the helpless: seek the strayed;
Comfort troubles; banish grief;
In the might of God arrayed,
Scatter sin and disbelief.

Be the banner still unfurled,
Still unsheathed the Spirit's sword,
Till the kingdoms of the world
Are the Kingdom of the Lord.

*Text as revised by the author
for 'Church Hymns' 1871*

Soldiers of Christ, arise!
And put your armour on,
Strong in the strength which God supplies
Through his eternal Son:
Strong in the Lord of Hosts,
And in his mighty power,
Who in the strength of Jesus trusts,
Is more than conqueror.

Stand then in his great might,
With all his strength endued:
But take, to arm you for the fight,
The Panoply of God:
That having all things done,
And all your conflict pass'd,
You may o'ercome, through Christ alone,
And stand entire at last.

Stand then against your foes,
In close and firm array:
Legions of wily fiends oppose
Throughout the evil day:
But meet the sons of night,
But mock their vain design,
Arm'd in the arms of heavenly light,
Of righteousness divine.

Leave no unguarded place,
No weakness of the soul;
Take every virtue, every grace,
And fortify the whole:
Indissolubly join'd,
To battle all proceed;
But arm yourselves with all the mind
That was in Christ, your Head.

*First of three parts of a text in
'A Collection of Hymns for the
use of people called Methodists'*

The Rector was always looking for opportunites of contact with his parishioners: beginning in 1855, he organised the New Year *Old Men's Dinner*. Many regular social events were set up in the Parish over the years. The Rector enjoyed lecturing and his subjects included *Geology, Visiting Rome*, and *Sir Humphry Davy*, who first suggested the possibility of nitrous oxide (laughing gas) as an anaesthetic and constructed the miners' safety lamp. In 1857, the *Oswestry and Welshpool Naturalists' Field Club* was founded: the Rector of Whittington was no nominal Vice-President, regularly joining them on field trips. In 1862, he read a paper to the Society on the *Botany of the Great Orme's Head at Llandudno* on the North Wales coast.

It is very important that the master or mistress should always *kneel* when reading prayers, and, both in posture and manner, set an example of reverence to the children.
The children should all be made to kneel facing the master or mistress, and to keep their eyes closed, and their hands together during the prayers. The responses should be made by the whole school, slowly, evenly, in one tone, and not too loud.

*William Walsham How:
'Prayers for Schools', 1861*

Several of the commoner limestone plants are there plentifully, such as Saxifraga tridactylites, Arabis hirsuta, and Geranium lucidum . . .

If you look under your feet in this breezy exposed spot, you will find at least three plants worth notice. The pretty Gnaphalium dioicum, the Cistus marifolius, and the delicate little Scilla verna . . .

Scrambling up to the steep shelves and levels of rock which face inland, and amongst the hawthorns and privets and brambles and blackthorns, we will poke about and see if we cannot discover *the* Orme's Head plant, Mespilus cotoneaster. Yes, here it is, just like one of the dwarf, round-leafed shrubby willows, a tough little shrub, with downy leaves, and pretty little waxy blossoms like the bilberry. Happily its roots are so deep, and so embedded in the rocks, that, although the visitors are cruelly destructive, I think they will not succeed in quite extirpating this plant from its only British dwelling-place.

From a paper 'Botany of the Great Orme's Head at Llandudno'
read to the Oswestry and Welshpool Naturalists' Field Club, 1862

God's free mercy streameth
Over all the world,
And his banner gleameth
Everywhere unfurled.
Broad and deep and glorious
As the heaven above,
Shines in might victorious
His eternal Love.

Verse 2 of 'Summer suns are glowing'

Behold the bending orchards
With bounteous fruit are crowned;
Lord, in our hearts more richly
Let heavenly fruits abound.

O, by each mercy sent us,
And by each grief and pain
By blessings like the sunshine,
And sorrows like the rain,

Our barren hearts make fruitful
With every goodly grace,
That we Thy name may hallow,
And see at last Thy face.

Closing verses of How's Hymn for Autumn
'The year is swiftly waning'

It is not surprising that so great a lover of nature should have chosen to contribute four hymns for the four seasons when he was working on *Church Hymns* in the eighteen-seventies. For Spring, he based the contribution on a poem by his sister, Frances Jane Douglas, entitled *April Verses*. It was set to a chant SPRINGTIME arranged by Arthur Sullivan and is printed to preface this article. His choice for Summer has an international dimension in its second verse. Today when winter darkens the Northern hemisphere, How's words are sung cheerfully by those who look to the Southern Cross. Tunes include RUTH, GHENT (ADORO TE No.2), PRINCETHORPE, GLENFINLAS and LYLE ROAD. Ralph Vaughan Williams harmonised a beautiful Somerset folk tune collected in Hambridge by Cecil Sharp when the autumn choice was reprinted in *The English Hymnal* in 1906 (DEVONSHIRE). It is also sung to AUTUMN. The tune CLARENCE was appointed for *Winter reigneth o'er the land*.

Shortly after the founding of the Field Club, How was able to see a new church dedicated to St. Andrew consecrated in his parish at Frankton. The same year, *Plain Words* on which he had started work many years earlier, was finally published. He eventually wrote four books of sermons by this title which were to sell hundreds of thousands of copies. The sixties began with his installation as an Honorary Canon of St. Asaph, an office he retained until his admittance in 1878 to the prebendal stall of Llanefydd with the Chancellorship of St. Asaph Cathedral. In 1861, he published his first book of poems. Other poems were to follow.

> Life is waning; life is brief;
> Death, like winter, standeth nigh:
> Each one, like the falling leaf,
> Soon shall fade, – and fall, – and die.
>
> But the sleeping earth shall wake,
> And the flowers shall burst in bloom,
> And all Nature rising break
> Glorious from its wintry tomb.
>
> So, Lord, after slumber blest
> Comes a bright awakening,
> And our flesh in hope shall rest
> Of a never-fading Spring.
> *Closing verses of 'Winter reigneth o'er the land'*

This poem is about Bishop Ellicott of Gloucester, Dean Alford, and Canon Wordsworth (afterwards Bishop of Lincoln)

A Bishop, a Dean, and a Canon, they say,
Were discussing a difficult passage one day.

Said the Canon, 'I rather
Agree with a father,
And fancy I see
A profound mystery,
Which confutes, when unravelled, with stringent austerity
Modern impugners of Catholic verity.'

Said the Dean, 'It is clear
There's a knotty point here;
And I really can't say
That I quite see my way:
The Germans no doubt
Have found it all out:
Ah no! But the Canon is wrong, I am sure;
So it's best, as we find it, to leave it – obscure.'

Said the Bishop, 'To me
The solutions seem three,
Which I'll call *a, b, c.*
In favour of *a*
There is much to say;
Something for *b,*
And a little for *c.*
Against *a* I find
Reasons strong to my mind;

But by stronger ones yet
b and *c* are both met.
And so when the three I impartially weigh,
I'm disposed to give my adhesion to *a*.'

It was thus that the Canon
Patriarchal ran on;
It was thus that the Dean
Halted doubting between;
It was thus that the Bishop
The meaning did fish up:
It was thus that Dean, Canon, and Bishop, they say,
Discussed that most difficult passage one day.

William Walsham How: 'The Three Pundits',
a poem in lighter mood written in the eighteen-sixties

In 1862, he mourned the death of his father who had tutored
him so faithfully. Between 1863 and 1868, at the request of
the *Society for Promoting Christian Knowledge* he prepared
his *Commentary on the Four Gospels* which sold around a
quarter of a million copies by the end of the century. In the
same year, there was published Earl Nelson's *Hymns for
Saints Days and Other Hymns, by a Layman.* It included
Earl Nelson's own text, with various verses for St. Andrew,
St. Thomas, St. Stephen, St. John the Evangelist, Innocents'
Day, the Conversion of St. Paul, St. Matthias, St. Mark,
St. Philip and St. James the Greater, St. Barnabas, St. John
the Baptist, St. Peter, St. James the Lesser, St. Bartholomew,
St. Matthew, St. Luke, St. Simon and St. Jude. The opening
line of Earl Nelson's hymn, sung usually to AURELIA or
HOLY CHURCH *From all Thy saints in warfare, for all Thy
saints at rest* has a striking kinship to How's world-famous
For all the saints who from their labours rest, usually sung
today to Vaughan Williams's equally famous tune SINE
NOMINE. Earl Nelson included How's text alongside his own
in his book: and How reciprocated by including both hymns
when *Church Hymns* was published in 1871. How's text
has also been sung to ENGLEBERG, LUCCOMBE and
ST. PHILIP. In *Church Hymns*, it was set as a chant.

. . . desires to put forward a
proof that a very strong
conviction that the freedom of
the Colonial Churches will
be their true strength, is
compatible with a very sincere
appreciation of the blessings of
an Established Church at home.
*William Walsham How
commenting in a sermon
he preached in Rome in,
March 1865*

For all Thy saints in warfare, for all Thy saints at rest,
To Thee, O blessed, Jesu, all praises be addressed.
Thou, Lord, dids't win the battle that they might conquerors be;
Their crowns of living glory are lit with rays from Thee.

Earl Nelson

In 1865 William Walsham How took a working holiday as
Chaplain to the English Church in Rome; the party included
his wife, his daughter Nelly and her governess. Letters home

remind us of his sense of fun. In 1866, his holiday took the form of six weeks in residence at the Canonry of St. Asaph. For yet another edition of Morrell and How's hymnbook, he wrote *Who is this, so weak and helpless*. It was revised for *Church Hymns* in 1871. Each of its four verses have the last half effectively juxtaposed against the first half. Tunes include CROSS AND CROWN, LLANSANNAN and ILSLEY.

Who is this, so weak and helpless,
Child of lowly Hebrew maid,
Rudely in a stable sheltered,
Coldly in a manger laid?
'Tis the Lord of all creation,
Who this wondrous path hath trod,
He is God from everlasting,
And to everlasting God.

Who is this – a Man of Sorrows,
Walking sadly life's hard way,
Homeless, weary, sighing, weeping
Over sin and Satan's sway?
'Tis our God, our glorious Saviour,
Who above the starry sky
Now for us a place prepareth,
Where no tear can dim the eye.

Who is this – behold Him shedding
Drops of Blood upon the ground?
Who is this – despised, rejected,
Mocked, insulted, beaten, bound?
'Tis our God, who gifts and graces
On His Church now poureth down;
Who shall smite in holy vengeance
All His foes beneath His throne.

Who is this that hangeth dying,
While the rude world scoffs and scorns;
Numbered with the malefactors,
Torn with nails, and crowned with thorns?
'Tis the God who ever liveth
'Mid the shining ones on high,
In the glorious golden city
Reigning everlastingly!

'Who is this, so weak and helpless'
as revised in 1871

. . . an English sculptor, a Mr. Adams . . . was working at a statue of Mr. Gladstone, in his Chancellor's robes. Mr. Gladstone being in England, a model was needful (the head having been taken before in England), so a regular Roman model was standing on a platform for him. You would have roared to have seen him. He was a handsome dirty Roman with beard and moustaches of course, and as Mr. Adams wanted legs and drapery, this fellow was divested of his trousers, and stood there with naked legs and feet of extreme shagginess and ruddiness, having on of his own only a shirt and a grey open waistcoat, but duly robed in a mock Chancellor's robe of state, which he had to hold in an attitude. I should like Mr. Wm. Lyttelton to have looked in. He would have shook the place down with laughing . . .

From a letter home
written in Rome,
20th March 1865

. . . By the way, you might be interested in a little matter showing the suspicion and the weakness of the present Roman government. There were races in the Campagna last Thursday, and the winning horse in the steeplechase, which was Prince Doria's, was ridden by an Englishman, a Mr. Spears, a horse of his own being ridden by his groom. Mr. Spears had lilac and green colours, and when he stripped to ride, people said they could not tell him from his groom, so he tied a white girdle round his waist. When he won the Italians were in raptures, shouting that he had the Italian colours, which are red, green and white. On reaching home he received notice from Cardinal Antonelli to leave Rome in twenty-four hours . . .

From a letter home
written in Rome,
11th April 1865

In 1867, How made his first serious attempt at salmon fishing; and he became widely known for his part in a debate on church ceremonial at the Wolverhampton Church Congress. For the Morrell and How supplement he also wrote a hymn, later to be much used in Mission Services, *O Jesu, thou art standing* which is sung to ST. CATHERINE, LLANGLOFFAN, LUX MUNDI and DAY OF REST.

> O love that passeth knowledge
> So patiently to wait!
> O sin that hath no equal
> So fast to bar the gate!
>
> O Jesu, Thou art pleading
> In accents meek and low,
> 'I died for you, My children,
> And will ye treat me so?'

From 'O Jesu, Thou art standing'

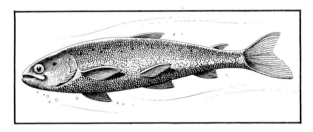

He chronicled his six-days-a-catching three fish in rhyme:

DAY 1

> Calmly bright
> Is the morning light;
> Lovelily blue are the mountain ridges;
> Gently ripple the waters
> Like the prattle of Erin's daughters;
> But oh! confound these venomous midges!

DAY 2

> Here it comes! raging and frantic
> Right off the face of the broad Atlantic,
> Tearing and dashing
> And shouting and splashing,
> All day long
> Steady and strong
> The only thing is to seek a retreat
> Under the lee of a stack of peat,
> While Patrick Fitzpatrick, to clear one's sorrow,
> Says, 'Sure there'll be beautiful sport, sir, the morrow!'

DAY 3

One minute more
We'd have been safely on shore:
But alas! and alas!
It ne'er came to pass.
I heard a great wail
That turned me all pale,
Moaning afar from the point surnamed Monaghan,
'Arrah! bad luck to him, sure, and he's gone again.'

DAY 4

As slashing a rise as a man could wish!
'Hurroor!' Pat cries, 'and it was a great fish!'
Rest him a minute, and then a fresh cast,
If you show it him neatly he'll take it at last.
But in working your fly on the rippling pool
You must keep your left eye on an Irish bull,
Till old Jimmy Carr, our friend at a pinch,
Repulses the baste from Ballinahinch.

DAY 5

Tried all the flies:
The fish *won't* rise:
Fishing voted a bore,
We repose on the shore,
And have a good snore,
While a brute of a cow with a morbid digestion
Eats the macintosh up without asking a question.

DAY 6

Off goes the reel
With a rattle and squeal.
Down through the rapids away the line spins,
It's ten minutes before you catch sight of the fins.
And says Pat as he plunges and tugs and bounds
'Sure he's every bit of twenty pounds!'
Six times or more
He's brought to the shore,
When off with a burst
As fresh as at first,
Till, seizing his moment, with dexterous hand
Pat cleverly gaffs him, and flings him on land.
Then, dancing around him, uproarious and frisky,
He crowns his success in a bumper of whisky!
   On a visit to Ballinahinch in Ireland with his cousin

His speech at Wolverhampton was described as epoch-making.
The Guardian wrote: *If it had not been for Mr. How's speech
it would have seemed as if the old English 'via media', with*

its long array of orators and divines, its massive learning and dignified integrity of character, had no place in a Church Congress of our time. He was still to serve as Rector of Whittington for many years: but the Wolverhampton speech marked him out as a potential bishop and he became widely known in Church circles. Preferment was however not a burning personal ambition.

Charley went to the cathedral service this afternoon. He has been very anxious to see the bishop, so we took him, and the bishop gave him a small wooden horse, so that he considers episcopy quite a desirable institution . . .

William Walsham How writing to his brother in 1866 about the Hows' four-year-old son.

My lord, – I stand up to express one conviction which I hold very strongly. It is this – that the strength and backbone of the Church of England lie in that very large party (if *party* that can be called which eschews and repudiates all party names and party practices) – that very large party (for I *must* use the word having no better) which has learnt many things from the great Church movement which has burnt its mark ineffaccably upon the history of this generation; but which is startled, and to some extent repelled, by the rapid and excessive development of that movement, which is making, perhaps no less ineffaceably, the present movement. This large party has been trained in a system which they find rudely questioned and shaken by some in these days. They have learnt to love the Church of England as they have learnt to know her. They have learnt to love the Prayer-book as they have seen it interpreted by wise and loving hearts for many years past. They are now asked to unlearn many old things, and to learn many new. I said that this party had gained much from the great advance in Church doctrine and practice in the present age, and they gladly acknowledge the debt. They have gained a clearer and firmer grasp of some very precious truths. They have gained the love of higher and more beautiful services, and of the musical offering of praise in choral worship. They delight in hearty congregational services. They love hymns heart-stirring and affecting, like Neale's and Faber's – hymns which can, and do, draw tears from eyes unused to weep. They hate all slovenliness and coldness and dryness. They are thankful to have escaped from the old reign of dry dignified proprieties. They seek, and I hope they attain to, life and warmth and love in their worship. They aim at short, stirring, and, where possible, extempore preaching. They accept without grudging much that will render their services attractive to the indifferent and elevating to the devout. They decorate their churches, and are not ashamed of the blessed symbol of our salvation. Above all, they are continually multiplying the opportunities of daily prayer in their churches, continually making more and more frequent the celebrations – especially the early celebration of the Holy Communion. They are learning – and thank those who teach them for the lesson – more and more to set forth *that* as *the* great act of worship in the Church of Christ . . .

. . . My lord, we love the name *Catholic* and we refuse to narrow it to a party watchword. We have long said to Rome: *You shall not have exclusive possession of this title*; we now say the same to others. We love the doctrine of the Church as we love nothing else, believing it to be *the truth as it is in Jesus*; we refuse to narrow it to mean Church doctrine as set forth in one particular development, and in one peculiar phraseology. We desire to treat candidly, and in a spirit of brotherly love, those with whom we find ourselves unable to agree in many things, and we desire to remain, what we hope we are now, plain, faithful, honest members of our ancient and purified, and therefore dearly beloved Church of England.

> *William Walsham How, speaking in a debate on Church Ceremonial at Wolverhampton Church Congress in 1867, when extreme positions were being taken by many on both sides of the argument.*

WILLIAM WALSHAM HOW

In the summer of 1868, however, his life was nearly cut short. The family were on holiday at Douglas in the Isle of Man when the parson became entangled while sea-bathing *in a quantity of floating seaweed which* he *shook off with a violent struggle* which left him exhausted. He thought there was no escape from drowning: and, but for his physical fitness providing the strength to cling to tiny rocks, he would doubtless have died. In 1869, he wrote *Great and glorious Father, humbly we adore Thee*, for which Durham High Church musician, the Reverend John Bacchus Dykes, provided the tune OSWESTRY.

> *. . . It is a solemn thing, my dear brother, to have been so near death. God grant I may not forget the thoughts and resolutions of yesterday! Do pray for me that I may give to God the life that He has again given to me far more thoroughly than I have done . . .*
>
> *From How's letter to a brother, 9th August 1868*

* PART I

Great and glorious Father, humbly we adore Thee,
p { Poor and weak and helpless sinners in Thine eyes;
{ Yet, in meek obedience, low we fall before Thee,
cresc. Trusting, pleading only Jesus' Sacrifice.

Bowed beneath Thy footstool, yet with boldness pleading
This the only plea on which our hope relies,
Unto Thee, O Father, all Thy mercy needing,
Make we this Memorial of Christ's Sacrifice.

PART II

To our brother sinners we repeat the story,
('Tis the Gospel story pictured to our eyes,)
Ever in this Service, till He comes in glory,
Showing forth the Saviour's priceless Sacrifice.

For His own dear members He is interceding,
Far above in light unseen by mortal eyes;
Yet is present now, His faithful children feeding,
Giving His own Self, their one true Sacrifice.

Then, O gracious Father, bent in reverence lowly,
We would taste the pledges we so dearly prize,
Food that none may dare to take with hands unholy,
cresc.   Feasting on the once accepted Sacrifice. *ff* Alleluia!

PART III

Hath He died to save us, in His love so tender,
And shall we repay Him nought but fruitless sighs?
Nay, our souls and bodies, all we have to render:
Father, for His sake accept our sacrifice.

f   Great and gracious Father, at Thy right hand glorious,
dim   As our souls to Thee in trembling worship rise,
cresc. Lo! the Lamb once offered reigneth now victorious,
f   And the Angel choirs adore His Sacrifice!

We too would adore Thee, Saviour, ever raising
Praises to the Lamb who reigns above the skies.
    { Oh, the mercy boundless! Oh, the love amazing!
ff { Glory be to Thee, our one true Sacrifice! Alleluia!

    * Part I is to be sung with either Part II or Part III
                The musical expression marks are How's own

It is an interesting text in that, beside being a hymn, each of its verses is intended to set forth one of the various aspects of Holy Communion. How was anxious to teach his congregation what they were about at the Sacrament and to stress eight emphases: our unworthiness to draw near; the memorial before God; the memorial before Man; Christ pleading his passion for us above, yet present in the

Sacrament; the receiving of the heavenly food; the offering of ourselves; the angelic worship; and adoration of the glorified Saviour. He also began work as a member of the Joint Committee of Convocation on the Revision of the Authorised Version of the Bible. His well established hymn *O Word of God incarnate* had been written in 1866. Tunes used include BENTLEY, NYLAND, AUTUMN, AURELIA and PEARSALL. In 1869, too, a future Bishop of Lincoln conducted a retreat at Whittington. Because at that time, retreats in the Church of England were associated with the extreme Ritual Party, this brought a storm of local protest, one letter even venturing to suggest that the idea was secretly to celebrate the Roman Mass. How, convinced of the value of retreats for middle-of-the-road members of the Church of England, was himself to conduct many during his future ministry.

> The Church from her dear Master
> Received the gift divine,
> And still that light she lifteth,
> O'er all the earth to shine;
> It is the golden casket
> Where gems of truth are stored:
> It is the heaven-drawn picture
> Of Christ, the living Word.
>
> *Verse 2 of 'O Word of God Incarnate'*

In 1870, the Cottage Hospital at Oswestry was opened: How wrote *O thou through suffering perfect made* and the juxtaposition of couplets in verse 4 seems to hint at suffering as a means of chastening the sinner.

> But, oh! far more, let each keen pain
> And hour of woe be heavenly gain,
> Each stroke of Thy chastising rod
> Bring back the wanderer nearer God.
> *Verse 4 of 'O Thou through suffering perfect made'*

The same thought is expressed in his *Pastor in Parochia*, which had been published in 1868. The hymn is sung to ST. SEPULCHRE. *The Society for Promoting Christian Knowledge* planned to publish a major collection of hymns, issued as *Church Hymns* in 1871. How was appointed co-editor of the literal texts, his partner being John Ellerton whose hymns include *The day Thou gavest Lord is ended*. The music editor, better known to many for his collaboration with W. S. Gilbert, was Arthur Sullivan: in the preface to a later printing, Sullivan thanks How for adding expression marks throughout the text to guide which lines should be sung softly, which passages crescendo or diminuendo through all the verses of 592 texts. The preface to a later edition of *Church Hymns* analyses the contents and shows the editors have ranged widely in their search for worthy material.

My children, I am going to ask you to do a very difficult thing. I want you to spend half-an-hour with God . . .
Opening advice to Confirmation candidates suggesting they should spend half-an-hour in personal communion with God, kneeling down and with bowed heads, during the period before and after the laying-on of hands, 1869

O Holy Father, Who chastenest us for our good, that we may be partakers of Thy holiness; Have mercy on this Thy servant, and bless to him such chastisement as in Thy love Thou art pleased to lay upon him . . .
William Walsham How: 'Pastor in Parochia': Part of a prayer for sanctification through sickness

118

Translated from the Latin of the first five centuries	17
Translated from the Greek	12
Translated from the Latin of the 6th to 16th century	30
Translated from the Latin (chiefly Gallican texts of the 17th and 18th centuries)	22
Translated from the German	30
Translated from other foreign languages	3
By American writers	6
English hymns of the 16th century	3
English hymns of the 17th century	11
English hymns of the 18th century	81
English hymns of the first half of the 19th century	95
English hymns by recent and living authors, previously published	239
English hymns appearing for the first time	43
	592

Analysis of contents of 'Church Hymns'

Many of the new texts were to meet gaps perceived by the editors in available material, and, as so often happens, How and Ellerton themselves wrote many texts for these gaps. How's included one for Church Guilds and Associations, linking the Transfiguration to the need of healing which the party found awaiting them at the foot of the mountain.

. . . got through fifty-seven pastoral visits last week, the most I ever did in any one week, except just when I was first making acquaintance with the parish . . .
William Walsham How to a new curate soon to join him.

He came from hours of rapture high
To care for human woe:
So Angels from God's presence fly
To succour men below.

O Jesu, be our life like Thine; —
Blest labour, doubly blest
By communings with things divine
Upon the mountain's crest.

Lord, we would pass from hours of prayer,
That lift our souls above,
To go where want and sorrow are
With lowly deeds of love.
Verses from 'Upon the holy Mount they stood'

Upon the holy mount they stood was sung to GLOUCESTER and ST. FLAVIAN. He joined forces with Bishop Thomas Ken in the hymn for St. Matthew's day, *Behold, the Master passeth by!* The first three verses are by How: most of the rest is from Ken's *Hymns for all the Festivals of the Year*, taking an extract from his effort to celebrate the life of St. Matthew. The tunes are BAVARIA or JAM LUCIS.

Behold, the Master passeth by!
Oh, seest thou not His pleading Eye?
With low sad voice He calleth thee —
'Leave this vain world, and follow Me'.

O soul, bowed down with harrowing care,
Hast thou no thought for heaven to spare?
From earthly toils lift up thine eye; —
Behold, the Master passeth by!

One heard Him calling long ago,
And straightway left all things below,
Counting his earthly gain as loss
For Jesus and His blessèd Cross.

That 'Follow Me' his faithful ear
Seemed every day afresh to hear:
Its echoes stirred his spirit still,
And fired his hope, and nerved his will.

God gently calls us every day:
Why should we then our bliss delay?
He calls to heaven and endless light:
Why should we love the dreary night?

Praise, Lord, to Thee for Matthew's call,
At which he rose and left his all:
Thou, Lord, e'en now art calling me, —
I will leave all, and follow Thee.

How and Ken:
'Behold, the Master passeth by!'

There were texts for the Annunciation of the Blessed Virgin, for St. Mark's Day, for Whitsuntide, for Epiphany, for catechising, beside general hymns. Most of these were not to become widely used but his Litany for the Rogation days, or Hymn of Supplication for the nation, *To Thee our God we fly* is still sung. Tunes include CROFT'S 136th, LATCHFORD, MANCHESTER, GRATITUDE, BEVAN, CHRIST CHURCH, DARWALL'S 148th and SAFE HOME.

To Thee, our God, we fly
For mercy and for grace;
Oh! hear our lowly cry,
And hide not Thou thy face.
O Lord, stretch forth Thy mighty hand,
And guard and bless our Fatherland.

Arise, O Lord of Hosts!
Be jealous for Thy Name,
And drive from out our coasts
The sins that put to shame. *Chorus*

.   .   .   .   .

Give peace, Lord, in our time;
Oh! let no foe draw nigh,
Nor lawless deed of crime
Insult Thy majesty. *Chorus*
Verses from 'To Thee our God we fly'

He also turned to the Latin: and like many others was inspired by the world-famous *Vexilla Regis* written by Venantius Fortunatus around 600. How and Ellerton considered some verses of this ancient Processional Hymn as wholly unsuitable for nineteenth-century congregations. How replaced the offending portions with material of his own. *The Royal banner is unfurled* was set to ELLESMERE.

The Royal banner is unfurled,
And lo! the Cross is reared on high,
Whereon the Saviour of the world
Is stretched in mortal agony.

Pierced by the spear He yielded forth
Water and Blood, a mingled tide,
That so a fount of priceless worth
Might flow for sinners from His side.
The opening verses of How's
hymn founded on the Latin
of Venantius Fortunatus

One of Walsham How's gifts as a preacher was his ability to use language that ordinary people could understand. Serving on a Convocation Committee about the Athanasian Creed which was trying to draft some wording for a Synodical Declaration about the meaning of certain phrases, he provided a paper for his colleagues emphasising the need for simple words in reacting to its condemnatory clauses, which some understood as consigning to everlasting death all, without exception, who did not hold the true Faith and even upon those who might err in a single item of required belief. How's involvement in an issue with which the Church of his day was wrestling shows his willingness to face up to theological difficulties as an essential element in his ministry.

The first parish mission How conducted was at Christ Church, Lancaster Gate, in London in 1872. At a mission later that year at North Malvern, he was so delighted by the incumbent's daughter that he wrote a poem about her in Latin. The same year he wrote *Behold a little child* to be published by the *Society for Promoting Christian Knowledge* in *Children's Hymns*. It is sung to BEVAN, ST. JOHN (CALKIN), SHEBBEAR COLLEGE and WESLEY.

> Where Joseph plies his trade,
> Lo! Jesus labours too;
> The Hands that all things made
> An earthly craft pursue,
> That weary men in Him may rest,
> And faithful toil through Him be blest.
>
> Among the doctors see
> The Boy so full of grace;
> Say, wherefore taketh He,
> The scholar's lowly place?
> That Christian boys with rev'rence meet,
> May sit and learn at Jesus' feet.
>
> Christ once Thyself a Boy,
> Our boyhood guard and guide;
> Be Thou its light and joy,
> And still with us abide,
> That Thy dear love, so great and free,
> May draw us evermore to Thee.

Three verses from 'Behold a little Child'
William Walsham How was later
to be known affectionately
as 'The Children's Bishop'

In 1873, How turned down the offer of a bishopric at Cape Town and the living of the famous London church of All Saints in Margaret Street. Of the latter, he wrote he was *too much out of harmony with the whole system there to be able to work there happily and usefully*. Further bishoprics at Natal, in Jamaica and in New Zealand were also turned down. How's inability to say *No*, except to preferment, meant that he accepted too many invitations. Even he was forced to admit he had set himself an impossible programme in the winter of 1874, describing his portion as *too full of work*. Apart from his parish duties, he conducted an evangelical retreat at Christ Church in the London district of Hampstead and another lasting more than a week at Stratford-on-Avon; he conducted two days of meditations for young ordination candidates; he preached in London's Cathedral of St. Paul:

little wonder when he crowded so much into seven or eight weeks that he wrote *it takes it out of me too much to be quite wholesome. It taxes spirit more than flesh with me.*

He spoke no grand or learned words, he used no studied art,
He simply spoke as one who tried to reach his brother's heart.
It was the old old story, that can never pall or tire
When the lips with grace are fervent and the heart with love on fire.
And the lady marked how, one by one, the tear-drops grew and fell,
While eagerly those wistful eyes were fixed as by a spell.
And then a hymn rose all around — no cultured choir's display,
For every voice and every heart seemed moved to sing that day;
And faster, faster, rained the tears, for with the well-known air
Came back her childhood's happy days, her childhood's home so fair.
She sees her father's thin white locks, her mother's loving eyes —
This night she cannot put aside the memory, if she tries:
She sees — she cannot help but see — the little sister sweet;
She hears upon the broad old stairs the little pattering feet;
They laid her in the old churchyard, beneath the sombre yew: —
And, *Oh! my God* the poor girl sobs, that I were laid there too!

> *William Walsham How: From 'Was Lost and is Found' an illustrated book, subtitled 'A Tale of the London Mission of 1874'*

And as to fasting, it is a means and not an end. It is meant to bring the body into a state helpful to a prayerful and watchful spirit. Let it be so used when it effects its purpose. But is it better to lie in bed till church time, as some do, because they cannot otherwise go through the long morning service fasting, or to take such simple food as may be found needful to enable both body and spirit to engage profitably in the worship of the Church without impairing their fitness for the ordinary duties of the morning? . . .

William Walsham How writing on the question of Fasting Communion in 'Church Bells'

He also gave a great deal of time with two other Committees of Convocation concerned with Liturgy; and was troubled that at least two important rubrics caused difficulty through lack of clarity, the more so when clergy were disciplined for disobeying that which was not adequately expressed.

By 1875, he had not learned to cut down his commitments. He led parish missions at Wolverhampton and Shrewsbury; he made over eleven hundred parochial visits in Whittington quite apart from brief courtesy calls; he led retreats at Bowden and Hawarden; he addressed lay workers at St. Paul's Cathedral; he spent four days in Bangor leading clergy meditations; and several days with candidates for ordination at Ely and Lincoln; he took part in Diocesan activities at St. Asaph and in the work of Convocation and its committees; he gave four addresses and one sermon in Worcester Cathedral; he travelled as far east as Great Yarmouth to preach; he attended and spoke at the Stoke Church Congress; he preached three times in one day at Bradford; he wrote for the magazine *Church Bells*; he joined twenty thousand others at London's Royal Agricultural Hall when Moody and Sankey were on the platform; and he persuaded the *Society for Promoting Christian Knowledge* that there was a need for a special hymnbook for Parish Missions. He was in this connection to come up against

problems of copyright with Sir Henry Baker, author of *Lord,
Thy word abideth* and Chairman of the proprietors of *Hymns
Ancient and Modern*, chiding him a little on this subject.

Whittington Rectory,
Oswestry
Jany 21. 1876.

I certainly *was* going to ask permission to use the 2 hymns
(Miss Noel's and Dean Alford's) in the obnoxious way you
condemn, & I cannot promise you not to do so still, if I learn
their addresses. But pray do not help me to these. I cannot, I fear,
enter into your feelings. It seems to me, if I had a good hymn
or tune, I cd have no other wish than to let it be used as widely
& freely as possible. But I must explain to you simply what I have
been about. I have conducted a good many Missions at which the
S.P.C.K. *Mission* Hymnbook was used, & I have found it scanty
& unsatisfactory. So I have prepared an enlarged edition (I
suppose I must call it so, as it is founded upon that book,) with
the help of several experienced missionaries. I have not said
anything about it to the Socy. yet, but I meant, when all was
ready, to ask them to print it. They are the proper people to print
such a book. So matters stand, & you know all about it. May I
observe that in most cases the Mission book has been used where
your book was the ordinary Church book, & since the Mission
book cd by no possibility be used for any other purpose or time,
it is obvious it cd in no way affect the use or sale of any book for
ordinary Church use. Indeed the use during a Mission of several
favourite hymns from your book wd only endear it the more to
the congregation.

*William Walsham How to Sir Henry Baker,
Chairman to the Proprietors of 'Hymns Ancient and Modern'
who controlled many copyrights Walsham How wished to use.*

. . . I should so dread it for
myself, such frequent mission
engagements, developing dispro-
portionately (it must be) the
emotional half of one's finely
strung nature . . .
*Archdeacon Norris to
William Walsham How*

Later in their correspondence, he seeks to use some of the
tunes in that collection which he thinks are especially
singable at Parish Missions but which are set there to other
words.

Whittington Rectory
Oswestry
Nov. 8. 1876.

Dear Sir Henry,
I hope you will not think me a pestilential fellow, in bothering
you so much, but it strikes me it may be worth while to mention
one thing in reference to the tunes for the Mission Hymns. For a
Mission you *must* have very easy popular & taking tunes. Now

there are some of the most suitable in all A & M the hymns for which are not in the Mission Book. The point is this — wd it not be well to assign some of these very popular tunes to other hymns in the Mission book, either instead of, or in addition to, the tunes given for each hymn in A. & M.? As an instance, I wd name Melita. We sang it at Berkhamsted several times to 'O Love, who formedst', & it was felt to be far better than the tune in A. & M. to these words. So again I shd myself like to assign Iam Lucis to one of the longer L.M. hymns. It is very grand with a vast congregation singing it. So I shd like to see St. Agnes given to one of the L. M.s — you see what I mean.

Believe me ever
Yours sincerely
Wm. Walsham How

Amongst the hymns How wrote especially for Mission Services is *O my Saviour, lifted,* sung to NORTH COATES and GLENFINLAS.

> Lift my earth-bound longings,
> Fix them, Lord, above;
> Draw me with the magnet
> Of Thy mighty love.
>
> Lord, Thy arms are stretching
> Ever far and wide,
> To enfold Thy children
> To Thy loving side.
>
> *Verses from*
> *'O my Saviour, lifted'*

Shall I tell you the name of the little bushes behind which the lion likes to hide? They are called Temptations. You will find them all along the way you go, on both sides. Sometimes they look very harmless and pretty, and are covered with gay flowers, or fruit which looks very sweet. Ah! my children, don't go too near. You think there can't be much harm in just picking one of these pretty flowers, or in just tasting one of those ripe berries. But what if the lion be crouching just behind that very bush? When you see Temptation, depend upon it the Tempter is not very far away.

William Walsham How: From 'The Roaring Lion' in 'Plain Words to Children' 1877

Many clergy were openly ignoring the discipline of their bishops; and in 1877, How organised a loyal address to those set in authority and secured over fifty signatures from fellow-priests. On seeing the wife of a Primitive Methodist local preacher in church one day, he was delighted with her explanation. *Well, sir, you see my old man be preaching at our chapel today, and I can't abide he!* During his long stay at Whittington, How was dissatisfied by his inability to be as successful as he would wish in the parish. He found it difficult to get close to the young men and sometimes was cowardly enough not to speak his mind when he should to the squirearchy. He told his curates they certainly should not use him as a model of an exemplary parish priest.

Of all the speculations affecting man's origin, the most prominent, as well as the most startling, is that which is propounded by the advocates of Evolution, who hold that all living creatures have been developed out of earlier and less perfect forms . . . There are some devout Christians who will say, *This and all such-like speculations are straight against the Bible and therefore utterly untrue and absurd. I cannot even consent to argue about them as tho' there were any possibility of their acceptance.* I confess I cannot use this language. I have too vivid a sense of the injury done to the cause of religion by the solid resistance of the Church in former days to the discoveries of Astronomy as opposed to the Bible . . .

From 'Hard Questions', a course of mid-day addresses at St. Peter's during the Mission at Chester, 1877

His wife's health was a worry to him; she suffered greatly with bronchitis and asthma. On 7th May that year, his diary describes her as very ill: six days later, he recorded that Frances came downstairs for the first time since October but for journeys.

The two following entries stand next to each other in the Register of Whittington Parish, Shropshire, in the year 1877:—
Sept. 13 — Ellenor Watkins, of Borth, aged 31
Oct. 9 — Ellenor Watkins, of Borth, aged one month

Sleep, sweet mother! Thy task is done;
It is time for thee to rest.
Trustfully leave thy little one
To lie on another's breast.
God's love, O mother, is greater than thine,
And He calls thee away to a peace divine.

Bright was the vision that met her eyes,
Yet it was not wholly fair;
And sweet were the glades of Paradise,
Yet she missed one sweetness there:
For Heaven itself would lack one grace
Till the mother might look on her little one's face.

And God looked down from His golden throne
On the mother's heart of love,
And He sent to the earth a shining one
To carry her child above;
And He laid it down on her yearning breast, —
And *then* the mother had perfect rest.

William Walsham How: 'Two Burials'

You may like to know the actual words I use daily: 'Into the hands of Thy fatherly goodness I commend my dear ones at rest, humbly beseeching Thee that they may be precious in Thy sight. Grant them light, peace, and a blessed resurrection . . . '

William Walsham How writing to his brother about lost loved ones in 1893

At the beginning of November 1877, he travelled with his wife to Cannes for the benefit of her health: her doctors had often counselled winters away from Whittington. How acted at Cannes as an assistant chaplain, and the couple stayed on through the winter months. Here, a letter arrived from London to test his thoughts about being appointed a Bishop with responsibility for its East End.

He was particularly troubled that any move from country to city might make his wife's bronchial troubles worse. As it was, nothing came immediately of the sounding as the person who had promised to put up some money to allow the Bishop of London to make the appointment did not think How was the right man for the job. That May, he was offered the Vicarage of Windsor with a Readership to the Queen. Again, he said *No*. In September, he was invited to a new appointment to help establish and oversee Mission work in the Diocese of Winchester: but he turned this down on the ground that the scheme had not been properly thought through.

John Stow, in his *Survey of London* (1598) described a church at the north-west corner of Aldgate as the *fair and beautiful Parish church of S. Andrew the Apostle, with an addition to be known from other churches of that name of the Knape or undershaft and so called S. Andrew Undershaft because that of old time, every year on Mayday in the morning it was used, that an high or long shaft (or Maypole) was set up there, in the midst of the street before the South door of the said Church, which shaft when it was set on end, and fixed in the ground, was higher than the Church steeple.* Sadly in 1549, a curate of nearby St. Catherine, believing that such fripperies as dancing round a maypole were sinful, made sure the maypole was sawn to small pieces — but the name of St. Andrew Undershaft remained.

ST. ANDREW UNDERSHAFT

The church has a beautiful pulpit finely carved and curiously adorned with cherubims, flowers, fruits, leaves and books. In 1879, the living of this church became vacant: it was a tiny parish, which could easily be served by a curate, and the Bishop of London took his chance to use the living to finance the Suffragan Bishop who would primarily serve East London. He now no longer depended on financial patronage: and in due course, the Queen approved the appointment of William Walsham How in this office. The letter from 10 Downing Street dated 4th July 1879 from the Prime Minister that he would *be styled suffragan of the See of Bedford, for the purpose of assisting the Lord Bishop of London in the duties of his diocese.* Bedford is many miles from East London: and the odd choice was to circumvent a law dating from the time of King Henry VIII which forbade a suffragan see being named in London! Still, the choice enabled Bishop Claughton of St. Albans, whom he had served as a curate in Kidderminster, to note the succession to a nonconformist Bedford saint, John Bunyan. While the possibility of the appointment was still secret, he wrote humorously to his son Harry about taking on a new parish of just 400 souls. His wife, on the other hand, knowing the truth, had written encouragingly to her husband from Barmouth. A home was made available to the family at Clapton Common by a Mr. Foster and they were soon to move into Stainforth House.

The Vicar of St. Matthew, Upper Clapton commented on the situation in East London at the time of Bishop How's arrival. Not everyone thought a country parson was the man for the job. *Very soon, however, were the clergy satisfied that in this they had been mistaken. The Bishop threw himself at once*

I have been offered a very good living further south, with only 400 population, and think of accepting it. What should you think of your old father settling down in a parish with that population to spend his declining years in idleness? I *really mean* that I shall probably take it.
William Walsham How, writing to his son, March 1879

I feel myself that the work at the east of London is what you could do, and that God is calling you to do it. We must not give one thought as to whether we should like to live there or not . . .
Frances How writing to her husband from Barmouth, March 1879

STAINFORTH HOUSE

. . . there is a nice garden, and a small field capable of supporting two cows. The house stands high, and on gravel, so is very healthy. It is quite rural at the back, looking down the slope of the ridge to the river Lea.
How describes the garden of Stainforth House

128

with ardour and enthusiasm into the work. Bishop John Selwyn of Melanesia wrote: *I went from smoke and dirt to sunny climes, you from one of the prettiest places on earth to what ? well, one of the grandest works a man could be*

called to. He enclosed a four-line doggerel. The consecration in St. Paul's Cathedral on 25th July was of a quartet of bishops: besides the Bishop of Bedford, those for the Anglican Church in Jerusalem, for Travancore and for British Columbia were consecrated.

How shall we reach these masses dense,
Beneath whose weight we bow?
At last a light breaks through the gloom
And we will show you — How.

The Cry of the East London Clergy:
Bishop Selwyn of Melanesia

In September, the Bishop finally left Whittington for London and lived for a few days in Whitechapel Vicarage. The Vicar had invited all the Board School teachers in the neighbourhood to bring the children to church one week-day after school. How expected a small turn-out, but the great parish church was full of some twelve hundred of the poorest children in London. It was a fitting occasion for one who was to earn the title 'The Children's Bishop'. Perhaps one of the hymns most associated with that title is *It is a thing most wonderful* sung to HERONGATE, SOLOTHURN, IT IS A THING MOST WONDERFUL, CRUX CRUDELIS and ALSTONE.

It is a thing most wonderful,
Almost too wonderful to be,
That God's own Son should come from heaven,
And die to save a child like me.

And yet I know that it is true:
He chose a poor and humble lot,
And wept, and toiled, and mourned, and died,
For love of those who loved him not.

I cannot tell how He could love
A child so weak and full of sin;
His love must be most wonderful,
If He could die my love to win.

I sometimes think about the Cross
And shut my eyes, and try to see
The cruel nails and crown of thorns,
And Jesus crucified for me.

But even could I see Him die,
I could but see a little part
Of that great love, which, like a fire,
Is always burning in his heart.

> It is most wonderful to know
> His love for me so free and sure;
> But 'tis more wonderful to see
> My love for Him so faint and poor.
>
> And yet I want to love Thee, Lord;
> O light the flame within my heart,
> And I will love Thee more and more
> Until I see Thee as Thou art.

Late one night, he went to address the men in the kitchen of a lodging-house of two hundred beds. *It was a curious sight, some of the men were smoking, some drunk, some snoring, many with hats and caps on, and one combing his head all the time with a bit of broken comb.* In those first few days he also attended the Feast of Tabernacles in a large Jewish synagogue.

The Church in East London, serving a population of 700,000 souls, was cruelly undermanned. The Bishop proceeded quickly to organise a response to his preliminary inspection. *The Worker* looking back at the position a decade later reported that there were churches enough, but clergy and paid church-workers were too few and the Church unequal to her task. The Bishop's response was *to fill up the gaps in the ministry, clerical and lay. A sufficient ministry is the first thing needful for church work . . . and each minister of such a ministry, whether in holy orders or not, whether male or female, ought to become a centre of energy and hope, a breadwinner of the necessaries of Church life.* The Bishop's means of meeting the financial challenge was to set up the East London Church Fund; it was launched in the very centre of the City of London, at the Mansion House, in June 1880. The Bishop was to preach in prosperous places to raise money for this fund. Its five pillars of action were wholly about person-power.

OF THE RECTOR OF SPITALFIELDS

'Christ pleased not Himself', the Master's lore,
Bowed at His feet, full well the servant learnt:
For in his breast a strong pure love that burnt,
That for unlovely souls but glowed the more.
Full many a wounded lamb he homeward bore,
As all night long he paced the desolate street,
Winning, with love most patient, far-strayed feet
From the dark paths that they had known before.
Keen-eyed to judge, in action quick and sure,
No trumpet-blower, scorning all display,
Of simple life, a brother of the poor;
Yet had he genial mood, and store of mirth,
And all the poor lads loved his kindly sway,
And knew they had one friend upon the earth.
W. W. How: Sonnet I

The Bishop rarely missed Morning Prayer at the parish church of St. Thomas in Upper Clapton; and was present for Holy Communion on Wednesdays and Fridays. His mornings were mostly taken up with correspondence with a mail averaging fifty letters a day. Even with a secretary, this was a heavy

130

OLD SWAN INN, STRATFORD BROADWAY *c.1890*

load. Besides the post, there were morning visitors. On Thursdays, he and his wife would entertain clergy and their wives to lunch. He also frequently visited clergy in their own homes: if there was illness, he was an early visitor and would assist by bringing the children to Stainforth House to relieve the pressure. His diary for an April afternoon in 1881 is typical. At 1.15 he addressed the Men's Meeting at St. Laurence Jewry Church: a committee at the Society for the Propagation of the Gospel at 2.30 was followed at 4.00 by a Diocesan Home Mission Committee. At 4.30 he was at the Deaconesses' Institution in East London. This busy afternoon was followed by a full evening beginning with a pastoral visit at 7.00 followed by Confirmation at St. Peter's, London Docks. Despite all his business, he found time during his East End ministry to write sonnets, some about the clergy of the diocese.

OF THE VICAR OF ST. PETER'S,
LONDON DOCKS, AFTER HIS DEATH

Like some tall rock that cleaves the headlong might
Of turgid waves in full flood onward borne,
So stood he, fronting all the rage and scorn,
And calmly waiting the unequal fight.
He fashioned his ideal — stately rite,
High ceremonial, shadowing mystic lore;
The Cross on high before the world he bore,
Yet lived to serve the lowliest day and night.
He could not take offence; men held him cold;
Yet was his heart not cold, but strongly just
And full of Christ-like love for young and old.
They knew at last, and tardy homage gave,
They crowned him with a people's crown of trust;
And strong men sobbed in thousands at his grave.

W. W. How: Sonnet IV

Neither did he overlook his duties in the Parish of St. Andrew Undershaft. The curate served the parish well, but the Bishop reckoned to preach twice a month and throughout the curate's holidays, to visit the schools regularly, and at least once a month to join his curate on a round of parochial visits. He also took a great interest in the splendid choir, who also had the benefit of an excellent organ. The church was beautified by windows of pre-Reformation heraldic figures. He found time for a newly established national society *Watchers and Workers*, and presided over its first annual meeting. The object was to form a guild of invalids who should write to one another, intercede for one another, and form correspondence classes for the study of the Bible and other subjects of mutual interest. The lonely might feel wanted again. It was proposed that he be elected a member of Convocation: as a suffragan Bishop, he had no automatic place: but some felt the ordinary clergy had insufficient representation already in the places where decisions were taken, and he withdrew from the election. He had always enjoyed the work of Convocation: but it was perhaps as well that there was not yet more to fit into his timetable.

> ## OF THE RECTOR OF ST. GEORGE'S IN THE EAST
>
> The genial friend, the ever-welcome guest,
> Of keenly flashing wit and strenuous mien,
> With home ancestral in the woodlands green
> Courting to rural joys and leisured rest;
> Yet this the dwelling-place he chose as best,
> Where all the wild sea-life of many a coast
> Flings on our river-marge its motley host
> To swell the surge of sin and strife unblest.
> What though from land to land he loves to roam
> Keen-eyed and eager-hearted as a boy,
> Yet evermore his heart is in his home;
> And there he rules with strong but gracious sway,
> And sad men catch the infection of his joy
> As cheery-voiced he greets them on their way.
>
> *W. W. How: Sonnet V*

He visited Rome in the Spring of 1882, and while there, received a letter from London asking him to give a sermon in St. Andrew Undershaft to the local corps of the Salvation Army. He duly consulted with himself as Bishop: and gave himself permission to make history — it is unlikely any bishop had preached thus before.

This workaholic bishop did believe in holidays: and in August, he and his family visited the Alps. Even on holiday, he did not completely switch off, for while there, he consecrated a new church, and preached before Prince and Princess Christian. Whilst climbing, the Bishop broke a small bone, and was confined on his return home, first to bed, and then to crutches.

In 1884, he was elected a member of Nobody's Club: and served on a Royal Commission on the Housing of the Poor, of which one member was the Prince of Wales. Meantime, Frances How was active in establishing a home, using the parlance of the time, for fallen girls aged between 13 and 21. She went and lived at the home for a spell to help get the work off the ground.

At the beginning of 1885, the Bishop of London died. Under Bishop Jackson, How had been allowed to use his full energies for the work of East London, seldom being called on for service elsewhere in the Diocese. He imagined this would continue: and turned down the offer of the Bishopric of Manchester so that he might stay with the work he thought vital. No sooner had he done so, however, than the new Bishop made it clear he was in future to assist him through-

> What is the squire's notion of a model parson? He is a man of great tact . . . He knows the world too well to give offence. He can shut his eyes when necessary. He has too much common sense to quarrel with his parishioners. especially with his rich ones. Well; this is not exactly one's idea of a brave faithful parish priest.
> *William Walsham How: From 'Dangers and Difficulties', one of a series of lectures on Pastoral Work delivered in the Divinity School, Cambridge, 1883*

> . . . indolence is often the parent of unmethodical ways, by which much is left undone that should be done, and much ill done that should be well done.
> *William Walsham How: From 'Dangers and Difficulties', one of a series of lectures on Pastoral Work delivered in the Divinity School, Cambridge, 1883*

out the whole Diocese. This angered How, who could not see how he could possibly cope with so high a workload. Correspondence between the two men led to the plainest of expressions: a meeting ensured there was no personal animosity but clearly from here on How would have much less freedom in how he allocated his days.

While at Stainforth House, How found opportunity for relaxation in his garden, which included a fern-house stocked with many favourites. Within a few minutes walk, the botanist, F. J. Hanbury lived and the Bishop was excited by the excellent herbarium there. The botanist invited How to join him one day in June: sadly the bishop declined saying every Sunday had its three engagements and every other day was pledged.

I only ask you to read your Bible, and see whether Joy ought not to hold a more forward place in our hearts than it generally does.
William Walsham How: From 'Holy Joy' in 'Words of Good Cheer' 1886

In 1886, on *a perfect day — beautifully bright and clear, and Oxford looking its best,* he received the honorary degree of Doctor of Divinity from his old University. That same year, Frances' health began to decline again — she too had been busy about the diocese and had a special concern of the need of clothing in many parishes. At the beginning of the following year, the Bishop records an interesting evening at Toynbee Hall between Champion the Socialist and Benjamin Jones, a leader of the Co-operatives. Jones contended that *until the people are Christian, Socialism is impossible, and when the people are Christian, it will be unnecessary.* Champion held that physical force was the only resource for his party, if their just claims were refused. The Bishop noted him as *awfully strong and dangerous.*

The following year, Queen Victoria celebrated her Golden Jubilee in June. The family went to Barmouth for their annual holiday in August. Mrs. How had been less well in recent months: and it was especially hoped she would be renewed by the break. However, once more bereavement was to strike there: and like the Hows' first-born, his wife died in West Wales.

Early in 1888, the Bishop's daughter-in-law was helping him with correspondence. She and her husband had moved into Stainforth House following How's bereavement. Now she saw his face whiten as he opened a letter. Lord Salisbury had offered him the newly-created see of Wakefield. At the age of sixty-four, the prospect was hard to bear. He said *Yes,* but wrote to a relative: *It is dreadful — about the most unattractive post on the bench, but one must not choose for oneself, and I dare not again refuse what others think I ought to do.* So the Bishop who ran to catch omnibuses, who would fly from Tottenham to Wapping, from Bromley to Whitechapel, to preside at a very humble parish festival . . . a new figure in the English hierarchy was to leave the East London he had come to love. On his last day, he boarded the tram as usual. The conductor asked if he could keep the ticket issued for his fare as a remembrance. The Bishop made sure he received a photograph.

HORSE-DRAWN TRAM IN EAST LONDON

The Work achieved in the first ten years
of the East London Church Fund

Large parishes, in which sub-division was inexpedient, have been supplied with additional curates, wholly or partly paid by the fund.

In parishes, where sub-division was considered expedient, mission districts have been formed and placed under mission clergy.

Incumbents who from old age or other adequate cause are unable any longer to do their duty to their parishes, have been enabled to retire; the Bishop of Bedford has taken over the charges of their parishes, and has placed over them curates licensed to himself.

An East London diocesan deaconess' home, with a series of branch homes, has been established at a cost to the fund of something more than £1000 a year.

Scripture readers, lay evangelists, and parish nurses, have been and are being provided here and there, as the needs of the various parishes require them, and the income of the fund permits the expenditure.

I came here straight from East London, where I have lived and worked for eight-and-a-half years, and no one can know East London, even superficially, and sit down content with what he sees. To me it has been a perpetual burden of sorrow and of shame to pass day by day by day among those crowds of poor, struggling, hope-forsaken, half-starved brothers and sisters. Can it be right? Can it be what God meant? Can it be after the mind of Christ?

> *William Walsham How,*
> *preaching at the*
> *Co-operative Congress in*
> *Dewsbury on*
> *20th May 1888*

For a fortnight, the Bishop and one of his sons fished off Llangedwin on the River Tanat. As they travelled on to his new home, they were whirled through the great Marsden train tunnel. *Now,* the Bishop addressed the black walls, *I am in my diocese — just look!* He was to write to a niece of his new see: *Alas! such things* (primroses) *are not for us in the West Riding, where smoke and acid fumes, and raw cold, destroy and dirty all vegetation.* He added positively that he liked *the human beings though: they are so full of energy and warmth and heartiness. They do nothing by halves. They are very independent, at times even seemingly rude, but will do anything for you once they like and trust you.*

On 27th May, 1888, the Bishop held his first Ordination. In the evening, he preached to a great congregation on Ephesians 4, 13, urging the necessity of clear dogmatic teaching but emphasizing too that without compromise on principles, working together with others seeking the spread of religion and fighting secularism, infidelity and materialism was important. The service over, the Bishop sent for a vestry chair on which to stand so he could address the crowd at the gates. He asked if he might be allowed to be bishop of them all. At the enthronement in Wakefield Cathedral, the Archbishop of York, comparing How's training with that of other priests, said it had been *nearer to the training of Christ himself during His painful ministry than any other could be.* He was to have the support of two family priests: a son and a son-in-law settled nearby and this was of great benefit during these last years of his life.

The Bishop set methodically to work on the organisation of the new Diocese. He caused some alarm amongst ultra Low Churchmen when he appointed High Churchmen to important posts. His open disapproval of evening Communions and encouragement of daily services caused a stir. Some incumbents who had seldom seen the Bishop of the huge Diocese of Ripon, out of which the See of Wakefield had been carved, did not find episcopal interest in their parishes congenial. Most incumbents however discovered the sympathy of his large heart, and the love and single-hearted earnestness which hall-marked the man. Save for the extreme Ritualists at one end, and Protestants who closed their

And was it there — the splendour I behold?
This great fjord with its silver grace outspread
And thousand-creeked and thousand-islanded?
Those far-off hills, grape-purple, fold on fold?
For yesterday, when all day long there rolled
The blinding drift, methinks, had some one said
'The scene is fair', I scarce had credited;
Yet fairer 'tis than any tongue hath told.
And *it was there!* Ah yes! And on my way
More bravely I will go, though storm-clouds lour
And all my sky be only cold and grey:
For I have learnt the teaching of this hour:
And when God's breath blows all these mists afar,
I know that I shall see the things that are.

> *Sonnet written at Trondhjen, Norway*
> *on 12th August 1888*

churches from week-end to week-end, providing but meagre spiritual opportunities for their people, he quickly won the support of the clergy.

As in East London, he set up a Commission to report on the spiritual needs of the diocese. It recommended five entirely new parishes, second churches in twelve parishes, thirty-four Mission Churches or Rooms, additional clergy in twenty-seven parishes, and at least lay-readers in seventeen others, the raising of all benefices to at least £200 a year involving increases in eleven parishes, a pension scheme to enable old and infirm clergy to resign, and the making of all Church Schools thoroughly good and efficient.

Less than two years after his enthronement, he was offered the Bishopric of Durham: he saw *no argument in favour of deserting the half-finished work of organising* his *young diocese* and remained at Wakefield. His loyalty to Yorkshire was helpful to the response he needed for funds to carry through the formidable tasks revealed by the Commission. He urged the importance of a Central Fund so that the most necessitous causes should not be overlooked by donors while schemes in their home town received support. This was a timely caution: there was great competition in the area between the new towns: and the municipal buildings are an example of an often selfish rivalry in keeping up with neighbours. Whilst a few substantial gifts helped meet some of the needs high-lighted by the Commission, the Bishop was disappointed that the response was not more widespread, perhaps because his work-load priorities did not allow him time to get to know the laity better.

I begin to feel we must never fret to see things very imperfect, but be thankful if only the good in them is more than the evil . . .
Bishop How

Mirfield Junction, a gloomy and draughty station, quickly became the place where the Bishop regularly waited for connections: and it seemed to him a See House near to this location would make the best use of his time. He made valiant efforts to change the minds of the Ecclesiastical Commissioners about building at Wakefield, but finally lost this cause. For three and a half years, during its continuation, he was able however to live at Thornhill, about six miles from Wakefield.

Despite his increasing years, the Bishop still had tremendous energy. One of his chaplains, recalling times when candidates were being prepared for ordination wrote: *His capacity for work was always enormous, and this came out forcibly in Ember weeks. He would generally go back into his study when the rest of us went to bed, and look over a pile of papers, making his comments upon them, and setting them in*

136

order for his interviews next day. He always expected other people to work as he did, and I remember well my consternation one night when, just before twelve o'clock, as I was gathering my papers together thinking I had finished for the night, he put his head in at my door and threw me a bundle of deacons' examination papers, asking me to look them over before I turned in and have them ready for them in the morning.

He came to love Yorkshire folk as much as he had loved the East Enders. In March 1891, he obtained a seat in the House of Lords, and made sure he was present when any great social or religious subject was discussed, even though the work left behind in the Diocese made the choice of this priority a hard one. He became involved with the detail of the Clergy Discipline Bill in 1891, and about denominational teaching in the Education Bill of 1896. Local or national funding of education (rate-aid or state-aid) was a live issue — he voted for rate-aid on the basis a National Exchequer would never agree to sufficient funds!

I have done with the Conservative Party. The action of the Cabinet in the matter of the Benefices Bill seems to me nothing short of the sacrifice of principle to expediency.
Bishop How writing from the House of Lords

In 1892, How was out of action three times, first falling while fishing, then jumping from a carriage drawn by a run-away horse, and finally falling down the Dean's steps at the Cathedral. Early in 1893, he tried to mediate without success during the Glass Bottle Industry strike. Later that year he tried again when the Colliery strike caused such hardship. *Oh,* he wrote, *how one longs to say to both masters and men, 'Sirs, ye are brethren'.*

He was still to escape for fishing holidays; and, if a spare moment occurred between appointments, the man who could not be idle would invite his Chaplain to his garden and point out the *little peculiarities of this plant and that.* In 1895, planning some botanising, he wrote to his old London friend, Hanbury, to ask what he might find at Ballinahinch by way of wild flowers. The following year he borrowed maps for a trip to North-West Scotland.

A Missionary Conference, involving some twenty-eight meetings in four days was arranged in London in 1894. He left a day early, *having had as much Missionary Conference as I can stand.* The same year, he wrote at length about what he saw as the practical short-comings of the most used hymn-book in Anglican circles *Hymns Ancient and Modern.* He was critical of the absence of tune names and metres which would make it easier to use the book with another tune with which a small congregation might be familiar. He became involved positively in the plans for a new edition of this collection, sending detailed comments as a corresponding adviser.

In returning you the first portion of the sheets of Hymns as suggested for a new and revised Edition of *Hymns Ancient and Modern*, I venture to make some remarks upon the printed letter bearing your name as Chairman of the Committee, which accompanied the sheets. I will be quite honest and confess that it is with some dismay that I read of the *deliberate opinion* of the Compilers *that a primary object of such revision should be to provide translations of the Office Hymns of the Sarum Breviary in the metre of the original*. I feel sure that this would be very fatal to the success of the book. The amount of translations of Office Hymns already in the book is quite as much as it can bear, many of such translations being a dead weight and rarely used, owing to their unattractive and unpoetical form. I do not think this is any great measure the fault of the translators. It is partly the fault of the original Latin hymns, which it cannot be denied are often very bald and poor, and partly the result of the extreme difficulty of making a translation really a good hymn. I believe it should be a principle (even tho' impossible of complete attainment) not to admit a translation unless it would be accepted by competent judges as a worthy hymn were it an original.

William Walsham How to Canon White,
Chairman of the Proprietors of 'Hymns Ancient and Modern',
16th September 1896

PAROCHIAL ADVICE *from Bishop How to the Proprietors of 'Hymns Ancient and Modern' - in his own hand.*

In 1897, the Bishop was asked to write the hymn for the Queen's Diamond Jubilee. Arthur Sullivan was commissioned to write the tune. It was a very hot summer and the Bishop felt increasingly unwell. On 1st August he celebrated Holy Communion in the chapel of the Home for Girls at St. John's, Wakefield. He preached in the Cathedral in the morning and at Wrenthorpe in the evening. He wrote to his brother that,

For heathen heart that puts her trust
In reeking tube and iron shard,
All valiant dust that builds on dust,
And guarding, calls not Thee to guard,
For frantic boast and foolish word –
Thy Mercy on Thy People, Lord!

Rudyard Kipling: The last verse of 'Recessional'

138

For every heart, made glad by Thee,
With thankful praise is swelling;
And every tongue, with joy set free,
Its happy theme is telling.
Thou hast been mindful of Thine own,
And lo! we come confessing
'Tis Thou hast dower'd our queenly throne
With sixty years of blessing.
Alleluia!

Oh Royal Heart, with wide embrace
For all her children yearning!
Oh happy realm, such mother-grace
With loyal love returning!
Where England's flag flies wide unfurl'd,
All tyrant wrongs repelling,
God make the world a better world
For man's brief earthly dwelling
Alleluia!

Lead on, O Lord, Thy people still,
New grace & wisdom giving,
To larger love, & purer will,
And nobler heights of living.
And, while of all Thy love below
They chant the gracious story,
Oh teach them first Thy Christ to know,
And magnify His glory.
Alleluia! Amen.

Sullivan's tune to the Jubilee Hymn with the
autograph of William Walsham How's words.

Children, have ye any meat? Have ye taken any spoil for the Master?
Lo! he stands upon the shore, the shore to which the fishers are steering their boat, dragging their net behind them. It is early morning twilight. He is unknown, unrecognised, as yet. But they are startled as a sudden Voice comes out from the shore, across the gleaming water, demanding what success.
And we too are *fishers of men*
. . . In a Retreat, the first question is, *What is the state of my own soul?* **and the second question is** *What is the fruit of my ministry?*
What account shall we give of *our* **fishing for men?**
William Walsham How: From 'The Miraculous Draught of Fishes', addresses given at Retreats, published posthumously in 'The Closed Door' 1897

though a little better, he had been off his food and feverish. He was alert enough, though to comment that he wished Rudyard Kipling had omitted the last verse in his *Recessional* hymn.

He travelled to Ireland for the family holiday to die at Dhulough Lodge on the West coast. He was buried beside his wife at Whittington, with the coffin propelled by men who had been schoolboys when Bishop Walsham How was Rector of their parish. In Convocation an oration compared him with many kinds of Bishops who had served the Church.

If we were to describe the place which Bishop Walsham How would be likely to take in the great order of prelates I have described, I think we should assign him a place beside Bishop Ken. God had bestowed upon him . . . certain special gifts — a sobriety of judgement, a happy mirthfulness of spirit, a kindly disposition, and untiring diligence. But there was another gift . . . of a rare and precious sort, the gift, I mean, of being able to interpret the piety of the people to the heart of the people . . . Added to this there was that happy gift of sacred song . . .

WILLIAM HAYES, d. 1777, abridged by A. H. D. Troyte.

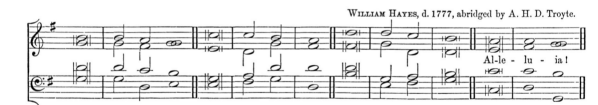

Al-le - lu - ia !

F 1 For all the Saints who from their| labours rest,
Who Thee by faith before the |world confessed,
Thy Name, O Jesu, be for |ever blest. Alleluia!

2 Thou wast their Rock, their Fortress, |and their Might;
Thou, Lord, their Captain in the |well-fought fight;
Thou in the darkness drear their| one true Light. Alleluia!

*3 For the Apostles' glorious |company, –
Who, bearing forth the Cross o'er |land and sea,
Shook all the mighty world, – we| sing to Thee, Alleluia!

*4 For the Evangelists, – by |whose pure word,
Like fourfold stream, the garden| of the Lord
Is fair and fruitful, – by Thy |Name adored. Alleluia!

*5 For Martyrs, — who with rapture-|kindled eye
Saw the bright crown descending|from the sky,
And, dying, grasped it, — Thee we|glorify. Alleluia!

6 Oh! may Thy soldiers, faithful, |true, and bold,
Fight as the Saints who nobly|fought of old,
And win, with them, the victor's|crown of gold. Alleluia!

7 Oh, blest communion! Fellow-|ship divine!
p We feebly struggle; they in|glory shine!
Yet all are one in Thee, for|all are Thine. Alleluia!

p 8 And when the strife is fierce, the|warfare long,
cres. Steals on the ear the distant|triumph-song,
f And hearts are brave again, and|arms are strong! Alleluia!

P 9 The golden evening brightens|in the west:
Soon, soon, to faithful warriors|cometh rest;
Sweet is the calm of Para-|dise the blest. Alleluia!

F 10 But lo! there breaks a yet more|glorious day;
The Saints triumphant rise in|bright array;
The King of Glory passes|on His way! Alleluia!

FF 11 From earth's wide bounds, from ocean's|farthest coast,
Through gates of pearl streams in the|countless host,
Singing to Father, Son, and|Holy Ghost — Alleluia!

William Walsham How
First printed in 1864

*   *These verses to be sung FF and in Unison on the Festivals of Apostles, Evangelists, and Martyrs, respectively.*

The expression marks against the text were added by How himself for the Annotated Edition of Church Hymns.

MEMORIAL PLAQUE, BARNES PARISH CHURCH

John Ellerton

John Ellerton came of a Yorkshire family. The surname almost certainly derives from a place in Swaledale, with an early English meaning of the farm by either the elder or the alder tree. He was, however, born in London on 16th December 1826 and baptized a month later in St. James', Clerkenwell. For eleven years, until the birth of George, he grew as an only child. Many years later, he was to recall that childhood in an article contributed to *All Saints Scarborough Parish Magazine*. He remembered Edward Irving who had been excommunicated in 1831 for heretical views about the humanity of Christ. This ex-Presbyterian constituted the *Catholic Apostolic Church* in 1835. Twelve apostles were nominated: the liturgy was characterized by elaborate ceremonial.

The Irvingite movement had instigated a much wider interest in Millenarian speculations: the staple reading of the religious folk amongst whom John Ellerton grew up was of prophecies and speculations about future catastrophic events. Ellerton was quite shocked when in 1841, his father granted a tenant a seven-year lease, when 1844 was pictured in a great coloured chart as the year the Millennium would begin.

John recalled being taken to great religious meetings at Essex Hall, often sponsored by the Church Missionary Society: it was a delight when a *real missionary* spoke in preference to the more tedious stock address by a London clergyman. In 1838 his father inherited from John's Uncle John a small property at Ulverston in the Furness Peninsular and a few miles south of Coniston Water and Windermere in the English Lake District. From here, he was sent to King William's College in the Isle of Man, involving trips each term from Liverpool across the Irish Sea.

In 1844, he suffered the double bereavement of his father and his young brother George. Leaving the college, he studied for a year at Brathay Vicarage, Ambleside, surrounded by rushing streams and wild fells. After the loss of husband and younger child, Ellerton's mother became even more devoted to John, and save for term-time at Cambridge, they were to share a home for nearly twenty years. When Ellerton began studies at Trinity College, his mother moved for a time to a smaller house owned by the family at Norham-on-Tweed. Jemima Frances Ellerton, herself a writer, published many short stories and *How Little Fanny learned to be useful* held its own

On the whole, the religious world at that time was rather gloomy. The great fight against slavery had been won, so completely won that some of the most earnest abolitionists began to think that the great Emancipation of August 1834 had been rather an extreme and hasty measure. There was no great social or theological battle to fight; religious people talked about Edward Irving and his followers . . .
I thought of him chiefly as an open-air preacher, for more than once on Sunday mornings, on my way to St. John's, Bedford Row, with my father, had I had a vision of that marvellous face and form, in the little movable wooden pulpit, sometimes in pouring rain, holding an umbrella over his head with one hand, as he poured forth his fervid oratory to a scanty group of hearers outside the walls of the great prison . . .
John Ellerton:
Recollections of Fifty
Years Ago.

Thine is the tranquil hour, purpureal Eve!
But long as god-like wish, or hope divine,
Informs my spirit, ne'er can I believe
That this magnificence is wholly thine!
– From worlds not quickened by the sun
A portion of the gift is won;
An intermingling of Heaven's pomp is spread
On ground which British shepherds tread!

William Wordsworth, whose home at Grasmere was a mile or so from Ambleside: 'Composed upon an Evening of Extraordinary Splendour and Beauty.'

144

as a favourite for half a century. John spent his vacations with his mother: and one summer, on holiday back in the Lake District, the weather was fine enough for whole days to be spent on a boat on Windermere devouring Wordsworth and Tennyson.

> The air is damp, and hush'd, and close,
> As a sick man's room when he taketh repose
>   An hour before death;
> My very heart faints and my whole soul grieves
> At the moist rich smell of the rotting leaves,
>   And the breath
>   Of the fading edges of box beneath,
> And the year's last rose.
>   Heavily hangs the broad sunflower
>   Over its grave i' the earth so chilly;
>   Heavily hangs the hollyhock,
>   Heavily hangs the tiger-lily.
>
> *From Alfred Tennyson's 'Song: A Spirit haunts the Year's last Hours'*

At Cambridge, Ellerton came into contact with a different calibre of Christian from those he had known at St. John's in Bedford Row. He met fellow-student Fenton Hort and a life-long friendship began. Many years later, they were to collaborate in making translations of Latin texts for *Church Hymns 1871*. One such, in the style of St. Ambrose, was *O Strength and Stay upholding all creation*, a hymn traditionally sung at the Ninth Hour.

> O Strength and Stay upholding all creation,
> Who ever dost Thyself unmoved abide,
> Yet day by day the light in due gradation
> From hour to hour through all its changes guide:
>
> Grant to life's day a calm unclouded ending,
> An eve untouched by shadows of decay,
> The brightness of a holy deathbed blending
> With dawning glories of the Eternal Day.

The Reverend John Bacchus Dykes, sometime Precentor of Durham Cathedral, wrote the tune STRENGTH AND STAY for the translation. It is also sung to MARLBOROUGH, WELWYN and PSALM 12 (LOUIS BOURGEOIS).

They also cooperated in writing *Joy! because the circling year* by reference to an ancient hymn probably of the seventh century, and sung particularly at Compline on Whitsun Eve. The last four lines of the first verse come from an earlier paraphrase by Bishop Mant of Killaloe. ALTENBURG, ST. GEORGE, LUBECK and SAVANNAH have been set as tunes. Whilst at college Hort and Ellerton set up *The Attic Society* which met in students' rooms to hear papers on any literary subject the members chose.

> Ellerton charmed us all by his poetic taste, and his contributions (sometimes original, and sometimes translations from classic authors) were rendered still more striking by the fine, deep, emotional tone in which he read them to us.
>
> *Reverend Gerald Blunt, Rector of Chelsea, recalling meetings of 'The Attic Society'.*

Joy! because the circling year
Brings our day of blessings here;
Day when first the Light divine
On the Church began to shine!
Like to quivering tongues of flame
Unto each the Spirit came;
Tongues, that earth might hear their call
Fire, that Love might burn in all.

So the wondrous works of God
Wondrously were spread abroad;
Every tribe's familiar tone
Made the glorious marvel known.
Hardened scoffers vainly jeered;
Listening strangers heard and feared;
Knew the prophet's word fulfilled;
Owned the work which God had willed.

Still Thy Spirit's fulness, Lord,
On Thy waiting Church be poured!
Once Thou on Thy saints didst shower
Mighty signs and words of power;
Humbler things we ask Thee now,
Gifts from heaven to men below;
Grant our burdened hearts release,
Grant Thine own abiding peace.

The ordinary outdoor-life of the University was of little interest to Ellerton. It was the opportunity to meet with new religious ideas that excited him. The chief influence came from the writings of the Reverend Frederick Denison Maurice. For the Chancellor's Medal, 1848, Ellerton wrote *The Death of Baldur*, based on the characters of Norse mythology. Asgard is the dwelling of the gods, centre of Earth. Baldur is one of Odin's children, a god beloved of many. Another child was Loki, the evil principle who sought to kill Baldur who was reverenced by many mortals. Ellerton described how Loki, disguised as a woman, comes to the hall

> I was first attracted by one or two of his pamphlets; then I fagged on at *The Kingdom of Christ*, but did not get as much out of it as I ought at the first time, probably because I was miserably ignorant of theology, and only had got up stock formulae of evangelicalism, which I had to produce in themes for a private tutor. But I think the books which helped me most were Maurice's *Lord's Prayer, Prayer Book* and *The Church a Family* . . . after three or four of his books you will be accustomed to his peculiarities, the strange *flashes* of deep insight, the reverent hesitation and fear of misstatements which makes people call him hazy; and his worst fault in the eyes of the common herd of readers is, that he refuses to tell you what your opinion is to be, but will have you think about a question, and generally leaves you with the impression that you have been talking nonsense very positively in all you have hitherto said about it.
>
> *Ellerton writing about Frederick Denison Maurice some years after leaving University.*

of Queen Frigga. He persuades her to tell the secret of what
alone can kill Baldur, the berry of the mistletoe. Thus,
leaving the palace, *she rose from out her loathely self and
cast her weazen slough*. Baldur is killed by Loki. No-one was
now able to lighten the place of the Gods for mortals. But in
Norse mythology, too, there is a resurrection story which
Ellerton tells in the final stanza of the poem.

> There came a woman to the shining gates
> Of Asgard, and to golden Fensalir
> The hall of Frigga. Frigga sate alone,
> A wan sad smile upon her face, like that
> A sungleam from a clouding sky lights up
> On some dark water; for her thoughts were far
> In deeps of time to come . . .

> — — — — —

> Even so
> For evil dreams had come to him, and fear
> Of some strange chance: whereat I took an oath
> Of all that is in earth, and sea, and sky,
> And every world; — of water and of fire,
> Of stones, and ores in the deep hill-caves hid,
> Of tree, and beast, and bird, and creeping thing,
> Yea of all deaths — all sickness, poison-drink,
> Sword-edge and spear-point; and they sware to me
> To harm him not. One living thing alone —
> Men call it mistletoe — it groweth east
> Of Valhall — I past by, too young methought
> To do him hurt: I laid thereon no ban.

> — — — — —

> Weep on, for we have lost him; nevermore
> The sunshine of his smile shall lighten up
> Asgard for us. But unto us, not him,
> The hurt is. Not for ever must we dwell
> In this our kingdom, but the Sons of Fire
> Must quell us, and the Evil Ones be strong,
> Till we and they have fallen. Then once again,
> Scathless and bright, shall Baldur fare from Hel,
> And here for ever under a clear sky
> Talk of old tales, and all those baleful times,
> As of a troublous dream long past away.
> *Selections from 'The Death of Baldur'*

In 1848 smallpox struck Ellerton and he was prevented from
sitting the Honours Examination; he received an aegrotat

degree awarded to someone having a certificate of illness. He spent 1849 in Scotland, tutoring and reading for Holy Orders. He was ordained deacon in the Cathedral Church of Chichester on St. Matthias' Day, 1850, and, his mother joining him, served as curate at Easebourne. Within the Parish stood the ruins of Cowdray House and the giant oaks which had for centuries graced Cowdray Park, a name also well-known today to polo enthusiasts. John Ellerton, who later admitted his one ambition was to have charge of a church possessing historical interest, was called as curate to St. Mary's, where Christians had worshipped for around 750 years. About 1248, a Priory was founded at Easebourne for ten Benedictine nuns and their prioress: St. Mary's was altered to provide two churches under one roof: the Nuns' Church of Presbytery and Quire, and the Parish Church consisting of the Tower and an L-shaped building, formed by a new nave and the western part of the old one. In 1535, at the Dissolution of the Monasteries, the nuns were evicted from the extensive priory buildings and their church was dismantled, its roof destroyed, leaving the remains to the mercy of the weather for nearly three hundred years.

Ellerton's biographer, the Rev. Henry Housman, his curate at Barnes, indicates that at Easebourne, the curate surrounded himself with his favourite authors, Plato, Clough, Kingsley, and above all, Maurice. Arthur Hugh Clough was in his early thirties; he had seen America as a child, was present with the free-thinking Ralph Waldo Emerson during the 1848 Paris Revolution, in Rome the following year during the siege of the Republic and in Venice in 1850. We learn of both Kingsley and Clough in the former's review of Clough's poem, originally called *The Bothie of Toper-na-Fuosich* which takes a group of undergraduates on a trip to the Highlands described in English hexameters. So Ellerton chose to read a poet who broke new ground both in subject and form. In *Ambarvalia*, published in 1849, Ellerton would have had the chance to read several poems which Clough in later life declined to have included in his *Complete Works*. In the extracts quoted, note the weaving between poetry and everyday life.

Mr. Clough has all the advantage of a novel subject, and one, too, which abounds in fantastic scenery and combinations, as it were, ready-made to his hands. On such ground he need only be truthful to be interesting. The strange jumble of society which the Highlands would present in the summer to such a party — marquises and gillies, shooters and tourists — the luxuries and fopperies of modern London amid the wildest scenery and a primitive people — Aristotle over Scotch whisky — embroidered satin waistcoats dancing with bare-legged hizzies — Chartist poets pledging kilted clansmen — Mr. Clough was quite right in determining to treat so odd a subject in a correspondingly odd manner.

Charles Kingsley reviews a proof-copy of 'The Bothie of Toper-na-Fuosich' in 'Fraser's Magazine' in 1849

Still, as before (and as now) balls, dances, and evening parties, . . .

Seemed like a sort of unnatural up-in-the-air balloon work, . . .

As mere gratuitous trifling in presence of business and duty, As does the turning aside of the tourist to look at a landscape, Seem in the steamer or coach to the merchant in haste for the city.

Arthur Hugh Clough: Ambarvalia

Charles Kingsley was born in 1819. By 1851 when Ellerton was ordained priest, the output from Kingsley's pen was considerable. Maurice in a preface to Kingsley's play *The Saint's Tragedy* writes *The clergy ought especially to lead the way in this reformation. They have erred grievously in perverting history to their own purposes. What was a sin in others was in them a blasphemy, because they professed to acknowledge God as the Ruler of the world, and hereby they showed that they valued their own conclusions above the facts which reveal His order. They owe, therefore, a great* amende *to their country, and they should consider seriously how they can make it most effectually. I look upon this Play as an effort in this direction, which I trust may be followed by many more. On this ground alone, even if its poetical worth is less than I believe it is, I should, as a clergyman, be thankful for its publication.* The story of St. Elizabeth, daughter of the King of Hungary, is available in many lives of the Saints. What is perhaps interesting for us as we review Ellerton's choice of reading is why Reverend Charles Kingsley chose to write the play.

If, however, this book shall cause one Englishman honestly to ask himself, *I, as a Protestant, have been accustomed to assert the purity and dignity of the offices of husband, wife, and parent. Have I ever examined the grounds of my own assertion? Do I believe them to be as callings from God, spiritual, sacramental, divine, eternal? Or am I at heart regarding and using them, like the Papist, merely as heaven's indulgencies to the infirmities of fallen man?* – then will my book have done its work.

If, again, it shall deter one young man from the example of those miserable dilettanti, who in books and sermons are whimpering meagre second-hand praises of celibacy – deprecating as carnal and degrading those family ties to which they owe their own existence, and in the enjoyment of which they themselves all the while unblushingly indulge – insulting thus their own wives and mothers – nibbling ignorantly at the very root of that household purity which constitutes the distinctive superiority of Protestant over Popish nations – again my book will have done its work.

If, lastly, it shall awaken one pious Protestant to recognise, in some, at least, of the Saints of the Middle Age, beings not only of the same passions, but of the same Lord, the same faith, the same baptism, as themselves, *Protestants*, not the less deep and true, because utterly unconscious and practical – mighty witnesses against the two antichrists of their age – the tyranny of feudal caste, and the phantoms which Popery substitutes

for the living Christ — then also will my little book indeed
have done its work.

From Charles Kingsley's preface to 'The Saint's Tragedy'

Ellerton may also have kept on his shelves the seventeen
Christian Socialist numbers of *Politics for the People*
published in 1848 with Kingsley writing under the
pseudonym *Parson Lot*. Then in 1851, the novel *Yeast*
was published in book form. It had caused an outcry from
the squirearchy when first issued in parts in *Fraser's Magazine*.
The miserable conditions of the agricultural labourer, the
game laws, and the Tractarian Movement all feature in the
novel.

You have sold the labouring man, squire,
Body and soul to shame,
To pay for your seat in the House, squire,
And to pay for the feed of your game.

You made him a poacher yourself, squire,
When you'd give neither work nor meat;
And your barley-fed hares robbed the garden
At our starving children's feet;

When packed in one reeking chamber,
Man, maid, mother, and little ones lay;
While the rain pattered in on the rotting bride-bed,
And the walls let in the day;

When we lay in the burning fever
On the mud of the cold clay floor,
Till you parted us all for three months, squire,
At the cursed workhouse door.

— — — — —

Our daughters with base-born babies
Have wandered away in their shame;
If your misses had slept, squire, where they did,
Your misses might do the same.

— — — — —

A labourer in Christian England
Where they cant of a Saviour's name,
And yet waste men's lives like vermin's
For a few more brace of game.

Selected verses from the song which
the squire was holding as he regaled
Tregarva in Charles Kingsley's 'Yeast'

It had come at last. The squire
was sitting in his study, purple
with rage, while his daughters
were trying vainly to pacify him.
All the men-servants, grooms,
and helpers, were drawn up in
line along the wall, and greeted
Tregarva, whom they all heartily
liked, with sly and sorrowful
looks of warning.
'Here, you sir, you —, look at
this! Is this the way you repay
me? I, who have kept you out of
the workhouse, treated you like
my own child? And then to go
and write filthy, rascally,
Radical ballads on me and mine!
This comes of your Methodism,
you canting, sneaking hypocrite!
— you viper — you adder — you
snake — you — !' And the squire,
whose vocabulary was not large,
at a loss for another synonym,
rounded off his oration by a
torrent of oaths . . .

From Charles Kingsley:
'Yeast'

They never supposed that truths which concerned their personal being had any thing to do with what they would have called mere worldly politics. They were inclined to leave all such subjects to persons whom they considered incapable of any high spiritual apprehensions. Those who were occupied with the world's business, were disposed, in their turn, to treat discussions about nature and grace, as the revival of an obsolete school-jargon, which seemed to them so much the more mischievous, because it was not confined to professional teachers, but was affecting the feelings and discourses of men and women in all classes and of all degrees of intellect.

The time has now come, I believe, when the separation between topics of great human interest is no longer possible; when men will not bear to be told that a word means *this* in political science and *that* in theological science; when they will trace out the connexion between the two, and if they find none, will suspect that both are practically dead.

> *Frederick Denison Maurice: 'The Church a Family' – from a sermon on the Service for Infant Baptism*

Maurice had preached twelve controversial sermons at Lincoln's Inn on the occasional services of the Prayer Book and published them under the title *The Church a Family* including thoughts on Infant and Adult Baptism, Marriage and the Burial Service. The parish records show that the young curate's pastoral duties included officiating at most of Easebourne's baptisms, marriages and funerals. With the help of his mother, he also started a night-school at a date when many who worked the land remained illiterate.

The Baptism for Infants, it is said, uses large, dangerous, unqualified language respecting the regeneration of little creatures incapable of repentance or faith; and then, by the awkward device of sponsors, tacitly confesses that these are necessary conditions to the attainment of the blessing. The Service for the adult assumes that repentance and faith have preceded the desire for Baptism, and yet it prays that the man then baptized may receive the gift of the Holy Ghost . . . But if it is all-important for the sake of God's truth, and for the sake of man's blessedness, to assert that the penitent and believing man does merely confess that to be true what *is* true according to God's eternal law; that the unbelieving and impenitent man does deny his own position to be that which it actually is; if it is needful to declare that repentance and faith whenever they shall appear proceed from God and not from the creature; if it is needful to signify that human instruments are employed by God to educate his children for a knowledge of their state; and that human beings may be the means of leading them to deny that state; then I claim the Service for the Baptism of Infants as one of the great witnesses which God has provided for us of a truth which we are every hour in danger of losing through our pride, and conceit, and self-exaltation, through our refusal to believe in God's character, in His actual redemption of mankind by His Son; through the low and grovelling notions which we form of the nature of our position, and of the glory and responsibility which God has put upon us.

> *Frederick Denison Maurice: 'The Church a Family' – from a sermon on the Service of Adult Baptism.*

The clergy at Easebourne also had troubles from an aristocratic past. During the eighteenth century, burials of the Montague family had taken place in the roofless Presbytery. In 1830, it was rebuilt as the Montague Memorial Chapel. Lord Montague, a staunch Roman Catholic, had remained in favour with King Edward VI and Queen Elizabeth I, both of whom visited Cowdray House. His tomb in Midhurst Church was a splendid example of a colourfully painted and brilliantly gilded Tudor memorial made of marble and alabaster, with an obelisk at each corner. In 1851, space was badly needed at the nearby Midhurst church and the Montague memorial was moved to Easebourne. But it would not conveniently fit into its new home. The figure of Lord Montague, wearing ruff and mantle and the collar of the Order of the Garter knelt between his wives with the children kneeling round them. For six months, the Montagues faced wind and weather, suffering much deterioration, until a way was eventually found of placing the memorial, previously free-standing, against a wall, with wives now side by side, and the obelisks with their alabaster bases relegated outside the Tower door.

MONTAGUE MEMORIAL, EASEBOURNE PRIORY

In 1852, Ellerton accepted the senior curacy at Brighton's parish church, dedicated to the fishermen's saint, Nicholas. For many years, the Vicar had wished to restore and modernise the building but had been unable to secure support or finance for his scheme. When the Duke of Wellington died, there was a wave of enthusiam across the land to erect memorials in his honour, especially if any local connection could be established. The Vicar recalled that the Duke had been a pupil of his grandfather who had brought him to worship in the Vicarage pew. Hence it was resolved that the restoration and enlargement of the Parish Church, wherein His Grace the Duke of Wellington at an early stage of his life was wont to worship would be an appropriate and enduring monument of our gratitude and veneration for his memory. The work was completed and the church re-opened on 8th April 1854: John Ellerton's name is among the list of

That in the opinion of this Vestry a Charter of Incorporation will be highly injurious to the interests of the Town and unjust to the Female Ratepayers in respect of their being disenfranchised, that it must of necessity increase the local taxation, and wish that every proper means be taken to prevent a Charter being obtained.

Minutes of the Vestry Meeting of the Parish of St. Nicholas, June 1852

Henry Harmer, sen., and Henry Harmer, jun., stealing fowls of Mr. Goodman, at Brighton. Mr. Creasey prosecuted. The elder prisoner *Ten months hard labour*, and the younger prisoner *Seven years transportation.*

Report on East Sussex Epiphany Sessions: Brighton Gazette 6th January 1853

This, our worshipping place, was well nigh desolate. The stones cried out of the wall, and the timber answered it. A variety of anomalies offended the eye. The bearings and fittings of the timbers were gone; and for the stone the carpenter substituted wood. The broken walls were defaced by unseemly boarding and plaster. The warden had written his name on the wall to descend to posterity, for none thought it would ever be repaired, or the writing effaced. Having spoken of the erection of galleries, the introduction of Graecian columns near the altar and other disfigurements . . .

Brighton Gazette of 13th April 1854 reporting the Vicar's sermon on the occasion of the re-opening of St. Nicholas Church, in which the state of the former building is described.

subscribers to the appeal. The same Spring, there was religious controversy in Anglican circles in Brighton by the insistence of the clergyman at St. Paul's Church in using the Auricular Confession in public worship, which others thought inconsistent and dangerous to the Protestant religion. John Ellerton's association was, however, with another of Brighton's Chapels-of-Ease, St. Peter's, where he had an Evening Lectureship. St. Peter's is now Brighton's principal Parish Church.

ST. NICHOLAS CHURCH, BRIGHTON

That with the experience of the corrupt practices at the late General Election this meeting is of the opinion that there is no security for the continuance of Free Trade and that no House of Commons can fairly and fully represent the honest opinions of the Electors unless chosen under the protection of a ballot, RESOLVED That petitions in favour of the Ballot from the Electors and Non-Electors of this Borough founded on the foregoing resolution be presented to Parliament and that the Members for the Borough be requested to support the same.

Minutes of the Vestry Meeting of the Parish of St. Nicholas, November 1852

Ellerton's first attendance as a committee member of the Brighton and District Provident Society is recorded in September 1852. A primary function of the Society was to rescue the industrious poor from the seven or eight local loanshops which advanced funds at interest of around 25% per annum, unhappily ensuring eventual ruin to many who came into their clutches. The Society had established a Loan Fund, receiving charitable deposits, and lending them at 4% to those who fell on hard times through no fault of their own.

Ellerton was appointed a Clerical Secretary in 1854: and chaired the proceedings occasionally in the absence of the Vicar. Great care had to be taken only to support genuine cases: charities depended on a good record if people were to continue to support them. At Ellerton's first meeting, there was the unhappy business of the clerk's embezzlement of a substantial sum.

Another role for the Society was to vet petitions for fund raising following a sudden disaster. The Committee could act quickly when need be: and, in 1856, two days after an accident, printed *the humble petition of Anne Collins . . . and Sarah Burchett (widows) . . . their husbands were in good health the day before yesterday . . . Collins was engaged in the cleaning of a cesspool, and was overpowered by foul air . . . Burchett accidentally passing by, descended to help Collins, and fell a victim to his humanity.* Two others who tried to save them are also mentioned: and a subscription invited to reward *a noble although unsuccessful* attempt to save the others.

At the Annual Meeting of the Society in 1855, Ellerton emphasized the vast importance of the Sick Relief Fund in *administering to the comforts and necessities of the afflicted poor*: by 1858, the Society was in trouble for its financial prudence in selling off its old correspondence as waste paper for a few shillings causing distress when somehow some of the papers were not destroyed. In 1859, though, it was minuted that *it is highly satisfactory to observe that in every branch of the Provident Society there is a continuance of prosperity, and this, not only in respect of the condition of the funds, but also in the number of district visitors, the families visited, the increased amount of deposits collected and repayments made.*

The National Schools for the education of poor children were also maintained by public collections, mostly made in the churches of Brighton. Ellerton was active in this field throughout his Brighton ministry. He arrived not long after a row between the committee and the staff of one of the schools. The staff had planned a treat for 550 children and had gone ahead with purchasing the necessities for the party and sought donations to meet the bill. The Committee members, hard put to raise funds for basic education, were angry that this was planned without their knowledge and consent: but decided the entertainment should go ahead to avoid breaking a promise to the children.

Over the years, tensions often arose between the Establishment, principally in the embodiment of the Committee, packed with the local clergy, and the teachers facing large classes and working long hours on low wages and tight budgets at the sharp end. Ellerton was often the mediator with the ability to see the situation from both sides.

The National School rules required the children be brought to Church on Sunday by their teachers. With many pews in the Brighton churches rented by the well-to-do there was often insufficient space for the children in the church nearest to the school. Moreover, not all the clergy were that keen on their congregation being swamped by charity children, and tried to hive them off elsewhere, sometimes to find that a

Great distress has prevailed throughout the country through the inclemency of the weather, and Brighton has shared in that distress, there being a larger amount of pauperism than was ever before known, the result entirely of the severe weather, which put a stop to building, and threw a number of bricklayers, carpenters and labourers out of employ.
Brighton Gazette,
1st March 1855

The Treasurer of the Soup Relief is sorry to have occasion to announce the insufficiency of the fund for this seasonable help to the necessitous poor to last longer than two weeks more at present rate of relief . . . the soup kitchens must soon be closed, unless renewed help is afforded.
Brighton Gazette
2nd February 1854

Being very desirous of welcoming the return, this day, of one of Brighton's greatest patrons, which I thought might be done by a peal on the bells in the venerable tower of St. Nicholas, I made some enquiry; and, to my great surprise, I found the bells could not be rung, for the best of all possible reasons — there were no bell-ropes.
From a letter of
13th June 1855 to
the Brighton Gazette

Who will say that an extension of education is not needed when we find Mr. Tuffnell, a Government Inspector, thus writing the result of his examination of the Brighton Workhouse Schools? *Examined the Girls' School, which appears in excellent order, and fairly instructed in all ordinary subjects. They write extremely well.*
Brighton Gazette,
17th November 1853

154

building grant they had received from the *Society for Promoting Christian Knowledge* contained a clause which did not give them the total discretion they would wish in how *free sittings* were allocated. For the teachers instructed to take children to a distant church, Sunday was far from a day of rest and one clergyman noted with some sense that *attending Divine Service twice on the Sunday is too much for them, and calculated to do more harm than good.*

There were little problems over the ink, which maybe had been charged for twice; of the pane of glass which a teacher dared to have replaced without the Committee's consent (the minute about it is dated December!); of the voluntary collector who spent £5. 18. 6 collected for the funds in an unsuccessful attempt to fend off bankruptcy, and the delicate matter of getting the guarantor of his good character to meet the deficit himself (besides the £5. 18. 6 there was £4. 10. 0 donated for the Prevention of Cruelty to Animals); of the teacher who allowed the school cellar to become full of unusable coaldust. There was controversy over whether the National School had behaved improperly in its relationship with the Blind School; there was criticism of school standards by the Brighton and Hove Philanthropic and Juvenile Street Orderly Society; there was the Bishop's plan to set up a Diocesan Inspector of Schools; the establishment of the principle of staff being entitled to three months' notice. A Recorder making forcible observations about teaching at a trial involving Brighton's Grand Jury was asked for a subscription towards the National Schools!

The appointment of a new master in 1856 showed the teacher needed varied qualifications. Besides the normal skills, he must instruct the children of the Central School in singing, and lead the choir in the Parish Church of St. Nicholas, where there is no organ, on Sundays at 9.00 and 2.45. He must also teach 20 boys supported by the Grimmett Foundation in Accounts and in the Art of Navigation. Besides involvement in educational administration, Ellerton followed up his work at Easebourne by starting a Night School in 1855; worked with the nephew of the Vicar and incumbent of St. Stephen's Church on a little manual *Prayers for Schoolmasters and Teachers* and undertook the compilation of *Hymns for Schools and Bible Classes* for use in the National Schools. He suggested tunes for the 66 hymns and authors selected included Cecil Alexander, Philip Doddridge, Robert Grant, Reginald Heber, Nicholas Hermann, William Walsham How, John Keble, Thomas Ken, Martin Luther, Richard Mant, Johann Meinhold, Henry Hart Milman, John Milton, James Montgomery, John Neale,

John Newton, Martin Rinkart, Isaac Watts and Charles Wesley.

The death of a child was not uncommon in Victorian Brighton. Ellerton's funeral hymn *God of the living* began life in this publication. He suggested two tunes, PALESTRINA from the beautiful little selection of *Metrical Tunes*, published by the *Society for the Improvement of Church Music* and ST. PHILIP'S from *Mercer's Church Psalter and Hymn Book*.

> God of the living, to Whose eye
> All worlds Thou madest open lie;
> All souls are Thine: we must not say
> That those are dead we mourn to-day;
> From this vain world of flesh set free,
> We know them living unto Thee.
>
> They are not dead, for Thou art just:
> To Thee we leave them, Lord, in trust,
> And bless Thee for the love which gave
> Thy Son to fill a human grave,
> That none might dread that realm unknown,
> Or fear to go where Christ hath gone.
>
> Still do we love them as of old,
> Still count them kept in Jesus' fold,
> Still do we share their faith and joy,
> Still join our voice in their employ,
> And Thee in them, O Lord most High,
> And them in Thee, we magnify.

While at Crewe, Ellerton revised the hymn extensively to provide a text suitable for use at funerals where the deceased had not been an active church-goer.

> God of the living, in whose eyes
> Unveiled Thy whole creation lies;
> All souls are Thine; we must not say
> That those are dead who pass away;
> From this our world of flesh set free,
> We know them living unto Thee.
>
> Released from earthly toil and strife,
> With Thee is hidden still their life;
> Thine are their thoughts, their works, their powers,
> All Thine, and yet most truly ours;
> For well we know, where'er they be
> Our dead are living unto Thee.

Not spilt like water on the ground,
Not wrapped in dreamless sleep profound,
Not wandering in unknown despair
Beyond Thy voice, Thine arm, Thy care;
Not left to lie like fallen tree;
Not dead, but living unto Thee.

Thy word is true, Thy will is just;
To Thee we leave them, Lord, in trust;
And bless Thee for the love which gave
Thy Son to fill a human grave,
That none might fear that world to see,
Where all are living unto Thee.

O Breather into man of breath,
O Holder of the keys of death,
O Quickener of the life within,
Save us from death, the death of sin;
That body, soul, and spirit be
For ever living unto Thee!

*Ellerton's final version of 'God of the Living'
as printed in 'Hymns Original and Translated'*

This revision fell into the hands of the proprietors of *Hymns Ancient and Modern* who wrote seeking amendments because of its suspect theology. Ellerton strongly defended his position calling the Medieval *Dies irae, dies illa (Day of wrath! O day of mourning)* to his defence.

From that sinful woman shriven,
From the dying thief forgiven,
Thou to me a hope hast given.
Worthless are my prayers and sighing,
Yet, good Lord, in grace complying,
Rescue me from fires undying.
With Thy favour'd sheep O place me,
Not among the goats abase me,
But to Thy right hand upraise me,
While the wicked are confounded,
Doom'd to flames of woe unbounded,
Call me with Thy Saints surrounded.
Low I kneel, with heart-submission,
Crush'd to ashes in contrition;
Help me in my last condition.

Ah! that day of tears and mourning!
From the dust of earth returning,
Man for judgement must prepare him;
Spare, O God, in mercy spare him!
Lord, all pitying, Jesu blest,
Grant them Thine eternal rest.

*A translation, mostly by W. J. Irons of the section of the 'Dies
Irae' to which John Ellerton refers in his letter. The original Latin
poem, from which the translation was made, dates from c.1250
and is probably by Thomas of Celano, the friend and biographer
of St. Francis of Assisi*

Ellerton's hymn was however not included until the 1889
Supplement to Hymns Ancient and Modern was published
and was dropped again from the 1904 edition.

Your letter has followed me here, or I would have replied to it
before. It is not for me to question Archdeacon Wordsworth's
judgement on a matter of theological statement; but I venture to
suggest, with much deference, that he has entirely mistaken the
real drift and purpose of my hymn. It was written many years
ago, but was entirely reset for Mr. Walsham How's book. Its
object was to put forward the Christian view of death, not as
regards those only of whom we can cherish the *sure and certain
hope* of rest in Christ, but as regards all those over whom we are
called to say the Burial Service, and therefore in whose case we
are likely to require an appropriate hymn. I do not wish to deny
that the unbelievers who *pass away* are indeed *dead*; but then
they were *dead while they lived;* I wish to lay stress on the fact
that our Lord does not call the mere dissolution of the body by
the awful name of death; that the soul is still living, not beyond
the reach, if God wills, of His infinite mercy. *You* who have not
scrupled at the last words of the *Dies Irae,* will not, I am sure
deny this, whatever the Archdeacon may do. Surely I say no
more than the Fathers imply again and again. I do *not deny* Hell,
or *assert* Purgatory; I merely say that the soul which departs from
the body does not depart from the range of God's love. Surely
it is recalling the worst side of doctrinal Calvinism to assert this
only of those few whom we can honestly call faithful Christians.
The belief that *all live with Him* is the only belief which can
justify the Church in expressing hope in the Burial Service over
all whatsoever their lives who are not formally excommunicate.
Most of our funeral hymns either presuppose that the deceased
was an eminent saint, or else say nothing which can give definite
hope and comfort to mourners at the very moment when their
hearts are most ready to receive the Gospel of God's love. I do
not put forward my hymn as one of any special merit; but such
as it is, it has a definite meaning. If I were to write one applicable
only to those who die with clear evidences of a state of grace,
I should only do badly what hundreds have done well . . .

158

If then you think it wise, in deference to the Protestant mind, to withdraw all suggestion of a possibility of mercy in the future life for the great mass of our parishioners, it would be I think better for you to cancel the hymn. I leave it entirely in your hands. Do whatever you think best for the Truth and for the Church. But I am afraid I cannot alter it without destroying it. Pray deal with the matter as you judge best; I shall feel you have acted for the best whatever be your decision.

John Ellerton writing from the Isle of Man to the
Proprietors of 'Hymns Ancient and Modern' in July 1868

In 1892 the *Commission of the General Convention of the American Episcopal Church* sought use of the text with thirteen others: but finally it was rejected. The 1933 edition of the British *Methodist Hymn Book* looked to Ellerton though for no less than three of the six hymns in the *Funerals* section, including this text. Tunes used include LAMBETH, GOD OF THE LIVING, ST. MATTHIAS and ST. CHRYSOSTOM.

Ellerton contributed two other texts to *Hymns and Songs for Bible Classes*. For Morning Assembly, his *Day by day we magnify Thee*, gives an insight into the virtues expected of a Victorian child. He suggested PEMBROKE and STUTTGART as tunes: SLINGSBY, DAY BY DAY and LAUS DEO have also been used. For the afternoon he wrote *The hours of school are over*, later given wider use as *The hours of day are over*. What adulation are the young expected to give their elders! He suggested KONINGSBERG for a tune: others used include CHENIES and KENT COLLEGE. In choosing his selection, Ellerton commented on a dearth of hymns between those mainly for little children, seldom of permanent interest; and those suitable for adults.

He clearly thought children could take quite strong stuff for Good Friday. For a Brighton class, he turned to a text by Joseph Anstice *Darkly rose the guilty morning*. Anstice, Professor of Classical Literature at King's College, London, dictated all his hymns to his wife during the last weeks of his life while he was

Day by day we magnify Thee —
When for Jesus' sake we try
Every wrong to bear with patience,
Every sin to mortify.

Day by day we magnify Thee —
Till our days on earth shall cease,
Till we rest from these our labours
Waiting for Thy Day in peace;

Verses from 'Day by day we magnify Thee'

For life, and health, and shelter
From harm throughout the day,
The kindness of our teachers,
The gladness of our play;
For all the dear affection
Of parents, brothers, friends,
To Him our thanks we render
Who these and all things sends.

But these, O Lord, can show us
Thy goodness but in part;
Thy love would lead us onward
To know Thee as Thou art;
Thy Son came down from heaven
To take away our sin,
Thy Spirit dwells among us
To make us clean within.

Verses from 'The hours of school are over'

still in his twenties. Ellerton revised and added to the text: and made further changes before the version in *Church Hymns*, 1871 was printed. A tune used is SON OF MAN.

Ellerton retained a special affection for St. Nicholas for the rest of his ministry. The scheme of the windows round the church introduced after he had left, with their couplets from Latin hymns, was his suggestion: and in 1882, he wrote the hymn for their Dedication Festival *Praise our God for all the wonders*. When he took part in a Parish Mission in Brighton in 1890, many elderly poor people flocked to see and hear a man they had come to love and respect when he served as a young curate.

He His Cross in patience bearing,
Meek His twisted thorn-crown wearing,
Friendless climbed that shameful hill;
Tasted not the drink benumbing,
Shrank not from the torture coming,
Suffered all to have their will.

God's own Son, of glory emptied,
Smitten, mocked, forsaken, tempted,
Died this day upon the Tree;
Dying, for His murderers pleaded:—
Lord, by us that prayer is needed;
We have pierced and stricken Thee!

*Verses by Ellerton and Anstice respectively
from 'Now returns the awful morning'*

Brought by long-forgotten teachers,
Many a legend fair and quaint,
Taught our simple sires to cherish
Memories of the Sailor-saint;
Told them how he loved the children,
How he succoured those in need,
How he burned with righteous anger,
Valiant for the Church's Creed.

So the seaman and the fisher
Called their Church upon the down
By his name who taught the sailors
In that old Levantine town;
Carved upon their font his story,
Raised his tower above the shore,
Found their rest beneath its shadow
When the storms of life were o'er.

*Verses from 'Praise our God for all the wonders'
written for the Dedication Festival of St. Nicholas
Church, Brighton, in December 1882*

In 1855, Lord Crewe determined to build a church for a parish peopled partly by the families of farmers and labourers on the Crewe estate, and partly by the new population settling as a result of the arrival of the railway works. The church was designed by Sir Gilbert Scott, who was largely responsible for the mid-nineteenth century Gothic revival in England renovating Westminster Abbey and Ely Cathedral, and designing London's Albert Memorial, and St. Pancras

Station. The church dedicated to St. Michael and All Angels was, unusually for Sir Gilbert, built in brick, red on the outside and lightish yellow for the interior. It consists of nave, chancel and apse and is adorned with a small spire.

ST. MICHAEL & ALL ANGELS, CREWE GREEN

The church was erected in 1859 on Crewe Green: and despite the expansion of Crewe, stands to this day in a rural setting of fields, oak trees, farms and cottages. A recent memorial is in thanksgiving for the life of Britain's Second World War Prime Minister, Sir Winston Churchill. The building is surrounded to-day by a continuous bed of flowers of considerable variety and lovingly tended.

To the parsonage opposite the church, John Ellerton brought his bride, daughter of one of his Brighton parishioners. John married Charlotte Alicia at St. Nicholas, Brighton on 19th May 1860. The parish register records the baptism of seven children of the marriage during the Ellertons' time at Crewe Green. Walter Maurice, born in 1870, was to become an Admiral.

Ellerton's appointment included that of domestic chaplain to Lord Crewe, whose family story is recorded as far back as the Middle Ages. The arrival of the railway had shattered the quiet of centuries: not since the Civil War when Crewe Hall was occupied by soldiery had peace been disturbed. The station at Crewe was built in the middle of no-where, established by its convenience as a meeting place of railway lines, which were still being added when Ellerton arrived. It is immortalised in the words sung by Marie Lloyd: *Oh, Mister Porter, what shall I do? I wanted to go to Birmingham, and they carried me on to Crewe!* Crewe, then, was one of Victorian Britain's New Towns.

The hall is a remarkably beautiful structure, and a fine example of the architecture of the period. It is characterised by a distinguished architect as *undoubtedly one of the finest remaining specimens of the English branch of the Italian cinque cento, which may be considered to have arrived at its full state of perfection during the reign of James I* . . .

It consists of two lofty stories, surmounted by a sculptured open parapet, concealing, in some degree, the high roof, from which rise the chimneys, representing detached octagonal columns, with their plinths, bases and capitals . . .

It presents an extraordinary variety of decorated ceilings, enriched plaster-work, and carved wainscot, the design and execution of which are masterly, fully equalling the choicest specimens of the French renaissance of the reign of Francis I . . .

At the extremity of the hall is the chapel of the mansion, small in size but of exquisite workmanship, being formed entirely of carved oak, to which Time has given the sombre tint that ever harmonises well with the sacred character of the structure. The chapel contains a painted window by Willement, and two noble paintings by Giordano. The roof is white and gold, with a single pendant; the gallery is for the servants, and there is a small place at the entrance for dependants.

S. C. Hall: 'The Baronial Halls of England', 1846

In 1862, the London and North Western Railway Company centralised its locomotive manufacture at Crewe: two years later a Bessemer steel works was set up. Sir Henry Bessemer had invented the process for converting molten pig-iron into steel in 1856. The Railway Company were monopoly employers, though beneficent by the standards of the day. They were however involved in every aspect of their employees' lives, providing housing, and feeling a responsibility in matters of education and religion. Some described the Directors as guilty of a smothering paternalism: a Board member said *even a railway company has bowels of compassion, although they are not on public exhibition.*

Crewe Hall — situate about four miles from the town of Nantwich — affords a striking example of the singular changes to which a baronial residence and its dependencies may be subjected in this utilitarian age. Formerly, it occupied the centre of a sequestered valley — now and then, when the wind was southerly, the ti-ri-la of the horn of a distant *stage* to Chester, fell upon the ear of the secluded villagers; it was almost the only sound that connected them with the business of actual life . . .

The picture at Crewe is now a new one; it is the largest of all the railway stations between Birmingham and Liverpool: the moaning of steam-engines never ceases there; a smoke perpetual gathers over the trees; travellers are rushing backwards and forwards every hour of the day; the noise unnatural is also unceasing and is audible for miles around, breaking the calm of night in the country, and making the day seem devoted to unhealthy and unpeaceful toil. The contrast between what this pretty hamlet was and is, becomes the more striking because, as yet, the station is some distance from the gigantic warehouses, engine-room, and coke-stores, which have suddenly grown into existence here.

S. C. Hall: 'The Baronial Halls of England', 1846

During the present dry weather the streets of Crewe are in a very disagreeable dusty condition, which is not only annoying to the pedestrians but injurous to the goods of the tradesmen. We would suggest to the ratepayers the desirability of purchasing a watering-cart.

Congleton Sandbach & Crewe Advertiser, 5th May 1861

Ellerton's preaching brought many from outside his actual parish to Sunday worship, including University men and pupils at the Railway works: many were received for the day at the Vicarage as guests of the Ellertons. Within Crewe itself — it should be remembered that Crewe Green was outside the boundaries — the population was growing fast; in 1851, the population was 4,571; in 1861 it had reached 8,159 and by 1871, the total was 17,810. Within the boundaries, too, no fewer than twelve new places of worship were opened between 1862 and 1870, including Anglican churches, principally financed by the Railway Company, three Primitive Methodist chapels, a Wesleyan Methodist chapel, Congregational, Presbyterian, Welsh Presbyterian and Unitarian churches.

It was the Unitarian Minister who issued an address to the inhabitants of Crewe explaining his own religious position and offering its advantages over others. The document was widely discussed in Ellerton's parish and he felt he must reply to a part of it which urged escape from the bondage of creeds. Significantly he writes of the Unitarian's statement: *I have neither the right nor the wish to criticize his specific teaching. I trust that he may be privileged to open to the love of God many a heart now closed against its influences: and to witness to the Divine Fatherhood in the consciences of many who have never yet realised that first and deepest of all truths. With regard to other, and, as I hold, co-ordinate truths, we must be content to part company until the time when all shall be made clear.*

But Ellerton does not shirk from defending the truth as expressed by the Anglican Church in their creeds and asks three questions. *Is it unfair to require the assent of a religious society to a Creed? Are Creeds contrary to the spirit of Christ's teaching? Are they an unreasonable bondage, a hindrance to free thought? I say — speaking for myself and for my own Church — distinctly No to all these questions.*

Ellerton has acknowledged earlier in his response that *this word Creed is a hard, ugly-sounding word, and carries with it a kind of savour of 'damnatory clauses' and trials for heresy . . . Yet after all it is a very simple matter. A Creed means nothing more than a form of words in which people express their religious belief.*

He believes it proper to invite a congregation to join in the statement of their beliefs in their common worship. But if someone feels *he cannot, what then? He is not obliged to retire, he is not constrained to remain. He may listen to the public ministry, he is at full liberty to think and say what he pleases about it, to speak his mind freely, so long as he does not interrupt the common worship.* He goes on to say that the Church of England is *provokingly lax,* and persists *in tolerating, with shameless impartiality, Ritualist, Rationalist, Calvinist, thinkers who in no other Church on earth could find a common home.*

MECHANICS' INSTITUTION, CREWE

In 1864, the Directors of the London and North Western Railway Company nominated John Ellerton for the Council of the Company's Mechanics' Institution at Crewe. Its object was defined as to supply to the working classes of Crewe the means of instruction in Science, Literature and the Arts. No political or religious subject could be taught. It was funded by the Railway Company and by fees charged. As well as educational classes, it was the place where newspapers could be read and books borrowed. Indeed the Institution provided the Library Service for the town until the mid nineteen-thirties, when a Local Authority Library was finally opened in Crewe. It was also a recreational centre, and the minutes for the period during which Ellerton was involved with the Institution mention an application to the Inland Revenue for

There is a great number of intelligent mechanics in Crewe who stand outside all church connection — either in indifference or hostility to Christianity.

Cheshire Observer, 1863

a Tobacco Licence and use of an American bowling alley. In 1859, the gymnasium was converted into a coffee and smoke room to afford the inhabitants of Crewe an opportunity for social intercourse but by 1863 it seems to have been restored to its original use. A dancing class was provided, with a fee payable by the men but ladies admitted free.

Ellerton served the Institution in four ways. First, he acted as an examiner for the annual prizes offered by the Railway to students. Second, he himself taught certain classes. Third, he served on the Education Committee and fourth he gave leadership as Vice President.

During his period of service, the library was reviewed and catalogued and the educational arrangements thoroughly reorganised. One of his last acts was to sign the petition to the University of Cambridge seeking links with the Institution which received a favourable response after he had moved on.

After a standard 58½ hour working week, often topped up by overtime, it says something for the railway employees that they were keen to attend classes: and especially those unconnected with their work. If the attendances at classes linked to literature and history remained small, it is surprising that they had any enrolments. Despite the ban on religious teaching, one of the subjects for the London and North Western Railway prizes was Scripture History. It was the only paper for which no tutor had been appointed: and Ellerton agreed to teach a class on Sunday evenings. The Institution was of course outside Ellerton's parish and the local Vicar complained to the Bishop that Ellerton was improperly poaching on his preserves. Whilst the Bishop did not uphold this view, Ellerton felt he should withdraw his offer to teach the subject and that the class should be offered to the local Vicar. The Vicar however refused to accept the ruling that the subject should be dealt with as a matter of historical fact, no teaching of religious dogmas being intended. He believed that it neither could nor should be taught in this way: and in the end, Ellerton took the class, although attendance was sparse.

Ellerton was appointed as Chairman of the Education Committee, an office which seems to have involved considerable executive activity between meetings. He gave up this post in favour of Mr. Warren Moorsom, son of a former Chairman of the Railway Company, on the grounds that someone living on the spot rather than some distance out of Crewe, would be more effective in the role. Soon however,

We, the Council of the Crewe Mechanics' Institution, desire to bring to your notice the great advantage that would accrue to the Members of our Society, and through them to the whole body of Artisans and Railway Servants, in this town, by the formation of a close connection between your ancient University and our young but prosperous and growing Educational System.

From an approach to the Vice-Chancellor, Council and Senate of the University of Cambridge by the Council of Crewe Mechanics' Institution

the Committee expressed unhappiness at the way Moorsom was dealing with certan matters, possibly because of his close association with the Railway's Management. Ellerton supported the new Chairman: but managed to do so in such a way as not to lose the goodwill of the remaining members. In due course, Moorsom resigned and Ellerton was an acceptable Chairman again to all concerned. This gift of reconciliation, without giving ground on principles, commended itself to the whole Council, who often had wide and acrimonious disagreements upon policy, and his appointment as a Vice-President at a crucial time helped wise decision-making. For most of the sixties, the Institution had lacked the space for expanding activities for an expanding population: but in 1869 the matter was brought to a head by a fire. The building was insured and the Railway Company advanced the £3,500 for new premises. So the Council was concerned with preparations for its new home which opened in 1871.

> Entering then Thy gates with praises,
> Lord, be ours Thine Israel's prayer; –
> 'Rise into Thy place of resting,
> Show Thy promised Presence there!'
> Let the gracious word be spoken
> Here, as once on Sion's height,
> 'This shall be My rest for ever,
> This My dwelling of delight.'
>
> *Verse 3 of 'Lift the strain of high thanksgiving', written for the re-opening of St. Helen's Church, Tarporley, Cheshire, 1869 (AUSTRIA)*

JOHN ELLERTON

During the past year the Council have also sustained the loss of the inestimatable services of the Rev. John Ellerton M.A. through his removal from the district. Mr. Ellerton was one of the most zealous friends of the Institution during the seven years he was connected with it. He was appointed a Vice-President in October 1870 and the skill and courtesy with which he performed the duties of that office are known to every member of the Council. The Council resolved to present him with a testimonial in the shape of books to be selected by himself . . . His portrait will also be added to those which hang upon the walls of the News-room.

From the Annual Report of Crewe Mechanics' Institution

Ellerton's interest in hymnody continued and in 1863, the Headmaster of Shrewsbury School, compiling his *Hymnologia Christiana* consulted him as an expert in the subject. In 1865, *The Churchman's Family Magazine* published a translation by Ellerton of the Latin hymn known by the closing line of each verse as the *Alleluia Perenne*. This ancient hymn was in use in the *Mozarabic Breviary* in Spain before the eighth century, was printed in Munich in the tenth century, and sung in England before the Norman Conquest. It was one of a number of hymns linked to some picturesque ceremonies marking the giving up of the word *Alleluia* during Lent: hence the contrast between the interrupted Alleluias of Earth and the perennial Alleluia of Heaven. In the church of Toul, the practice of burying Alleluia in a coffin with full funeral services survived to the end of the fifteenth century.

The proprietors of *Hymns Ancient and Modern* had noted Ellerton's translation and wanted to use it with some changes in the Appendix to the Original Edition of their book. Ellerton's reply is preserved.

> As to the *Alleluia Perenne* (which I did not send, but to which, if you like it, you are very welcome), if I had seen Mr. Blew's translation and that in Mr. Shirmer's hymnal, I scarcely think I should have printed mine. Still, *I think* I have caught the true meaning, though my interpretation is different from theirs. The *cives aetherei* of the first verse I take to be the Church on Earth, the *perpetui luminis accola* (referring I suppose to St. Luke: 1. 19ff) to be the Angels, and the *vos urbs examina* to be the Church Triumphant. So I ventured to translate *hinc vos* by *Ye next* explaining it to mean that the Alleluia begun by the Church on earth in the first verse, is caught up by the Angels in the second, and by them carried to the heavenly Jerusalem, where, as a part of the ceaseless praise of the redeemed, it is offered before the throne of God. But I fear I have wearied you . . .

When *Sing Alleluia forth in duteous praise* was published in *Church Hymns* 1871, Ellerton had amended his translation, for which Arthur Sullivan chose his own tune HOLY CITY. William H. Monk, the music editor of *Hymns Ancient and Modern* also wrote the tune ALLELUIA PERENNE especially for the hymn as did B. Luard–Selby later when organist of Rochester Cathedral (CIVES COELI). It is also sung to ST. SEBASTIAN.

> Sing Alleluia forth in duteous praise,
> Ye citizens of heaven; in sweet notes raise
> *An endless Alleluia!*

Ye Powers who stand before the Eternal Light,
In hymning choirs re-echo to the height
An endless Alleluia!

The Holy City shall take up your strain,
And with glad songs resounding wake again
An endless Alleluia!

In blissful answering strains ye thus rejoice
To render to the Lord with thankful voice
An endless Alleluia!

Ye who have gained at length your palms in bliss,
Victorious ones, your chant shall still be this —
An endless Alleluia!

There, in one grand acclaim for ever ring
The strains which tell the honour of your King —
An endless Alleluia!

This is the rest for weary ones brought back!
This is the food and drink which none shall lack:
An endless Alleluia!

While Thee, by whom were all things made, we praise
For ever, and tell out in sweetest lays
An endless Alleluia!

Almighty Christ, to Thee our voices sing
Glory for evermore; to Thee we bring
An endless Alleluia!

In 1866 soon after the completion of extensive repairs, Crewe Hall suffered destruction by fire. Ellerton wrote *Saviour, again to Thy dear name we raise* for a Festival of Parochial Choirs at nearby Nantwich, revising and abridging it for the Appendix to *Hymns Ancient and Modern, 1868*. Tunes to which it is sung include ADORO TE, BENEDICTION, PAX DEI, MAGDA, ELLERS and JOLDWYNDS. The following year he provided *Our day of praise is done*, in which he took four stanzas from a hymn of Charles Coffin translated by Rev. W. J. Blew (1808 - 1862) and added others of his own.

Too faint our anthems here;
Too soon of praise we tire:
But Oh, the strains how full and clear
Of that eternal choir!

Yet, Lord, to Thy dear will
If thou attune the heart,
We in Thine Angels' music still
May bear our lower part.

'Tis Thine each soul to calm,
Each wayward thought reclaim,
And make our life a daily psalm
Of glory to Thy Name.

From 'Our day of praise is done'

Written again for a Choral Festival at Nantwich, it is sung today to FRANCONIA, ALLINGTON and HOLYROOD. It was recast so as to be primarily his own work save for the line of thought, for use in Reverend R. Brown-Borthwick's *Supplemental Hymn and Tune Book*. His *This is the day of light* (THE DAY OF PRAISE, DULWICH COLLEGE, CHISELHURST, DOMINICA, SANDYS, HOLYROOD) was first published in the *Selection of Hymns compiled for use in Chester Cathedral*.

> This is the day of Peace!
> Thy Peace our spirits fill!
> Bid Thou the blasts of discord cease,
> The waves of strife be still.

In 1868, Ellerton made a translation, also for R. Brown-Borthwick's book, from the Latin of Venantius Fortunatus, beginning *Welcome, happy morning! age to age shall say* for which Brown-Borthwick wrote the tune SALVE FESTA DIES. Joseph Barnby's tune is similarly named. It is also sung to FORTUNATUS.

> Venantius Honorius Clementianus Fortunatus, born in the north of Italy about AD530, educated at Ravenna, became enormously popular in the latter years of the sixth century as a poet and orator. He lived for many years a wandering life, chiefly in the south of France, the guest of great men and noble ladies, and the favourite of everybody. From this somewhat frivolous and careless career he was aroused to higher aims, partly, it is said, by the influence of a pilgrimage to the shrine of St. Martin at Tours; but doubtless more especially by the friendship of a living and no less saintly Bishop of the same city, the illustrious Gregory of Tours. At length he settled at Poictiers, attracted mainly by the presence there of St. Rhadegund, the Queen of Clotaire, who, after the strange fashion of the sixth century, had left her husband to become the foundress of a convent there. The relations of Venantius with Rhadegund were very intimate, and did not wholly escape scandalous comment; but his life was now of deepening earnestness and sanctity, and there is not the slightest ground for questioning the purity of the aims and motives which bound together these remarkable friends. Fortunatus became Bishop of Poictiers in 599, and died there, ten years afterwards, in 609.
>
> *John Ellerton's notes about Venantius Fortunatus in the Annotated Edition of 'Church Hymns'*

The original Latin is selected from 114 lines of elegaic verse addressed to Felix, Bishop of Nantes in Brittany. It was sung throughout Europe during the Middle Ages, with varying choices of verses, becoming the most popular of all Processional hymns of that period. Ellerton reviewed the several versions and mostly chose to use those common to all of these. In the fourteenth and fifteenth centuries, it was frequently translated into German: and it is said to have been sung by the martyr Jerome of Prague as he suffered at the stake. Ellerton notes that a letter from Cranmer to Henry VIII indicates a translation the former has made into English verse, *and wished it to be included in a book of 'Processions' for such festival days as the Reformed Church retained, to be set forth by royal authority.*

Welcome, happy morning! age to age shall say;
Hell to-day is vanquished; Heaven is won to-day!
Lo! the Dead is living, God for evermore!
Him, their true Creator, all His works adore!
Welcome, happy morning! age to age shall say.

Earth with joy confesses, clothing her for Spring,
All good gifts returned with her returning King:
Bloom in every meadow, leaves on every bough,
Speak His sorrows ended, hail His triumph now.
Hell to-day is vanquished; Heaven is won to-day!

Months in due succession, days of lengthening light,
Hours and passing moments praise Thee in their flight;
Brightness of the morning, sky and fields and sea,
Vanquisher of darkness, bring their praise to Thee.
Welcome, happy morning! age to age shall say.

Maker and Redeemer, Life and Health of all,
Thou from Heaven beholding human nature's fall,
Of the Father's Godhead true and only Son,
Manhood to deliver, manhood didst put on.
Hell to-day is vanquished; Heaven is won to-day!

Thou, of Life the Author, death didst undergo,
Tread the path of darkness, saving strength to show;
Come, then, True and Faithful, now fulfil Thy word;
'Tis Thine own Third Morning! Rise, O buried Lord!
Welcome, happy morning! age to age shall say.

Loose the souls long prisoned, bound with Satan's chain;
All that now is fallen raise to life again;
Show Thy Face in brightness, bid the nations see;
Bring again our daylight: day returns with Thee!
Hell to-day is vanquished! Heaven is won to-day!

John Ellerton seemed to be satisfied with neither the book published by the *Society for Promoting Christian Knowledge* called *Psalms and Hymns* (1855) with its 1863 *Appendix* nor with *Hymns Ancient and Modern* (1861) with its 1868 *Appendix*. He therefore drew up a prospectus for circulation amongst his friends in London for his own publication of a general Hymn Book.

I feel sure that an examination of the best mediaeval hymns will convince you that there is no real reason for their exclusion . . . This leads me to refer to another case, the absence of many popular hymns by living authors . . . I should most respectfully suggest to the Committee whether it would not be worth while, even as a money speculation, to lay out a certain sum in the purchase of copyright . . .

The character of too many hymns in the Society's present book is certainly a rather dull and colourless mediocrity . . .

The great position of the S. P. C. K. gives it a matchless opportunity for investigating and using foreign hymnody . . .

No one would banish *Rock of Ages* or *Sun of my Soul*; on the other hand, such a hymn as Cowper's *Oh for a closer walk with God* belongs to a particular state of mind, and ought not to be put into the lips of a whole congregation. It is therefore out of place in a Hymnal for congregational use . . .

A selection of points from John Ellerton's letter to the Society for Promoting Christian Knowledge: 3rd July 1868

When, in 1635, this chapel was consecrated, how little did its pious founder anticipate that within less than ten years his stately rooms would ring with the noise of civil war; his hall be filled with coarse and brutal soldiers . . .

It is not the material dwelling, however fair and splendid, which is really the House: it is the group of human lives which those outward walls bind together . . .

. . . finally, that each may strive to be a living and a polished stone in the true House of which I spoke — itself the noblest part of this noble dwelling — yet itself but one chamber in the vast eternal Mansion which God is ever building up with His true children.

From Ellerton's sermon preached in the Chapel of Crewe Hall on the occasion of its re-opening after the 1866 fire on 16th October 1870. The architect Edward Barry reproduced the Old Hall but added a great deal of mid-Victorian detail

At this point a member of the Tract Committee of S.P.C.K. a Revd. Berdmore Compton wrote Ellerton of their plans to issue a major supplement to their book, with the intention of following this up with a new book, *Church Hymns* and seeking permission to use *Sing Alleluia forth in duteous praise* and *Saviour, again to Thy near name we raise*. This led Ellerton to write at length beginning: *If I can be of any use to you in your task of improving the present S.P.C.K. hymnal, I shall have much pleasure in assisting this work.* He abandoned his own plans to be a publisher and served as a member of a working party on the new book. Its other members besides Berdmore Compton were Rev. William Walsham How, author of *For all the saints who from their labours rest* and Rev. R. Brown-Borthwick, Vicar of All Saints, Scarborough. The result of their work was presented to the Tract Committee on 25th October 1870 with a proviso that they could withdraw it in the event of the Society proposing alterations which would, in the compilers' opinion, impair its value as a whole. Arthur Sullivan was later to accept the invitation to act as Music Editor.

Alongside his parish work, his involvement with the Mechanics' Institution and his editorial work in connection with *Church Hymns*, Ellerton wrote no fewer than 26 hymns and translations in 1870 and 1871. They included one of the few hymns about St. Paul written for the Feast Day celebrating his conversion, *We sing the glorious conquest* (Tunes: MISSIONARY, LLANGLOFFAN, AURELIA and ELLACOMBE).

> We sing the glorious conquest
> Before Damascus' gate,
> When Saul, the Church's spoiler,
> Came breathing threats and hate:
> The ravening wolf rushed forward
> Full early to the prey;
> Bo lo! the Shepherd met him,
> And bound him fast to-day!
>
> Oh, Glory most excelling
> That smote across his path!
> Oh, Light that pierced and blinded
> The zealot in his wrath!
> Oh, Voice that spake within him
> The calm reproving word!
> Oh, Love that sought and held him
> The bondman of the Lord.
> *Opening verses of 'We sing the glorious conquest'*

He also wrote texts for the Feasts of St. Bartholomew and St. Barnabas and the celebration of the Circumcision of Jesus: he wrote words for use in times of scarcity — 1870 was the year of Starvation in Paris — in which he links human sinfulness to absence of provisions; he wrote too for times of pestilence, mentioning the insanitary conditions which led to so much illness especially amongst the poorer members of society.

> Not in vain the mighty promise,
> From beneath the Bow of Peace,
> Told us, while the earth remaineth,
> Seed-time, harvest, shall not cease.
>
> But our sins have stayed Thy blessing,
> Our rebellions drawn Thy sword;
> Pity now Thy mourning people;
> Think upon Thy Covenant, Lord.

So the sunshine of Thy bounty
Once again shall dry our tears;
And Thy gracious hand restore us
All our canker-eaten years.

The last three verses of a hymn for a time of scarcity,
'God, Creator and Preserver!' sung to LANGDALE

Forgive the foul neglect that brought
Thy chastening to our door;
The homes uncared-for, souls untaught,
The unregarded poor.

From A Hymn in time of Pestilence, 'O Lord of
life and death, we come', sung to WINDSOR

He also penned three verses about war which were later joined to verses written by another author in 1842 beginning *God the all-terrible! King who ordainest* sung to ULTOR OMNIPOTENS and RUSSIA (REPHIDIM).

God the all-righteous One! Man hath defied Thee;
Yet to eternity standeth Thy word;
Falsehood and wrong shall not tarry beside Thee;
Give to us peace in our time, O Lord!

God the all-pitiful! Is it not crying –
Blood of the guiltless like water outpoured?
Look on the anguish, the sorrow, the sighing;
Give to us peace in our time, O Lord!

God the all wise! By the fire of Thy chastening,
Earth shall to freedom and truth be restored;
Through the thick darkness Thy kingdom is hastening;
Thou wilt give peace in Thy time, O Lord!

He also took a very small fragment *of a long and famous alphabetical Latin hymn on the life of our Lord, by Caelius Sedulius, an Irish ecclesiastic, who came to Rome about the middle of the fifth century, and made himself a great name for learning. This hymn became exceedingly popular, and the author was ranked among the four founders of Christian hymnody in medieval expositions.* Ellerton mentions that in his translation *From East to West, from shore to shore* he had to omit two or three verses too plainspoken for modern ears. His version in *Church Hymns* for Common Metre was later retranslated for *Hymns Ancient and Modern* for Long Metre.

Behold, the world's Creator wears
The form and fashion of a slave;
Our very flesh our Maker shares
His fallen creature man to save.

For this how wondrously He wrought!
A maiden, in her lowly place,
Became in ways beyond all thought,
The chosen vessel of His grace.

Verses from the Hymn for Christmas Morning
'From East to West, from shore to shore'

Tunes are ST. LEONARD and THIS ENDRIS NIGHT (c.m.) and ST. VENANTIUS, COLLINS STREET and TRINITY COLLEGE.

He translated an original Latin hymn of German origin, for the Festival of the Name of Jesus. He wrote for the re-opening of the nave in Chester Cathedral and for the consecration of an extension to a graveyard, for the annual Diocesan Choir Festival, for services in early morning and mid-afternoon and for Sundays and weekdays. His funeral hymn *When the day of toil is done* (IRENE: PRESTON) was first sung in his church at Crewe Green on the death of the chief manager of Crewe Railway Works at the early age of 35. In his sermon, Ellerton remembered soldiers and sailors who often gave their lives in the days of their youth and then continued: *And surely it is just as heroic, just as honourable, to be found faithful to death in any other service to which a man has been called; to care more for doing our daily work well, than for doing it easily; to treat it not merely as a means of getting bread, but as a task which it is a duty to God to do thoroughly, and a sin against God to do carelessly.*

> Name beloved, Name of Jesus!
> Name beyond what words can tell;
> Name that comforts, Name that pleases
> Every heart which knows it well;
> Name that man from guilt releases,
> Name that breaks the bonds of hell!
>
> *From a translation of the Gloriosi Salvatoris*
> *beginning 'To the Name that speaks salvation',*
> *sung to ST. LAWRENCE and ORIEL*
>
> When the heart by sorrow tried
> Feels at length its throbs subside,
> Bring us, where all tears are dried,
> Joy for evermore!
>
> *From 'When the day of toil is done'*

Perhaps the best known text from Reverend Gerard Moultrie (1829 - 1885) is his translation from the Greek of the Liturgy of St. James *Let all mortal flesh keep silence, and with fear and trembling stand,* usually sung to the French Traditional Carol tune, PICARDY. Amongst other writings was a poem beginning *Brother, now thy toils are o'er.* This has been preserved in its own right as a six-verse hymn in the *English Hymnal* with just the opening line amended. *Now the labourer's toils are o'er* is usually sung to PRESSBURG (NICHT SO TRAURIG) or REDHEAD NO.76.

John Ellerton was inspired by the Moultrie text when he wrote *Now the labourer's task is o'er* for *Church Hymns 1871*. Ellerton wrote that the whole hymn, especially the third, fifth and sixth verses, owed many thoughts and some expressions to Moultrie's beautiful poems. Ellerton's version is sung to HEBRON, LUARD, and REQUIESCAT. Here are the two texts side by side.

Now the labourer's toils are o'er	Now the labourer's task is o'er;
Fought the battle, won the crown:	Now the battle day is past;
On life's rough and barren shore	Now upon the farther shore
Thou hast laid thy burden down:	Lands the voyager at last.
Grant him, Lord, eternal rest,	Father, in Thy gracious keeping
With the spirits of the blest.	Leave we now Thy servant sleeping.
Angels bear thee to the land	There the tears of earth are dried;
Where the towers of Sion rise;	There its hidden things are clear;
Safely lead thee by the hand	There the work of life is tried
To the fields of Paradise:	By a juster Judge than here.
Grant him, Lord, eternal rest,	Father, in Thy gracious keeping
With the spirits of the blest.	Leave we now Thy servant sleeping.
White-robed, at the golden gate	There the Angels bear on high
Of the new Jerusalem,	Many a strayed and wounded lamb,
May the host of Martyrs wait;	Peacefully at last to lie
Give thee part and lot with them:	In the breast of Abraham.
Grant him, Lord, eternal rest,	Father, in Thy gracious keeping
With the spirits of the blest.	Leave we now Thy servant sleeping.
Friends and dear ones gone before	There the sinful souls that turn
To the land of endless peace,	To the Cross their dying eyes,
Meet thee on that further shore	All the love of Christ shall learn
Where all tears and weeping cease:	At His feet in Paradise.
Grant him, Lord, eternal rest,	Father, in Thy gracious keeping
With the spirits of the blest.	Leave we now Thy servant sleeping.
Rest in peace: the gates of hell	There no more the powers of hell
Touch thee not, till he shall come	Can prevail to mar their peace;
For the souls he loves so well, —	Christ the Lord shall guard them well
Dear Lord of the heavenly home:	He who died for their release.
Grant him, Lord, eternal rest,	Father, in Thy gracious keeping
With the spirits of the blest.	Leave we now Thy servant sleeping.
Earth to earth, and dust to dust,	'Earth to earth, and dust to dust;'
Clay we give to kindred clay,	Calmly now the words we say;
In the sure and certain trust	Left behind, we wait in trust,
Of the Resurrection day:	For the Resurrection day.
Grant him, Lord, eternal rest,	Father, in Thy gracious keeping
With the spirits of the blest.	Leave we now Thy servant sleeping.

The Ellerton text was to become one of the most used funeral hymns for several decades. His hymn *Praise to our God, whose bounteous hand* (HILDERSTONE, OAKLEIGH and IVYHATCH) still sometimes voices public thanksgiving.

> Praise to our God; His power alone
> Can keep unmoved our ancient Throne,
> Sustained by counsels wise and just,
> And guarded by a people's trust.
>
> Praise to our God; who still forbears,
> Who still this guilty nation spares;
> Who calls us still to seek His face,
> And lengthens out our day of grace.
>
> Praise to our God; though chastenings stern
> Our evil dross should throughly burn;
> His rod and staff, from age to age,
> Shall rule and guide His heritage!
> > *From 'Praise to our God, whose bounteous hand'*

On weekdays we still need to ask *Behold us, Lord, a little space* (ST. BERNARD, FARRANT, FERRY, GRETTON, ST. FLAVIAN, and BYZANTIUM).

> Thine is the loom, the forge, the mart,
> The wealth of land and sea,
> The worlds of science and of art
> Revealed and ruled by Thee.
> > *From 'Behold us, Lord, a little space'*
> > *one of the first texts to mention science*

The words of *The Lord be with us as we bend* (HOLY TRINITY, GLENLUCE and NORTH REPPS) are still remembered occasionally when used as the closing hymn of a service in late afternoon or early evening.

> The Lord be with us as we walk
> Along our homeward road;
> In silent thought or friendly talk
> Our hearts be still with God.
> > *From 'The Lord be with us as we bend'*

Above all, Ellerton gave us in this burst of creativity *The day Thou gavest, Lord, is ended*. The text was sparked off by the first line of a rather poor hymn published anonymously in *Church Poetry* 1855. Professor J. R. Watson, Professor of English at Durham University, making a close analysis of

Ellerton's text in *The Bulletin of the Hymn Society of Great Britain and Ireland, September 1983* believes *the effect of the hymn to depend upon a sensitive and moving use of word, phrase, image, line and verse to convey a complex two-fold movement: both a recognition of man and all his limitations, and a sense of man's great imagination, of his imaginative perception of the world beyond himself, and of its Creator. The result is a masterpiece.* It was originally published by Mr. John Hodges of Frome in *A Liturgy for Missionary Meetings* and revised for *Church Hymns*, 1871. One of the tunes there was ST. CLEMENT; other tunes used include RADFORD and LES COMMANDEMENS DE DIEU. It is also sung to JOLDWYNDS.

> The day Thou gavest, Lord, is ended,
> The darkness falls at Thy behest;
> To Thee our morning hymns ascended,
> Thy praise shall hallow now our rest.
>
> We thank Thee that Thy Church unsleeping,
> While earth rolls onward into light,
> Through all the world her watch is keeping,
> And rests not now by day or night.
>
> As o'er each continent and island
> The dawn leads on another day,
> The voice of prayer is never silent,
> Nor dies the strain of praise away.
>
> The sun, that bids us rest, is waking
> Our brethren 'neath the western sky,
> And hour by hour fresh lips are making
> Thy wondrous doings heard on high.
>
> So be it, Lord; Thy throne shall never,
> Like earth's proud empires, pass away;
> But stand, and rule, and grow for ever,
> Till all Thy creatures own Thy sway.
> *The version in 'Church Hymns', 1871*

In 1872, Ellerton turned to the Latin of Charles Coffin for inspiration. Coffin lived from 1679 until 1749, serving as a priest in the Diocese of Rheims, then as the Principal of the College of Dormans-Beauvais, and finally as Rector of the University of Paris, of which the college is a part. When Ellerton was translating, he looked at the work of earlier translators and is indebted in part to the work of Reverend Isaac Williams whose *Hymns from the Parisian Breviary* were published in 1839. Ellerton's *Morn of Morns, the best and first* sung to VIENNA is based on one such Parisian text.

> Morn of morns, the best and first!
> When the light from darkness burst;
> When the world's true Light broke through
> . Death's stronghold, and rose anew?

The same year, Ellerton was appointed Rector of Hinstock, a Shropshire village nestling in sandstone hills. The church had not been long built and was very plain with absolutely no chancel; it was dedicated to St. Oswald, the seventh century King of Northumbria who was converted to Christianity while exiled in Iona, and died a martyr on the battlefield in contest with the heathen Penda of Mercia. After the business of Brighton and Crewe and before the business of Barnes, Ellerton was shunted for over four years to this quiet retreat. After two years, however, the Bishop made use of his experience in education by appointing him as Diocesan Inspector for Salop-in-Lichfield. He wrote the article *Hymns* in the *Dictionary of Christian Antiquities*, a task which involved many cross-country journeys to consult libraries in Cambridge. Much of his basic research to be used in compiling the Notes to *Church Hymns* was undertaken during this spell as a country parson. In conjunction with his friend, William Walsham How, not too far away at Whittington, he compiled *Children's Hymns and School Prayers*. This included his own *Again the morn of gladness*, not previously published. Tunes used have included WIR PFLUGEN and TUSSER.

As to copyright of other hymns, I confess I do not like parting with it; it takes away the feeling that one's hymns — such as they are — are a gift to the Church — I have never refused permission even to Unitarians — But I will certainly gladly undertake not to allow any one to print the hymns I have written for you, for say the next four or five years, without leave obtained from you. That I hope will prevent any unfair course being taken.
> *John Ellerton writing from Hinstock to Sir Henry Baker, Chairman of the Proprietors of 'Hymns Ancient and Modern'. Epiphany 1875*

Again the morn of gladness,
The morn of light, is here;
And earth itself looks fairer,
And heaven itself more near:
The bells, like angel voices,
Speak peace to every breast,
And all the land lies quiet
To keep the day of rest.
Glory be to Jesus!
Let all His children say;
He rose again, He rose again
On this glad day!

The Church on earth rejoices
To join with these to-day;
In every tongue and nation
She calls her sons to pray:
Across the Northern snowfields,
Beneath the Indian palms,
She makes the same pure offering,
And sings the same sweet psalms.
Chorus

Selected verses from 'Again the morn of Gladness'

For the laying of the corner-stone of the Chapel of Ease at Cote Brook, a hamlet in Tarporley parish, he wrote *Thou Who once for us uplifted* with a verse linked to the chapel's

By Thy Cross, that day of sorrow,
Stood Thy loved Apostle John,
Till he heard the Cry that witnessed
All Thy mighty labours done;
Till he saw the cruel spear-point
Pierce the Breast he leaned upon.

The verse of 'Thou Who once for us uplifted' written for the dedication of St. John and the Holy Cross

Hark that cry that peals aloud
Upward through the whelming cloud!
He, the Father's only Son,
He, the Christ, th'anointed One,
He doth ask Him – even He –
Why hast Thou forsaken Me?

Verse 3 of 'Throned upon the awful Tree'

O Saviour, Guest most bounteous
Of old in Galilee,
Vouchsafe to-day Thy presence
With those who call on Thee;
Their store of earthly gladness
Transform to heavenly wine,
And teach them, in the tasting,
To know the gift is Thine.

Verse 2 of 'O Father all creating'

dedication to St. John and the Holy Cross. Another amongst the seven hymns of this period was the solemn *Throned upon the awful Tree* sung to AUS TIEFER NOTH, NICHT SO TRAURIG, GETHSEMANE, ARFON and PETRA (REDHEAD NO. 76), and a wedding hymn written by request of the Duke of Westminster for the marriage of his daughter *O Father all creating* sung to GENESIS, DAY OF REST, DANK SEI GOTT IN DER HOHE and KOMM, SEELE, and *Thou who sentest thine Apostles*, preserved in Ellerton's hand. The tune BRYNTIRION was set in *The English Hymnal*.

In 1876, Ellerton was appointed Rector of Barnes, which nestles in that horseshoe of the Thames famous to this day as the course for the annual Oxford and Cambridge Boat Race. The congregation was used to teaching of a high order from the pulpit and their new rector was not to disappoint them. He came to a parish where riches lived side by side with poverty; and which was changing fast as London burst its seams and new homes were built in Barnes. Ellerton presided over most of the Vestry Meetings during his incumbency: and the agendas reflected the urbanisation of the parish. Barnes had been linked to London by the toll bridge at Hammersmith; and the Toll Bridges (River Thames) Bill of 1876 proposed the abolition of tolls, and an average annual maintenance charge of the sizeable sum of £700 mostly to fall on the Parish of Barnes. The same Vestry approved a total budget for £175 for all church expenses including £35 for the organist. A Vestry Meeting which had primarily been involved with the important task of the relief of the poor and the administration of several charities was to begin 1877 with a meeting requisitioned by fifty ratepayers. The Richmond Rural Sanitary Authority, however, had apparently not complied with Clause 176 of the Public Health Act of 1875 in applying to set up a sewage works on Barnes Common, a useful technicality for those appointed to represent the Parish at any Public Enquiry. It was not the first time that the Vestry Meeting was concerned with sanitation: ten years earlier the question of the dreadful effects of near proximity of wells and cesspools had been on the agenda: what was new

. . . that he was a man of deep learning and of varied and extended reading, no educated listener could fail to discover, although his sermons were remarkably free from parade of erudition or excess of ornament. But it was not his mastery of English, his many-sided culture, and his transparent sincerity that gave to his sermons the attractiveness to which we refer. It was rather that rare and indefinable *something* which radiates from poetic natures, and makes other hearts burn within them.

Professor Henry Attwell K.O.C. and member of the Barnes congregation recalling Ellerton's ministry.

in Ellerton's decade was the quantity of new legislation affecting the parish.

A fortnight later, Barnes Common was under threat again. The South Western Railway Company wanted to build a railroad across this *watering place for cattle*. For many years the Common had been a happy hunting ground for many of nearby London's naturalists: but if the Common were to be preserved as an important local amenity, its marshy banks and swampy hollows would clearly need to be improved and properly managed. Ellerton missed the March Vestry, concerned with the purity of gas and the testing of gas appliances: but in April £250 was taken from the Poor Rate to manage the Common. Managing the finances in 1877 was far from easy. The magistrates were expected to order the Conservators of the Common to clean out the pond on the Green (estimated cost £100 — it was eventually to cost £275). But the James Hedgman School Charity *to provide clothing for children or aiding children to attend school, for gutter children or for the poorest of the poor without distinction of creed and country* produced £1282 that year, of which £82 was used for the relief of the poor and £1,200 to reduce the Poor Rate. The Poor Rate in its turn had found £206 to oppose the railway unsuccessfully and £87 in winning the sewage fight.

Resolution:
That this Vestry desires most emphatically to express its disapproval of the proposal to take a portion of Barnes Common for the purpose of establishing a Sewage Manure Works.
Vestry Meeting:
1st February 1877

Resolution:
That the Vestry of Barnes desires that Barnes Common may be preserved in its integrity for the purpose provided for by the *Metropolitan Commons Supplemental Act 1876* and it regards the Bill which has been presented to Parliament by the London & South Western Railway Company for various powers, as an attempt to violate the above mentioned Act, and the Vestry desires that the most strenuous opposition shall be offered to any portion of the Common being taken for the purposes of the London and South Western Railway Company.
Vestry Meeting:
15th February 1877

	Males	Females	Houses
1871	1,863	2,324	714
1881	2,660	3,341	1,000
1891	3,792	4,653	1,493

Census Returns for the Parish of Barnes

BARNES PARISH CHURCH, *as rebuilt in 1985*

The Church of St. Mary began life about the time of Richard I (just before 1200). When Ellerton arrived, the building, with its walls of stone and flint, had been altered so often that only a very small portion of the original remained. Changes have continued to date, but, following fire damage, the latest building integrates new and old effectively and won a civic award in 1985. The bells which in Ellerton's day called people to worship were struck in 1575, 1616 and 1667.

I am quite of your mind that we do not want it to be a book of baby hymns, still less of hymns written down for 'infant minds' by people who are well-meaning but do not understand children. By all means have a large infusion of strong and vigorous hymns such as are generally used in church; *so long as the sentiments they convey are such as children can be expected to appreciate.* If you do not make that limitation what is the *raison d'etre* of a *children's* book as distinguished on the one hand from an *infant* book, and on the other from an adult book?
John Ellerton writing to Mrs. Carey Brock about 'The Children's Hymnbook'

Mrs. Carey Brock had been entrusted with the acting editorship of the new *Children's Hymnbook*, and, hearing she was anxious to consult him, Ellerton immediately wrote offering any help he could give, as well as making available any of his own hymns. He was to be drawn into the project in a major way and in due course the *Society for Promoting Christian Knowledge* credited him with being one of its advisers. Early on he especially wrote *This day the Lord's disciples met* for a Whit Sunday contribution to the collection.

I think you will be obliged to fix a limit, say, the usual age for Confirmation, and determine not to have a hymn that is above the comprehension or beyond the spiritual experience (which is *far* more important) of the average Confirmation candidate. I know, of course, that many young people, especially well-educated girls, enjoy at thirteen or fourteen such hymns as *Lead, kindly Light* or *Abide with me* or *Lord of our life, and God of our salvation*, but the question is rather, Are these hymns good to be put before the *average* child, even at fourteen? Well-educated (I mean *spiritually* well-educated) girls can get the books in which these hymns are to be found. But to me it is simple *misery* to hear a noisy Sunday School singing *Abide with me* — I don't mean a class of upper girls; I know there are many exceptions. So there are with adults. I knew a costermonger's wife who was sustained through a terrible operation by repeating to herself over and over again Novalis' wondrous hymn *What had I been if Thou were not*; but it does not follow that I should put the hymn in a book for the poor.
Correspondence from John Ellerton to Mrs. Carey Brock on the 'Children's Hymn Book'

During 1878, besides such local concerns as the proposed construction of a tramway from Hammersmith Suspension Bridge to the White Hart with the cars propelled by horses or hot-air engines, disputes over who should pay what for maintenance of local roads, with consideration of counsel's opinion, and the establishment of a publicly elected Board to run the local National School, an iron church to cater for the growing population in Westfields with seating for 200 was erected. Like his church at Crewe Green, it was dedicated to St. Michael and All Angels and Ellerton wrote *In the Name which holy angels* especially for the occasion. He preached each year in the iron church in evenings throughout Advent and Lent.

In 1878, too, Ellerton joined the Tract Committee of the *Society for Promoting Christian Knowledge* and a colleague described him as *our authority in matters of poetry and music . . . looked up to by all as a sound theologian.* He served on the Committee until his death, and the editing of the *Manual of Parochial Work* was his most major task. Back in 1872, Ellerton had asked that same committee to encourage his preparation of an annotated edition of *Church Hymns*, but there was concern that such a volume would be too expensive. They apparently consented to the project and used the promise of an explanation in this future edition to defuse a difficult situation about omitting without the author's consent a verse of Bishop Christopher Wordsworth's hymn *Hark, the sound of holy voices chanting at the crystal sea* in *Church Hymns 1871*. The controversial verse reads:

> All who had the pleasure of working with him remember with affection his gentle and quiet manner, and the touches of humour which he not unfrequently threw into his observations.
>
> *A fellow-member of the Tract Committee of the Society for Promoting Christian Knowledge.*

Now they reign in heavenly glory, now they walk in golden light;
Now they drink, as from a river, holy bliss and infinite:
Love and Peace they taste for ever; and all truth and knowledge see
In the beatific vision of the Blessed Trinity.

Hark, the sound of holy voices, chanting at the crystal sea.

By Bishop Christopher Wordsworth (1862) being his hymn for All Saints' Day in the *Holy Year*. In ii. 2, the sequence of words has been slightly altered (by the compilers of *Hymns Ancient and Modern*) to avoid the obsolete accentuation of the word *Confessor*. It ran thus in the original: *King, Apostle, Saint and Martyr, Confessor, Evangelist*. It was doubtless considered that the old distinction between *Cónfessor* (one who *witnesses for the faith a good confession* short of actual martyrdom) and *Conféssor* (one who *receives confessions*) was too subtle for modern congregations; and the compilers of *Church Hymns* have acquiesced in this decision. In the earlier editions of *Church Hymns* the fifth verse of this hymn *Now they reign in heavenly glory* &c. was omitted in deference to the judgment of one of the Episcopal Referees of the Society for Promoting Christian Knowledge, who held that the verse was liable to be misunderstood as countenancing the popular error that the Blessed are already in the full fruition of their future and ever-lasting glory — the *Beatific Vision*. It is scarcely needful to say that so accurate a theologian as the Bishop of Lincoln had no sympathy with this view. His Lordship, while pressing for the restoration of the verse, explained that the whole hymn from beginning to end, was to be regarded as the utterance in triumphant song of a vision of the *final* gathering of the Saints, not an exposition of their *present* condition in the Intermediate state. The Tract Committee of the Society therefore desired that the verse should in subsequent editions be restored; but should, in deference to those who might still think it liable to misconstruction, be bracketed for optional use.

John Ellerton's Notes published in the annotated edition of 'Church Hymns' (1881)

Whilst at Barnes, the preparation of the Annotated Edition was described by Ellerton as his hobby. It was nine years after his original proposal that it was finally published and the modest volume had grown into a mighty tome. Perhaps his own membership by then of the Tract Committee helped to gain support for its publication. Ellerton's notes about cach hymn are fascinating and the two quotations give a flavour of his work. It will be seen how wide ranging was Ellerton's experience as a hymnologist as well as a hymn-writer.

Sweet the moments, rich in blessing. Recast by Walter Shirley (grandson of the first Earl Ferrers, and brother of the second; born 1725, died 1786, Rector of Loughrea, Galway), printed in 1774 in *Lady Huntingdon's Collection*, which he revised at her request; based on a hymn by James Allen, born in Wensleydale, Yorkshire, June 24, 1734; a man of independent means, who, at the age of eighteen, while preparing for college, connected himself with Benjamin Ingham, one of the most erratic of the preachers of the Methodist revival, who was successively a Clergyman of the Church of England, as associate of the Wesleys in Georgia, then a Moravian, next an adherent of Lady Huntingdon, whose sister he married, and finally the founder of a sect bearing his own name. Allen, after a time, separated from Ingham, built a chapel on his own estate in Wensleydale, and preached in it until his death in 1804. In 1757 he had edited, in conjunction with Ingham and a few other friends, a hymn-book entitled (in a phrase borrowed from Charles Wesley) *A Collection of Hymns for those that seek, those that have found Redemption in the Blood of Christ*, commonly known as the *Kendal Hymn Book*. Two of his coadjutors were named Christopher and William Batty, and to one of these this hymn has been sometimes ascribed; but the above is its true history. Allen's hymn is of six eight-line stanzas, and begins *While my Jesus I'm possessing*. Shirley's alterations were so great and important as to amount to a rewriting of the hymn: as written by Allen, it never could have won its hold, so well-deserved, upon the affection of all English Christians: in fact, much of it is simply repulsive.

Part of John Ellerton's notes in the annotated edition of 'Church Hymns' (1881) revealing the breadth of his general knowledge of hymnody.

Vestry Meetings continued to be full of controversy for the rest of Ellerton's time at Barnes. There were problems over unauthorised cesspools on the common, the Vestry's Clerk's duties and salary (including confrontation with Whitehall), battles with the Charity Commissioners. Grazing rights were disputed, polls were challenged as invalid or irregular, and house numbering brought conflict with the Post Office. There were petitions against a proposed closure of Hammersmith Bridge, which would leave the residents with just a ferry while a new bridge was constructed. Fire engines, the effect of a proposed Thames lock at Isleworth, a major report from the Common Conservators, with a minority report from a dissenting officer, the need for flood protection . . . all these were part of the Rector's lot: no wonder he often worked late into the night on his writing and correspondence. In caring for his parishioners, he had the help of his curate, Reverend Henry Housman: but Ellerton took a full share of parish duties whilst maintaining an academic output which would have taxed many with a quiet living in a cathedral close.

. . . views with alarm the increase of water arising from the high tides which overflows the Road adjacent to the River Bank and part of the High Street, and the damage done to certain of the inhabitants by the said water, and is of opinion that the works now being executed by the Duke of Devonshire at Chiswick is likely to affect more or less the whole parish . . .

. . . express their strong sense of the great inconvenience that will arise to the inhabitants of this Parish by the proposed closing of Hammersmith Bridge, and the substitution of only a ferry-boat accommodation from sunrise to sunset and they beg most respectfully to urge upon the Secretary of State for the Home Department the absolute necessity that accommodation for foot passengers and vehicles be provided.

. . . inform the Thames Conservancy that the Parish are willing that the Draw Dock be done away with . . . provided sufficient accommodation be made for unloading Barges.

Resolutions of Vestry Meetings arising from the presence of the River Thames

In the strongest possible way He sanctioned the use of wine, not for health or medicine, but as help in social enjoyment. I think that those of us who are setting themselves to take part in the great battle against drink in this country must be careful to lay this to heart. The consideration of this must keep us at once humble as regards our own practice, and charitable in our judgement of others. We are getting accustomed to the truth that no man who is the slave of drink can be reclaimed except by total abstinence . . . Their Master, when needful, watched and fasted, denied Himself . . . but . . . the self-righteousness which often taints the abstainer is emphatically and forever condemned by this history . . .

– – – – –

Our Lord put a large quantity of wine, it would appear, at the disposal of those who had invited Him to the feast. He entrusted them with it. And surely this is in perfect harmony with the ordinary working of God. He gives wealth, and high station, and beauty, and eloquence, and genius, and artistic power, and the fascination of personal influence, in various ways and in diverse measure, to His children. Yet how much harm each of them has wrought in the world! . . . And yet they are His gifts; they are the wine of life . . . that we are to use them as our Master used the wine; that we are to manifest His glory.

From 'The Holiest Manhood and Its Lessons for Busy Lives:
Sermon preached at Barnes Church'

While it is right to begin and close the day with an act of prayer, it is often unadvisable to attempt too much in our morning prayer, when probably the shortness of time at our disposal tends to distract us: and it is still worse to put off our chief act of prayer to so late an hour as to ensure our liability to the influences either of a drowsy or an over-excited brain.

From the Introduction to
'Our Infirmities'

Some natures are especially *sensitive*. There are people whom we call thin-skinned; which means, that every outward influence, even the smallest, reaches them at once, and disturbs the balance of their minds. Irritability of temper is one of their great crosses, – mourned over, repented of, striven against, but tormenting them still – a very thorn in the flesh; such natures need, that they may conquer their infirmity, not merely special prayer and continual watchfulness, but some definite rule of self-government. The habit of deliberation has to be cultivated; the grace of patience has to be specially sought; the soul must be trained to meet the surprises of its enemy.

– – – – –

With others the leading characteristic is a *sanguine* temperament. These are eager and impulsive, throwing themselves into the present, allowing each new impression to obliterate the last one; thus they miss the wholesome teaching of experience, and are easily discouraged, and repeatedly disappointed. Yet this enthusiasm of nature is in itself a precious gift of God, capable of being the spring of noble sacrifices and great victories for Him. The enthusiasts are the pioneers of practical Christianity, they revive dormant energies in others, they kindle the dying fires of love and zeal, they try bold experiments, they strike out new paths of good, they rouse other people to withstand advancing evils.

– – – – –

I at least will never say to the eager and enthusiastic, *How foolish you are; you will soon get tired of this scheme of yours; you will only make a failure of it, and be sorry for it*. For when one of these impulsive people proposed to walk upon the water to meet his Master, we know that the Master did not say *Thou fool*; did not bid him *Stay* but *Come*.

From 'Our Infirmities' (Six Short Instructions delivered at Barnes/Cambridge 1879/1880): 'Infirmities of Natural Temperament'

Another battle with the authorities was for the appointment of a third Guardian of the Poor: the need for a third Victorian social worker was evident locally if not higher up. Eventually the case was successfully made and the staff strengthened. During this whole period, Ellerton continued to write hymns. Whilst visiting his friend, the Reverend Gerald Blunt in June 1880, he wrote *O Thou whose bounty fills the earth* (sung to BYZANTIUM) which stood alongside his host's *Here, Lord, we offer Thee all that is fairest* (sung to ABINGDON) in *The Children's Hymn Book* and other

collections. The way that death is overtly mentioned in
Victorian children's hymns is again noticeable in these texts.

> O Thou whose bounty fills the earth,
> Accept the gifts we bring;
> For all their beauty, all their worth,
> From Thy perfection spring.
>
> These flowers that on our borders blow,
> Or bloom beside the way,
> And fill with fragrance and with glow
> This holy place to-day;
>
> They make us happy, for they tell
> Of love unseen but sure;
> Let others, then, be glad as well:-
> The suffering and the poor.
>
> To beds of anguish and of death
> We send our store of flowers,
> To whisper with their fragrant breath
> Our Father's love, and ours.
>
> Take, Lord, our gifts, though this fair show
> To-morrow will be o'er;
> Yet that great Love of Thine, we know,
> Abides for evermore.
>
> *John Ellerton*

> Here, Lord, we offer Thee all that is fairest,
> Bloom from the garden, and flowers from the field,
> Gifts for the stricken ones, knowing Thou carest
> More for the love than the wealth that we yield.
>
> Send, Lord, by these to the sick and the dying;
> Speak to the hearts with a message of peace;
> Comfort the sad, who in weakness are lying;
> Grant the departing a gentle release.
>
> Raise, Lord, to health again those who have sickened,
> Fair be their lives as the roses in bloom;
> Give of Thy grace to the souls Thou hast quickened,
> Gladness for sorrow and brightness for gloom.
>
> We, Lord, like flowers, must bloom and must wither;
> We, like these blossoms, must fade and must die:
> Gather us, Lord, to Thy bosom for ever;
> Grant us a place in Thy house in the sky.
>
> *Abel Gerald Blunt*

186

But borne upon the throne
Of Mary's gentle breast,
Watched by her duteous love,
In her fond arms at rest:—
Thus to His Father's house
He comes, the heavenly Guest.

There Joseph at her side
In reverent wonder stands,
And, filled with holy joy,
Old Simeon in his hands
Takes up the promised Child,
The Glory of all lands.

Verses from John Ellerton's
'Hail to the Lord who comes'

Praise Him, though our anthems rise
Over chill and sodden fields:
Still His care our need supplies,
Still our poor from dearth He shields;
Winds of God across the deep
Waft the Harvest-laden sails;
Sign of Love that knows no sleep,
Pledge of Truth that never fails.

From 'Praise our God, whose open hand'
written in September 1881 after a wet harvest

Thy kindness spreads with golden wheat
Broad miles of Western plain,
And makes green English orchards sweet
With Autumn's wealth again;
Thy sun and shower bring back the hour
Of Cana's gracious sign,
Where warm on Southern vineyard slopes
The mellow clusters shine.

We bless Thee for the fruitful fields,
The seasons' changing round,
The store which every region yields,
The year with plenty crowned:
All praise be Thine for Corn and Wine,
High gifts, by Thee decreed
For Symbols of a Food divine
Our Meat and Drink indeed.

Part of Ellerton's Hymn written in
August 1882 to a commission from the
Church of England Temperance Society
(and which they rejected as unsuitable)

Ellerton's hymn for the Purification of Saint Mary the Virgin, still sung today, *Hail to the Lord who comes* set to OLD 120th and HAIL TO THE LORD, was also written in 1880: but is presumably the text about which Ellerton, in correspondence with Reverend Godfrey Thring, editor of *The Church of England Hymn Book* commented *You were quite right to abuse my Purification Hymn. I know it is very bad.* In 1881 the harvest failed: and the *Guardian* published that August *Praise our God whose open hand*, a hymn for a bad harvest. He received a sheaf of letters and telegrams asking permission to copy it. His assignments for 1882 included a commission to write a harvest hymn for the Church of England Temperance Society. They did not publish it; perhaps its assertion that both corn and wine are God's *high gifts* presented them with a dilemma. He wrote hymns that year, too for the Golden Jubilee for Christ Church, Coventry, and for the opening of a Workman's Coffee Tavern. Bishop Bickersteth and Canon Walsham How consulted him as co-editors with Ellerton of a hymn book for a mission to London planned for 1884. Most of the work fell on the Barnes Vicar — and the book ended up as a sizeable collection of 211 hymns. A personal contribution was the processional *Onward, brothers, onwards.*

During the cold Spring of 1884, Ellerton suffered a severe attack of pleurisy; and his mortal life was in serious jeopardy. The Parish of Barnes in Vestry assembled desired *to convey to its Rector its sincere regret at his indisposition and to express an earnest wish for his speedy restoration to perfect health and after his necessary rest and change of air* would *hail with delight the resumption of his ministerial duties.* It was not to be. The opinion of the Vestry about police supervision on the Thames between

Teddington and Barnes would not be his burden: he resigned his post and in the Autumn of 1884, with the annotated edition of *Church Hymns* and *The Children's Hymnbook* both successfully launched, he began to recover his strength at Veytaux at the extreme eastern end of Lake Geneva. *How can I tell you of the view up the lake, with colours indescribable — the grey old castle rising sheer out of the bluest of water, with little white waves washing its walls — the wooded hills, in such hues of scarlet, purple, crimson and gold as no paint-brush could draw — the stern pine-clad ridge behind — the Rhone valley opening up at the head of the lake, with the central distance filled with the most beautiful of all the mountains, the seven-topped 'mystery' wonderful 'Dent Du Midi'?*

> Glory in the highest! Ah, what sounds arise
> Now from earth responsive to the peaceful skies?
> Sounds of midnight revel, oath, and jest, and brawl:—
> Say, is this our welcome to the Lord of all?
> *From 'A Christmas Carol for Temperance Workers'*
> *Advent 1884*
>
> What is earth itself? an Inn
> Where we wait our time to go;
> Business, pleasure, care, and sin
> Through the doors pass to and fro.
> *From 'A hymn for the Opening*
> *of a Workmen's Coffee Tavern'*

He found a French hymn, *Pourquoi reprendre, O Père tendre*, in the hymnbook of the Swiss National Church used at Veytaux. The author was Vinet, *the greatest man by far of modern French and Swiss Protestantism, whose words*, recalled Ellerton *are the striking motto of Maurice's 'Theological Essays'*. He described the hymn as a great comfort when, depressed and weary on his arrival, he was hardly able to find comfort from nature. From Veytaux, he went rather reluctantly to Pegli in Italy as a winter chaplain for the Society for the Propagation of the Gospel. By February, the poet could write again. In the next three months, he visited Genoa several times, writing eloquently from there about the Hostelry or Inn of the Poor, and was enraptured by Florence.

As for the walks, they are endless, and ever fresh in deliciousness. Each day reveals some new vision of mountain glory, and the very road into Montreux is never twice alike. Moreover, there are charming groups of picturesque chalets, fountains, wood and rock at every turn; but to say that is only to say that this is Switzerland.
John Ellerton writing from Veytaux

> Thou too hast known the thronging of the crowd,
> The *many coming* as the hours went by,
> The weary head in deep exhaustion bowed,
> The broken sleep, the sudden midnight cry.
>
> All these are Thine, O Bearer of our woes;
> No rest for Thee our suffering manhood gave;
> Through Thy three years no leisure for repose,
> Till that last Sabbath in Thy garden-grave!

I am rapidly discovering the pleasure of returning to my old vocation of a country parson; and certainly this delightful summer weather presents the life to us all on its brightest side. It is very pleasant to have what I have always longed to have — an old church with some historical interest about it, and thoroughly English looking; and I never see its shingled spire peeping through the elms and limes, or its grey tower with a foreground of corn-fields and a background of dark trees, without a fresh pleasure in thinking of it as something full of true English beauty and charm, of which one can never tire.

John Ellerton writing to his friend Professor Henry Attwell of Barnes about life at White Roding

Yet Thy compassion knows my feebler frame,
Mine is the rest my Master would not take;
And if my work indeed be in Thy Name
These quiet hours are hallowed for Thy sake.

— — — — —

So when Thy call shall bid me to return
With strength renewed, to labour in my place,
My lips shall overflow, my heart shall burn
With new revealings of Thy boundless grace.

Verses from John Ellerton's 'Hymn of the Worker on a Holiday'

When he returned to England in 1885 *with strength renewed, to labour in my place*, it was to the country living of White Roding in Essex that he was presented.

ST. MARTIN'S CHURCH, WHITE RODING, ESSEX

His colleague in editing *Church Hymns*, now Bishop Walsham How had represented to the patron that *the best living hymnwriter* was without a benefice. Ellerton was delighted to find a very good organ in the church; and a mixed choir to lead the singing at services. His predecessor had lost his sight and there was much to be done to put the house into good order and set the garden straight. But the parish work was light. The minutes of White Roding Vestry Meetings for his entire ministry there were little longer than for a single meeting at Barnes. The new valuation list for the Poor Rate involved some discussion and in April 1889, it is recorded that *the Rector handed to the Church Wardens a cheque for*

£50 being the contribution of a friend towards a heating apparatus for the better warming of the Church. A year later the final bill of just under £57 was reported. These were large sums for White Roding: the Church Wardens' accounts show a total income of just under £10 for 1887/88, with less than £4 from Church Offertories and £2 from John Ellerton himself.

In 1885, the Proprietors of *Hymns Ancient and Modern* invited Ellerton to act as a consultant as they planned a Supplement: and in May 1886 his help was asked *in arriving at a final decision as to the admission or rejection of the hymns which have been suggested: to strengthen, in fact, as an Assessor* their *Final Court of Appeal.*

> I feel rather a difficulty in altering old hymns of mine which have been many years in use, except for real and great faults. Any hymn which appears for the first time in H.A.M. I am most thankful for my colleagues to pull about to any extent. It is a great thing to get good and thoughtful criticism on them.
>
> *John Ellerton writing to Cosby White, Chairman of the Proprietors of 'Hymns Ancient and Modern' on 3rd July 1888*

> I have two Editions of Watts, one bears date 1777; another dated 1818 but professing to be specially accurate and full, and attested by the imprimatur of the six leading Dissenting Ministers of the day as the best edition yet published. I have compared these with a curious book by a Mr. Rust, a selection in which he has verified the text of every hymn he gives, except where marked. In all three of these verse 3 line 2 of the Sunday hymn reads *To David's holy Son.* So I think there is no doubt about it.
>
> In the next line, I should have been glad if Watts had written *Make haste to help us Lord, and bring* but as Watts wrote *Help us O Lord, descend and bring* I doubt if the alteration is really necessary. I am afraid I am guilty in my own Sunday hymn of saying *Come down to meet us here.* It is not theologically accurate perhaps, but is it not defensible as connected with the idea of the *Throne.* I have no doubt that *Look down* is a more Scriptural expression than *Come down* or *Descend* and it is easy to pass the limits of what is lawful in applying to the Divine Being imagery drawn from human actions. Yet I scarcely think Watts passes these limits here, though alas! he often does. Yet I like our own line better, and should never vote against the alteration.
>
> *John Ellerton writing to Rev. G. Cosby White about a line in Isaac Watts' paraphrase of part of Psalm 118. The alteration discussed has been made in many modern printings of 'This is the day the Lord hath made'*

Until publication in 1889, he was busy helping the Proprietors, not just in selection, but in translating hymns from the Latin. Of the 165 hymns chosen for the Supplement, thirteen were by Ellerton to bring his total, including those in the main book to twenty-six. The additions included *Shine Thou upon us, Lord,* a hymn for dedication services for Church workers, which still is used to

this end today. Tunes include SUPPLICATION, HYMN OF
EVE (UXBRIDGE) and ANNUE, CHRISTE.

> Live Thou within us, Lord;
> Thy mind and will be ours;
> Be Thou beloved, adored,
> And served, with all our powers;
> That so our lives may teach
> Thy children what Thou art,
> And plead, by more than speech,
> For Thee with every heart.
>
> *From 'Shine Thou upon us, Lord'*

He also collected together a definitive edition in *Hymns,
Original and Translated* of his many texts, dedicating the
volume published in 1888 to *the Right Honourable Lord
Crewe in remembrance of nearly thirty years of unbroken
friendship and continued kindness.*

O Father, bless the children
Brought hither to Thy gate;
Lift up their fallen nature,
Restore their lost estate;
Renew Thine image in them,
And own them, by this sign,
Thy very sons and daughters,
New-born of birth divine.

O Holy Spirit, keep them;
Dwell with them to the last,
Till all the fight is ended,
And all the storms are past.
Renew the gift baptismal,
From strength to strength, till each
The troublous waves o'ercoming
The land of life shall reach.

*Written at White Roding 1886
for use at Infant Baptism*

The years bring change. The fires of youth grow old:
We half forget the names we once revered,
Smile at the hatreds and the loves of old,
And dwell in peace among the things we feared.
Glory to Thee, the One Unchanging Name:
Thou art the same!

*Verse 2 of a 'Hymn for New
Year's Eve' written in 1889*

Ellerton continued to write hymns during his ministry at White Roding, including his offering for Infant Baptism *O Father, bless the children*, sung sometimes to ST. KENELM, a Hymn for New Year's Eve, a children's text for Queen Victoria's Jubilee, and near the end of his time for the Parish Festival in 1891, a hymn about their patron, Saint Martin, *To-day we sing to Christ our King*. He also wrote a sonnet sending New Year Greetings of Good Luck in the Name of the Lord to his friends. But it was mostly prose which flowed from Ellerton's pen during his last incumbency. His book *The Great Indwelling* searches the mystery of the Holy Communion in relation to the whole spiritual life. He enlivened *The Children's Almanack; The Twilight of Life*, thoughtfully printed in large type, looks positively at some of the trials of old age, with bodily powers in decline. His love of translation led him to his own version of Thomas à Kempis' *Imitation of Christ*.

English children, lift your voices
To our Father's throne on high!
Many a land to-day rejoices,
Many a coast prolongs the cry —
God, save the Queen!

Dusky Indian, strong Australian,
Western forest, Southern sea,
None are wanting, none are alien,
All in one great prayer agree —
God, save the Queen!

Part of Ellerton's 'Children's Hymn
for Queen Victoria's Jubilee, 1887'

To-day we sing to Christ our King
His valiant soldiers' praise;
The men who bore from shore to shore
The Faith in ancient days;
Of Martin's work for God we tell,
Through patient years sustained,
Till thousands heard the Gospel word,
And life eternal gained.

When first to these lone woods and fields
Our conquering fathers came,
They gave their new-built house of prayer
Saint Martin's honoured name;
Because from him their sires had learned
The tale of Jesus' love,
And so from idol forms had turned
To worship God above.

Eight hundred years have passed away
Since this old church was new;
And still to-day the Creeds we say
Which Martin taught for true.
Then speed Thy Word, O conquering Lord,
From rise to set of sun,
Till land and sea shall bow to Thee,
And praise the Three in One!

Written for the Parish Festival, 1891.
Saint Martin, patron saint of White
Roding Church, died and was buried at
Candes Monastery; in 473 his relics were
removed to Tours. The translation
of his remains was celebrated on
4th July in the Prayer Book Calendar.

But the old do not, I think, always value aright the good which comes from attaching themselves to the young. And yet this power and love of drawing the younger ones round one is to me almost a measure of the degree to which the ideal of old age has been reached. One cannot think well of the old people who do not make children *take to them* or do not care to try . . .

From 'The Twilight of
Life: Words of Counsel
and Comfort for the Aged'

O Friends, from under skies of ashen grey
What tokens can we send you o'er the snow,
While not a flower as yet has leave to blow,
And early we shut out the short dark day?
Yet thoughts are free through curtained panes to go
And find you out and bring you unawares
Memories of brighter days, and silent prayers,
With power, methinks, to set your heart aglow.
Fain would we send you, ere the year expire,
Some word that tells you of our hearts' desire.
Hark! from their tower the midnight bells proclaim
In changing tones the One Unchanging Name:
Then in that Name, O friends, both far and near,
Good luck we wish you in the new-born year.

A Sonnet sending New Year Greetings from
White Roding based on Psalm 129, 3. 'We wish
you Good Luck in the Name of the Lord'

Ellerton wrote many popular articles on the lives of hymn-writers: John Cosin, Thomas Ken, Isaac Watts, Philip Doddridge, the Wesleys and Toplady, William Cowper and John Newton, Reginald Heber and Henry Hart Milman, James Montgomery, Henry Francis Lyte, Charlotte Elliott, Frances Ridley Havergal, John Keble and John Henry Newman, Edward Caswall and Frederick William Faber, Christopher Wordsworth, Horatius Bonar and Cecil Frances Alexander all featured in his catholic choice of subjects.

Recent legislation has enabled Dissenters to claim the interment of members of their own communion in all cases by ministers of their own, when desired. A wise clergyman will not merely cheerfully obey the law, but will show all courtesy and kindly feeling to those who avail themselves of its permission.
A Manual of Parochial Work 1892

A major task was the edition of a *Manual of Parochial Work, for the Use of the younger Clergy* published in 1888 with a Revised Edition in 1892. Ellerton himself contributed chapters on the Liturgy, Music and Night Schools in a volume which ranged from the Pastor's personal life-style to bell-ringing, counselling, sick and pastoral visiting, day and Sunday Schools, church fabric, the treatment of Romanism, Dissent and Unbelief, Temperance work and finance.

Christmas Day is a day more for worship and praise than for instruction. At the Evening Service, Carol singing in church is much appreciated, especially by the poor. The Carols should be preceded by a very few words of address from the parish priest, and each one given out by him, with perhaps a short explanation of its origin or meaning.

— — — — —

Why should the linen for Holy Communion be washed, or the sanctuary be made clean and fair for service, by those who care nothing for the Sacrament, and never enter the chancel as worshippers?

— — — — —

The Pew-Opener of history and fiction is happily disappearng, as pew-doors vanish, and the small coins of strangers find their way into the alms-bags instead of into her ever-ready palm.

— — — — —

Temporary decorations, as for Christmas, Easter, or a Harvest Thanksgiving, should be carried out on a definite system, not left to individual caprice. . . . But it is a mistake to leave everything to be done by a few zealous ladies, and to ignore the poorer members of the congregation . . .

— — — — —

On the one hand, attempts at reading the Bible with dramatic effect seldom fail to annoy and disgust the listeners. But the custom which during the last thirty or forty years has sprung up under the plea of reverence, of reading the Lessons in a uniform tone, like an important but uninteresting legal document, is not less objectionable. To read such chapters as 1 Corinthians 6 or 2 Corinthians 11 without marking the irony or the impassioned pleading of the Apostle, or 1 Kings 18 or 22 without noting the changes of tone in the speakers, — not to mention many other instances, — is simply to conceal from the people the real meaning of Holy Scripture.

Advice contributed by John Ellerton
to 'A Manual of Parochial Work'

In December 1891 as the area was struck by the greatest influenza outbreak in living memory, Ellerton suffered a stroke and went to Torquay to recuperate. As he recovered, he greatly enjoyed Julian's recently published *Dictionary of Hymnody*. In May 1892, he suffered a second stroke and a few months later, when a successor had been found, he resigned the living of White Roding. That same year, he was nominated to a prebendal stall at St. Albans, with the honorary title of Canon. However, after attending worship for the last time at the Feast of Epiphany on 6th January 1893, his condition deteriorated though he lingered on, whispering from time to time half-remembered lines of beloved hymns, until his death on 15th June that year.

On Tuesday, 20th June, he was buried to the singing of six of his own hymns. Rather less than three years later, his wife was called across the divide. Husband and wife are buried together in Torquay's old cemetery, beneath a tall Celtic Cross. On the long sides of the grave are four lines from his text *God of the living*:

> All souls are thine: we must not say
> That those are dead who pass away;
> From this our world of flesh set free,
> We know them living unto Thee.

INDEX OF PERSONS

INDEX OF PLACE NAMES

GENERAL INDEX

Note: The individual first lines of hymns by Cowper, Ellerton, Heber, How and Ken are not listed in this index but they can be found quite quickly by referring to the composite entry, e.g. Hymns of Cowper.

INDEX OF TUNES

This index lists tunes mentioned in the text: it does not claim to be a comprehensive list of all the tunes to which the texts mentioned have ever been set.